PATHWAYS

SECOND EDITION

Listening, Speaking, and Critical Thinking

BECKY TARVER CHASE

CHRISTIEN LEE

NATIONAL GEOGRAPHIC

L E A R N I N G

Australia • Brazil • Mexico • Singapore • United Kingdom • United States

NATIONAL GEOGRAPHIC
L E A R N I N G

Pathways 3: Listening, Speaking, and Critical Thinking, 2nd Edition

Becky Tarver Chase and Christien Lee

Publisher: Sherrise Roehr

Executive Editor: Laura Le Dréan

Managing Editor: Jennifer Monaghan

Senior Development Editor: Jennifer Bixby

Director of Global and U.S. Marketing:
Ian Martin

Product Marketing Manager: Tracy Bailie

Media Research: Leila Hishmeh

Senior Director, Production: Michael Burggren

Manager, Production: Daisy Sosa

Content Project Manager: Mark Rzeszutek

Senior Digital Product Manager: Scott Rule

Manufacturing Planner: Mary Beth Hennebury

Interior and Cover Design: Brenda Carmichael

Art Director: Brenda Carmichael

Composition: MPS North America LLC

For product information and technology assistance, contact us at
Cengage Learning Customer & Sales Support, cengage.com/contact
For permission to use material from this text or product,
submit all requests online at **cengage.com/permissions**
Further permissions questions can be emailed to
permissionrequest@cengage.com

Student Edition: 978-1-337-40773-1
SE + Online Workbook: 978-1-337-56253-9

National Geographic Learning
20 Channel Center Street
Boston, MA 02210
USA

National Geographic Learning, a Cengage Learning Company, has a mission to bring the world to the classroom and the classroom to life. With our English language programs, students learn about their world by experiencing it. Through our partnerships with National Geographic and TED Talks, students develop the language and skills they need to be successful global citizens and leaders.

Locate your local office at **international.cengage.com/region**

Visit National Geographic Learning online at **NGL.Cengage.com/ELT**
Visit our corporate website at **www.cengage.com**

Printed in China
Print Number: 03   Print Year: 2019

Contents

Scope and Sequence

Speaking & Presentation	Vocabulary	Grammar & Pronunciation	Critical Thinking
• Quoting Statistics • Asking Rhetorical Questions **Lesson Task** Designing a Store Layout **Final Task** Giving a Persuasive Presentation	Participial Adjectives	• Real and Unreal Conditionals • Question Intonation	**Focus** Recognizing Pros and Cons Predicting, Analyzing, Synthesizing, Reflecting, Personalizing, Making Inferences, Brainstorming
• Making Suggestions • Presenting with Others **Lesson Task** Discussing Conservation and Extinction **Final Task** Creating and Presenting a Proposal	Using Context Clues	• Adjective Clauses • Syllable Stress before Suffixes	**Focus** Deciding on Criteria Evaluating, Personalizing, Interpreting a Flowchart, Ranking, Synthesizing, Reflecting, Brainstorming, Organizing Information
• Expressing Probability • Expressing Your Opinion Strongly **Lesson Task** Discussing a Case Study **Final Task** Presenting a Viewpoint	Noticing Clues to Meaning	• *Enough* and *Too* • Linking	**Focus** Categorizing Information Predicting, Personalizing, Evaluating, Applying, Categorizing, Organizing Ideas
• Answering Questions Effectively • Making Eye Contact **Lesson Task** Creating a Legend **Final Task** Presenting a Business Report	Using Digital Tools	• Passive Voice • Word Stress for Emphasis	**Focus** Being Creative Evaluating, Brainstorming with a Mind Map, Reflecting, Personalizing, Categorizing, Organizing Ideas
• Using Numbers and Statistics • Looking Up While Speaking **Lesson Task** Discussing Small Businesses **Final Task** Presenting a Socially Responsible Business	Suffix *-ive*	• Indirect Questions • Pronouncing Large Numbers	**Focus** Personalizing Evaluating, Analyzing, Synthesizing, Interpreting Statistics, Organizing Ideas

Scope and Sequence

Speaking & Presentation	Vocabulary	Grammar & Pronunciation	Critical Thinking
• Using Descriptive Language • Body Language **Lesson Task** Presenting a Design **Final Task** Presenting a Process	Multiple Meanings	• Making Comparisons • Effective Pausing	**Focus** Making Inferences Personalizing, Evaluating, Synthesizing, Analyzing, Applying, Reflecting
• Using Analogies • Storyboarding **Lesson Task** A Group Presentation about the Environment **Final Task** Planning a Video	Using Word Maps	• Tag Questions • Intonation with Tag Questions	**Focus** Considering Other Views Predicting, Personalizing, Evaluating, Brainstorming, Making Inferences, Ranking, Synthesizing, Organizing Ideas, Reflecting
• Using Phrases to Signal Reasons • Practicing and Timing Your Presentation **Lesson Task** Discussing Claims about Public Health **Final Task** A Presentation on Medicine and Health	Word Families	• Adverb Clauses of Reason and Purpose • Linking Vowel Sounds with /y/ and /w/	**Focus** Evaluating Claims Making Inferences, Evaluating, Personalizing, Applying, Brainstorming, Organizing Ideas
• Participating in Group Discussions • Introducing Your Talk **Lesson Task** Participating in a Group Discussion **Final Task** Presenting about Life in the Past or Future	Phrasal Verbs	• Using Demonstratives • Stress in Phrasal Verbs	**Focus** Drawing Conclusions Personalizing, Categorizing, Ranking, Organizing Ideas, Evaluating, Reflecting, Analyzing
• Defending an Opinion • Interacting with the Audience **Lesson Task** Presenting Survey Results **Final Task** Presenting Research	Identifying Latin Prefixes and Suffixes	• *Used to* and *Would* • Using Punctuation Marks	**Focus** Making Judgments Analyzing, Personalizing, Synthesizing, Categorizing, Making Inferences, Evaluating, Applying, Judging, Organizing Ideas

Pathways Listening, Speaking, and Critical Thinking, Second Edition

uses compelling National Geographic stories, photos, video and infographics to bring the world to the classroom. Authentic, relevant content and carefully sequenced lessons engage learners while equipping them with the skills needed for academic success.

Explore the Theme provides a visual introduction to the unit, engaging learners academically and encouraging them to share ideas about the unit theme.

D ▶ 1.8 Watch the video. Answer the questions. Then discuss your answers with a partner.

UNDERSTANDING MAIN IDEAS

1. What main idea(s) does the video express?
   a. The Colorado River is important but endangered.
   b. The Colorado River should have a different name.
   c. both a and b

2. How did the director express the main idea(s)?
   a. through the words spoken by the narrators
   b. through the images shown in the video
   c. both a and b

NEW Integrated listening and speaking activities help **prepare students for standardized tests** such as IELTS and TOEFL.

UPDATED *Video* sections use relevant National Geographic **video clips** to give learners another perspective on the unit theme and further practice of listening and critical thinking skills.

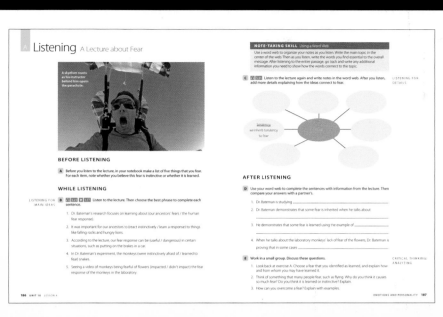

A Listening A Lecture about Fear

A skydiver reacts as his instructor behind him opens the parachute.

BEFORE LISTENING

A Before you listen to the lecture, in your notebook make a list of five things that you fear. For each item, note whether you believe this fear is instinctive or whether it is learned.

WHILE LISTENING

LISTENING FOR MAIN IDEAS

B 🔊 1.33 ▶ 1.7 Listen to the lecture. Then choose the best phrase to complete each sentence.

1. Dr. Bateman's research focuses on learning about (our ancestors' fears / the human fear response).
2. It was important for our ancestors to (react instinctively / learn a response) to things like falling rocks and hungry lions.
3. According to the lecture, our fear response can be (useful / dangerous) in certain situations, such as putting on the brakes in a car.
4. In Dr. Bateman's experiment, the monkeys (were instinctively afraid of / learned to fear) snakes.
5. Seeing a video of monkeys being fearful of flowers (impacted / didn't impact) the fear response of the monkeys in the laboratory.

NOTE-TAKING SKILL Using a Word Web

Use a word web to organize your notes as you listen. Write the main topic in the center of the web. Then as you listen, write the words you find essential to the overall message. After listening to the entire passage, go back and write any additional information you need to show how the words connect to the topic.

C 🔊 1.33 Listen to the lecture again and write notes in the word web. After you listen, add more details explaining how the ideas connect to fear.

LISTENING FOR DETAILS

AFTER LISTENING

D Use your word web to complete the sentences with information from the lecture. Then compare your answers with a partner's.

1. Dr. Bateman is studying _____
2. Dr. Bateman demonstrates that some fear is inherited when he talks about _____
3. He demonstrates that some fear is learned using the example of _____
4. When he talks about the laboratory monkeys' lack of fear of the flowers, Dr. Bateman is proving that in some cases _____

E Work in a small group. Discuss these questions.

CRITICAL THINKING: ANALYZING

1. Look back at exercise A. Choose a fear that you identified as learned, and explain how and from whom you may have learned it.
2. Think of something that many people fear, such as flying. Why do you think it causes so much fear? Do you think it is learned or instinctive? Explain.
3. How can you overcome a fear? Explain with examples.

186 UNIT 10 LESSON A

EMOTIONS AND PERSONALITY 187

Typical participial adjectives are formed from the past (usually -ed) or present (-ing) participle of a verb. These two forms have different meanings and can be confused.

Typically, past participial adjectives describe an emotion or feeling that somebody has:

*He felt **frustrated** that the item was out of stock.*
*Many people were **bored** during the discussion.*

Present participial adjectives describe something that causes an emotion or feeling:

*He said that the item being out of stock was **frustrating**.*
*The discussion was **boring** to many people.*

NEW *Vocabulary Skills* help students develop essential word building tools such as understanding collocations, word forms, and connotation.

Listening passages incorporate a variety of listening types such as podcasts, lectures, interviews, and conversations.

WHILE LISTENING

LISTENING FOR MAIN IDEAS

B 🔊 1.33 ▶ 1.7 Listen to the lecture and take notes. Then use your notes to complete a sentence summarizing what you heard.

A geology professor described _____

C 🔊 1.34 Listen again to part of the lecture and take notes. Then use your notes to complete the diagram by writing the correct letter in each space. One answer has been done for you.

Formation of the Tsingy de Bemaraha

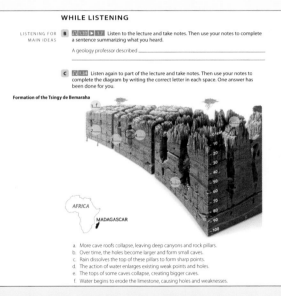

AFRICA
MADAGASCAR

a. More cave roofs collapse, leaving deep canyons and rock pillars.
b. Over time, the holes become larger and form small caves.
c. Rain dissolves the top of these pillars to form sharp points.
d. The action of water enlarges existing weak points and holes.
e. The tops of some caves collapse, creating bigger caves.
f. Water begins to erode the limestone, causing holes and weaknesses.

NEW *Slide shows* for selected listening passages integrate text and visuals to give learners a more authentic listening experience.

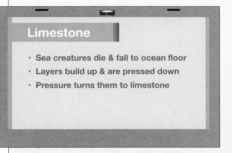

Limestone

· Sea creatures die & fall to ocean floor
· Layers build up & are pressed down
· Pressure turns them to limestone

LISTENING SKILL Recognizing a Speaker's Attitude

🔊 1.6 Speakers often express an attitude—or how they feel—about certain things. Recognizing attitude can help you better understand a speaker's message. There are three main ways you can recognize a speaker's attitude:

1. A speaker may state what he or she is feeling directly.
   I'm really excited we're going shopping tomorrow. (excitement)

2. A speaker may express his or her attitude indirectly.
   It's too bad you can't come shopping tomorrow. (disappointment)

3. A speaker's intonation may help you recognize his or her attitude. For example, a falling intonation can indicate disappointment.
   She can't come shopping tomorrow.

E 🔊 1.7 Listen to four excerpts from the interview. Write the excerpt number next to the attitude of the speaker.

RECOGNIZING A SPEAKER'S ATTITUDE

a. _____ confident   c. _____ thoughtful
b. _____ surprised   d. _____ uncertain

UPDATED Explicit listening and note-taking skill instruction and practice prepares students to listen and take notes in academic settings.

AFTER LISTENING

NOTE-TAKING SKILL Reviewing Your Notes

While you are listening and taking notes, it can be difficult to decide what the most important ideas are. This is why it is important to review your notes after you finish listening. First, add any information to make your notes clearer. Then, to review what you have learned, add a section at the bottom of your notes titled *Main ideas*. In that section, list three or four main ideas from the listening.

F Review your notes and make any additions to make them clearer. Then list three or four main ideas at the bottom of your notes. In a small group, compare your main ideas.

Speaking lessons guide learners from controlled practice to a final speaking task while reinforcing speaking skills, grammar for speaking, and key pronunciation points.

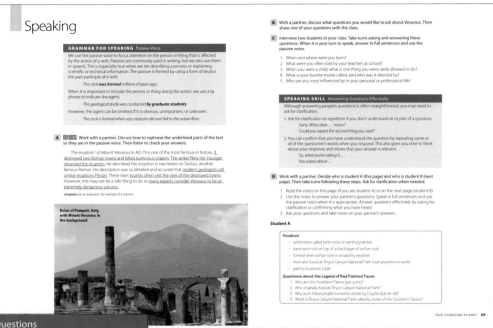

A Speaking

GRAMMAR FOR SPEAKING Passive Voice

We use the passive voice to focus attention on the person or thing that is affected by the action of a verb. Passives are commonly used in writing, but we also use them in speech. This is especially true when we are describing a process or explaining scientific or technical information. The passive is formed by using a form of *be* plus the past participle of a verb.

*This rock **was formed** millions of years ago.*

When it is important to include the person or thing doing the action, we use a *by* phrase to indicate the agent.

*This geological study was conducted **by graduate students**.*

However, the agent can be omitted if it is obvious, unimportant, or unknown.

This rock is formed when sea creatures die and fall to the ocean floor.

A 1.17 Work with a partner. Discuss how to rephrase the underlined parts of the text so they are in the passive voice. Then listen to check your answers.

The eruption¹ of Mount Vesuvius in AD 79 is one of the most famous in history. It destroyed two Roman towns and killed numerous citizens. The writer Pliny the Younger observed the eruption. He described the eruption in two letters to Tacitus, another famous Roman. His description was so detailed and accurate that modern geologists call similar eruptions Plinian. These days tourists often visit the sites of the destroyed towns. However, this may not be a safe thing to do as many experts consider Vesuvius to be an extremely dangerous volcano.

¹**eruption** (n): an explosion, for example of a volcano

Ruins of Pompeii, Italy, with Mount Vesuvius in the background

B With a partner, discuss what questions you would like to ask about Vesuvius. Then share one of your questions with the class.

C Interview two students in your class. Take turns asking and answering these questions. When it is your turn to speak, answer in full sentences and use the passive voice.

1. When and where were you born?
2. What were you often told by your teachers at school?
3. When you were a child, what is one thing you were rarely allowed to do?
4. What is your favorite movie called, and who was it directed by?
5. Who are you most influenced by in your personal or professional life?

SPEAKING SKILL Answering Questions Effectively

Although answering people's questions is often straightforward, you may need to ask for clarification.

1. Ask for clarification or repetition if you don't understand all or part of a question:
Sorry. What does … mean?
Could you repeat the second thing you said?

2. You can confirm that you have understood the question by repeating some or all of the questioner's words when you respond. This also gives you time to think about your response and shows that your answer is relevant.
So, what you're asking is …
You asked about …

D Work with a partner. Decide who is student A (this page) and who is student B (next page). Then take turns following these steps. Ask for clarification when needed.

1. Read the notes on this page (if you are student A) or on the next page (student B).
2. Use the notes to answer your partner's questions. Speak in full sentences and use the passive voice when it is appropriate. Answer questions effectively by asking for clarification or confirming what you have heard.
3. Ask your questions and take notes on your partner's answers.

Student A

Hoodoos
• sometimes called tent rocks or earth pyramids
• have hard rock on top of a thick layer of softer rock
• formed when softer rock is eroded by weather
• more are found at Bryce Canyon National Park than anywhere in world
• park is located in Utah

Questions about the Legend of Red Painted Faces
1. Who are the Southern Paiute (pie-yute)?
2. Who originally lived at Bryce Canyon National Park?
3. Why were these people turned to stone by Coyote (kai-oh-di)?
4. What is Bryce Canyon National Park called by some of the Southern Paiute?

OUR CHANGING PLANET **69**

PRESENTATION SKILL Asking Rhetorical Questions

A rhetorical question is one that does not require an answer. When giving a presentation, rhetorical questions can be useful in several ways:

1. They can help you create a connection with the audience.
We've all wanted an app like this, haven't we?

2. They can persuade the audience to agree with your view.
Don't you think this new app sounds amazing?

3. They can introduce a point that you will then discuss.
Why is the app going to be popular? Let me tell you.

Presentation skills such as introducing your talk, presenting with others, making eye contact, and interacting with your audience, help learners develop confidence and fluency in communicating ideas.

A **Final Task** allows learners to consolidate their understanding of content, language, and skills as they collaborate on an academic presentation.

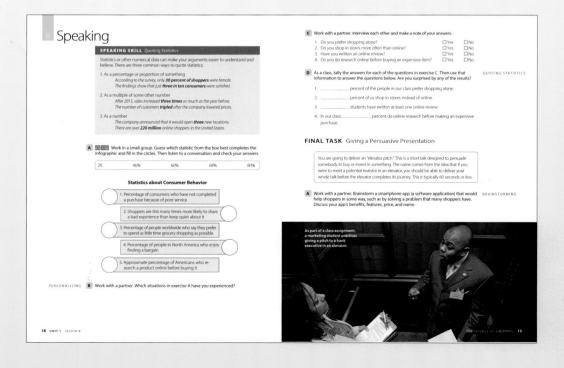

B Speaking

SPEAKING SKILL Quoting Statistics

Statistics or other numerical data can make your arguments easier to understand and believe. There are three common ways to quote statistics:

1. As a percentage or proportion of something
*According to the survey, only **30 percent of shoppers** were female.*
*The findings show that just **three in ten consumers** were satisfied.*

2. As a multiple of some other number
*After 2015, sales increased **three times** as much as the year before.*
*The number of customers **tripled** after the company lowered prices.*

3. As a number
*The company announced that it would open **three** new locations.*
*There are over **220 million** online shoppers in the United States.*

A 1.12 Work in a small group. Guess which statistic from the box best completes the infographic and fill in the circles. Then listen to a conversation and check your answers.

20   46%   60%   68%   80%

Statistics about Consumer Behavior

1. Percentage of consumers who have not completed a purchase because of poor service
2. Shoppers are this many times more likely to share a bad experience than keep quiet about it
3. Percentage of people worldwide who say they prefer to spend as little time grocery shopping as possible
4. Percentage of people in North America who enjoy finding a bargain
5. Approximate percentage of Americans who re-search a product online before buying it

PERSONALIZING **B** Work with a partner. Which situations in exercise A have you experienced?

C Work with a partner. Interview each other and make a note of your answers.

	Yes	No
1. Do you prefer shopping alone?	☐ Yes	☐ No
2. Do you shop in stores more often than online?	☐ Yes	☐ No
3. Have you written an online review?	☐ Yes	☐ No
4. Do you do research online before buying an expensive item?	☐ Yes	☐ No

D As a class, tally the answers for each of the questions in exercise C. Then use that information to answer the questions below. Are you surprised by any of the results?   QUOTING STATISTICS

1. _____ percent of the people in our class prefer shopping alone.

2. _____ percent of us shop in stores instead of online.

3. _____ students have written at least one online review.

4. In our class, _____ percent do online research before making an expensive purchase.

FINAL TASK Giving a Persuasive Presentation

You are going to deliver an "elevator pitch." This is a short talk designed to persuade somebody to buy or invest in something. The name comes from the idea that if you were to meet a potential investor in an elevator, you should be able to deliver your whole talk before the elevator completes its journey. This is typically 60 seconds or less.

A Work with a partner. Brainstorm a smartphone app (a software application) that would help shoppers in some way, such as by solving a problem that many shoppers have. Discuss your app's benefits, features, price, and name.   BRAINSTORMING

As part of a class assignment, a marketing student practices giving a pitch to a bank executive in an elevator.

18 UNIT 1 LESSON B

THE SCIENCE OF SHOPPING **19**

THE SCIENCE OF SHOPPING 1

A woman looks at a window display of expensive jewelry in Shanghai, China.

THINK AND DISCUSS

1 The woman in the photo is window-shopping. Do you enjoy window-shopping? Why or why not?

2 Look at the title. What do you think this unit will be about?

Look at the photos and read the information. Then discuss the questions.

1. What information in the timeline surprises you?

2. Do you think shopping has changed positively over the years? Why or why not?

3. How do you think shopping might change in the future? Explain.

TWO CENTURIES OF SHOPPING

1890
Window Shopping
Shoppers look into the new glass display window of Marshall Field's department store in Chicago, Illinois, USA.

1796
Department Stores
The first department store, Harding, Howell and Company opens in London, U.K.

1893
Mail Order
Sears, Roebuck & Co. launches their first mail-order catalog, and continues filling orders until 1993.

1927

Convenience Stores
The first convenience store is opened in Texas, USA, by the Southland Ice Company and is later known as 7-11.

1956
Shopping Malls
Southdale Center, the first indoor shopping mall, opens in Minnesota, USA.

1962
Big Box Retail
The first Walmart store opens in Arkansas, USA, starting a trend of "big box" retailers, so called because they look like a big box.

1998

Vending Machines
Vending machines become very popular in Japan. In 1998, there are over 5.4 million machines there.

2010

Online Shopping
Online shopping and payments become more and more popular.

2017
Grab and Go
Amazon opens a new type of store that allows shoppers to pay electronically and leave the store without waiting in line to pay.

Vocabulary

A farmers' market in Venice, Italy

A Look at the photo and discuss the questions in a small group.

1. What are some of the advantages and disadvantages of shopping at a market like the one in the photo?
2. Have you visited an outdoor market? If so, how was the experience? If not, would you like to shop at an outdoor market?
3. Do you think markets like this will still exist 50 years from now? Why or why not?

B 🎧 1.2 Listen to the words. Choose the best word to complete each definition. Then work with a partner to check your answers in a dictionary.

addictive	assume	bump	complex	purchase
alter	bargain	commercial	consumer	retail

1. _____ (adj) hard to understand or analyze

2. _____ (adj) related to business

3. _____ (adj) so enjoyable that one wants more of it

4. _____ (n) a person who buys goods or services for personal use

5. _____ (n) an item that one buys

6. _____ (n) something bought for a cheaper price than usual

7. _____ (n) the sale of goods or services directly to people

8. _____ (v) to believe without checking if it is true

9. _____ (v) to change

10. _____ (v) to hit with your body, especially by accident

C 🎧 **1.3** Complete these sentences with a word in **blue** from exercise B. Use the correct form of the word. Then listen and check your answers.

1. In the United States, many teenagers' first work experience is a job in
   retail or in a restaurant.

2. Although the store only _alter_ the location of a few of the
   departments, many customers disliked the changes.

3. Ben had _assume_ that the store closed at six and was disappointed when
   he got there and found the door locked.

4. Customers frequently _bump_ into and knocked over the sign because
   of its inconvenient position.

5. Most people do not use a credit card when they make a very large
   purchase such as a new car.

6. During the end-of-year sale, hundreds of customers visited the department store
   hoping to find a great _bargain_ or two.

7. Many _consumer_ use their phones to check prices online before
   purchasing anything in a store.

8. In a survey of people who have bought items through online sites like eBay, some said
   they felt online shopping was so _addictive_ that they couldn't stop doing it.

9. According to the plans, the new apartment building will have _commercial_
   space for offices, restaurants, and stores on the first floor.

10. The store's refund process was so _complex_ that many customers decided
    it was easier to keep an item than to return it.

D Work in a small group. First, choose five questions that you all find interesting. Then discuss them. Explain and support your reasons.

1. Do you assume that an item with a high price is always good quality? Explain.
2. In your view, which kinds of commercial buildings generally have the best design: stores, restaurants, or office buildings?
3. Would you agree that working in retail is good experience for a teenager?
4. In what ways do stores encourage consumers to buy things they do not really need?
5. Where do you shop to get the best bargains? What bargains have you found recently?
6. What is one past purchase that you regret buying? Explain.
7. When you have to study something complex, what study techniques do you find effective?
8. What do you say when you bump into someone? Are there times when an apology isn't necessary?
9. Who is most likely to make you alter your behavior and why: your family, your friends, or celebrities?
10. Would you agree that anything which is enjoyable could become addictive?

A Listening An Interview about Consumer Behavior

Shoppers ride on escalators in Bashundhara City, Dhaka's biggest shopping center, Bangladesh.

BEFORE LISTENING

A With a partner, make a list of things that consumers often do before, during, and after shopping, such as making a shopping list or trying items on. Then join with another pair and compare your lists.

WHILE LISTENING

CRITICAL THINKING: PREDICTING

B 🎧 1.4 Work in a small group. Before listening to an interview with an environmental psychologist, discuss what you think her job involves. Then listen to the first part of the interview to check your answer.

LISTENING FOR MAIN IDEAS

C 🎧 1.5 Listen to the whole interview. What do the speakers mainly discuss? Choose two answers.

 a. how some stores try to influence their customers' behavior
 b. what causes some people to become addicted to shopping
 c. what factors might cause shoppers to take certain actions
 d. which stores are more popular with shoppers than others
 e. why shoppers are likely to touch or feel inexpensive items

LISTENING FOR DETAILS

D 🎧 1.5 Listen again and take notes. Then check (✓) the five statements that match what the psychologist says.

 1. ✓ Consumers generally behave in complex ways when shopping.

 2. ✓ For shoppers, being bumped is sometimes bad, but sometimes OK.

3. _____ Shoes and shirts are common items that people buy online.

4. ✓ Buying items at bargain prices can improve a person's mood.

5. ~~_____~~ Shopping is a much more addictive activity than anything else.

6. _____ Stores are good at making people feel many positive emotions.

7. ✓ Shopping when feeling bad can lead to increased spending.

8. ✓ A number of different factors can affect how shoppers behave.

LISTENING SKILL Recognizing a Speaker's Attitude

🎧 1.6 Speakers often express an attitude—or how they feel—about certain things. Recognizing attitude can help you better understand a speaker's message. There are three main ways you can recognize a speaker's attitude:

1. A speaker may state what he or she is feeling directly.

   I'm really excited we're going shopping tomorrow. (excitement)

2. A speaker may express his or her attitude indirectly.

   It's too bad you can't come shopping tomorrow. (disappointment)

3. A speaker's intonation may help you recognize his or her attitude. For example, a falling intonation can indicate disappointment.

   She can't come shopping tomorrow.

E 🎧 1.7 Listen to four excerpts from the interview. Write the excerpt number next to the attitude of the speaker.

a. _____ confident   c. _____ thoughtful

b. _____ surprised   d. _____ uncertain

AFTER LISTENING

NOTE-TAKING SKILL Reviewing Your Notes

While you are listening and taking notes, it can be difficult to decide what the most important ideas are. This is why it is important to review your notes after you finish listening. First, add any information to make your notes clearer. Then, to review what you have learned, add a section at the bottom of your notes titled *Main ideas*. In that section, list three or four main ideas from the listening.

F Review your notes and make any additions to make them clearer. Then list three or four main ideas at the bottom of your notes. In a small group, compare your main ideas.

G Work in a small group. Discuss how it makes you feel that "stores are trying to alter" your behavior. Also discuss how you might shop differently now that you know this.

Speaking

GRAMMAR FOR SPEAKING Real and Unreal Conditionals

The present real conditional describes something that is always or generally true. Notice that the two verbs in the sentence are both simple present.

> If I **buy** something on sale, I **feel** happy.

The future real conditional describes a real or possible situation that has results in the future. Notice that the *if* clause is simple present while the result clause is future.

> If the price **drops**, I **will buy** it.

The present unreal conditional describes something that is not true but can be imagined. Notice that the *if* clause is simple past and the result clause uses *would* + verb. Note that *were* is used for both singular and plural forms in the *if* clause of present unreal conditionals.

> If the price **were** cheaper, I **would purchase** it.
> If I **had** money, I **would buy** a new laptop.

A Work in a small group. Discuss these questions. Use conditionals in your answers.

1. If you need to buy clothes, where do you usually go shopping? Why?
2. If you have some free time next weekend, will you go to a mall? Why or why not?
3. If you could go anywhere on vacation, where would you go? Why?
4. What restaurant would you go to if you wanted to have a special celebration? Why?

CRITICAL THINKING:
ANALYZING

B Work with a partner. Look at the chart and complete the steps.

1. Imagine that you receive $10,000. How would you use the money? On what three things would you spend the money?
2. How are your ideas similar to or different from the information in the chart below?
3. Ask other students in the class what they would do with the money. Then share what you learned and create a chart showing the most popular ideas.

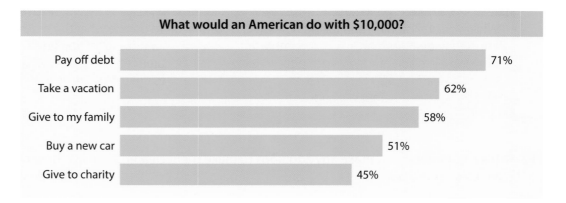

What would an American do with $10,000?

Pay off debt	71%
Take a vacation	62%
Give to my family	58%
Buy a new car	51%
Give to charity	45%

PRONUNCIATION Question Intonation

🎧 1.8 Questions in English typically have one of two common intonation patterns:

1. Rising intonation—the speaker's tone rises on the stressed syllable of the last content word. Rising intonation is common in *yes/no* questions.

   Is the store on the corner still open?

2. Falling intonation—the speaker's tone rises and then falls on the stressed syllable of the last content word. The content word depends on the focus of the question. Falling intonation is common in *wh–* questions.

   What did you buy yesterday? (focus on *buy*)

   What did you buy yesterday? (focus on *yesterday*)

C Complete the steps to practice question intonation.

1. In the chart below, write three questions about money or spending habits. Include real and unreal conditionals. Mark the intonation pattern in each question.
2. Interview other students in your class and note their answers.
3. Share what you learned from the interviews with a partner. In general, would you expect to see differences in how males and females answered your questions?

Questions	Interviewee 1	Interviewee 2	Interviewee 3

CRITICAL THINKING Recognizing Pros and Cons

When you are making a decision or debating what to do, it can be helpful to discuss the pros and cons of a situation or action. Talking about the pros and cons can help you:

- make a better and more informed decision about the best action to take
- argue for (or against) a particular action more easily and effectively

EVERYDAY LANGUAGE Discussing Pros and Cons

One advantage/disadvantage of . . . is that . . .
The upside/downside of . . . is that . . .
On the one/other hand, . . . is an obvious strength/weakness.

D Work with a partner. Discuss the pros and cons of each of these situations.

1. paying for items with a credit card
2. going shopping with friends
3. eating out at restaurants
4. taking a vacation overseas

E Work in a small group. Think about how stores can change shoppers' behavior. Complete the chart with some pros and cons of each action. Then compare your ideas with those of another group.

How to Change Shoppers' Behavior	Pros	Cons
Train sales clerks to smile more to put shoppers in a better mood.		
Bake fresh bread in a supermarket to make shoppers hungry.		
Post "limit 2 per customer" signs to suggest items are in limited supply.		
Move the registers so shoppers must walk through the whole store to pay.		
Put chairs outside the fitting rooms so people can sit while they wait.		

LESSON TASK Designing a Store Layout

A You have been asked to design the layout of a new store that will sell clothes for children, men, and women. Work in a small group to complete the steps.

1. Discuss what the store should include and where. Think about how the layout might affect the behavior of customers.
2. Draw your store plan on a separate piece of paper. Label each area on the floor plan.
   - women's clothing
   - men's clothing
   - children's clothing
   - fitting rooms
   - check-out area
   - entrance/exit
3. Share your design with the rest of the class. Explain what you will include and where and why. Then listen to the ideas of other groups.

B As a class, discuss the following questions.

CRITICAL THINKING: SYNTHESIZING

1. Of the store layouts in exercise A, which one is the most attractive? Why?
2. Which of the layouts would be least likely to appeal to people your age? Why?
3. Which of the layouts is the most unusual? Do you think the layout would work well in an actual store? Why or why not?

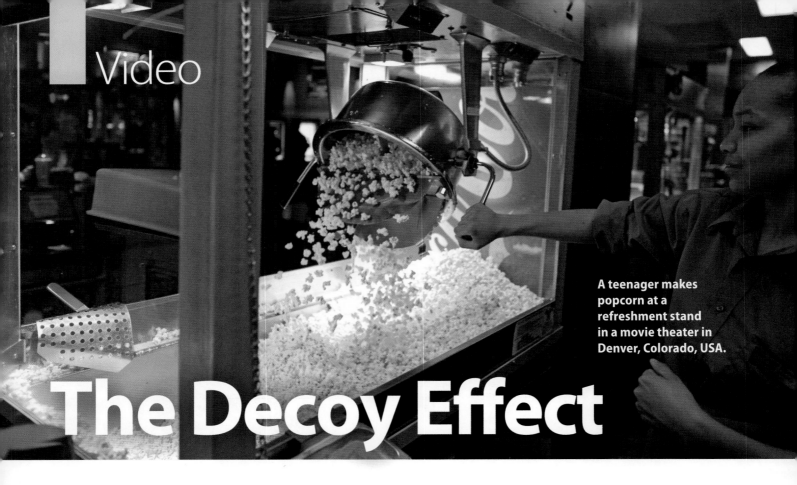

A teenager makes popcorn at a refreshment stand in a movie theater in Denver, Colorado, USA.

The Decoy Effect

BEFORE VIEWING

A Complete these definitions of words and phrases from the video with the best option from the box. When you have finished, check your answers with a partner.

appealing	decoy	influence	out of line
concession stand	head over	irresistible	rip off

1. If something is _____, it is so attractive that it is impossible not to like it.

2. A(n) _____ is a place that typically sells food inside a larger business.

3. A(n) _____ is something that people feel costs more than it should.

4. If a person decides to _____ somewhere, he or she goes or visits there.

5. If a person or thing can _____ something, it can have an effect on it.

6. If something is _____, it goes beyond what most people would accept.

7. A(n) _____ is a thing or person designed to trick a person or animal.

8. If something is _____, people think it is nice, interesting, or desirable.

B Work in a small group. You are about to watch a video about refreshments that are sold at movie theaters. What refreshments are usually sold in your country? Do you buy refreshments at a movie theater? Why or why not?

WHILE VIEWING

C ▶ **1.1** Watch the video. Then, in a small group, choose the answer that best defines "the decoy effect."

UNDERSTANDING MAIN IDEAS

a. Customers are more likely to choose good value items if no decoy options are available.
b. Offering customers one more option can have a strong effect on which option they prefer.
c. If customers have several similarly priced options, they usually prefer the cheapest one.

D ▶ **1.1** Watch again. Complete the notes with one word or a number from the video.

UNDERSTANDING DETAILS

1st Experiment	• Customers had choice between sm. and lg. popcorn
	• Experiment showed that $_____ size was most popular 1
	• Some customers felt other size was a lot of _____ 2
2nd Experiment	• Consumers had choice of sm., _____, or lg. popcorn 3
	• Experiment showed that $_____ one was most popular 4
	• Consumers explained that this size was a good _____ 5

AFTER VIEWING

E Work with a partner. Practice orally summarizing the video. Try to do it without looking at the notes in exercise D.

> *This video showed two experiments to illustrate the decoy effect in a movie theater. In the first experiment, . . .*

F Work with a partner. Discuss the questions. Then share your ideas with the class.

CRITICAL THINKING: REFLECTING

1. A decoy is a thing designed to trick a person or animal. Does this change how you feel about companies using the decoy effect? Why or why not?
2. Will you change your shopping behavior after learning about the decoy effect? If yes, what will you do differently? If no, why not?
3. What else do businesses do to encourage consumers to spend more?

B Vocabulary

A 🎧 1.9 Read and listen to the conversations. Notice the words in blue. Then complete each definition with one of the answers in the box.

an important task	information discovered through research
as much as is necessary	support and commitment
a necessary but boring task	identifying as either male or female
causing somebody to be upset	to do something such as an experiment
not currently available to buy	to do things with other people

A: You didn't mark your **gender** on this application form, Bob.
B: I must have forgotten. Filling out applications is such a **chore**. Would you mind checking the box next to "male" for me, please?

1. The noun *gender* means _____.

2. The noun *chore* means _____.

A: Is it true that you met Lionel Messi yesterday? For real?
B: Yeah! And it was great, especially because I speak some Spanish, so I could **interact** with him better than the other people with me.

3. The verb *interact* means _____.

A: How did your experiment go, Ahmed?
B: I can't say for sure yet, but I came up with a good way to **conduct** it, I think, so I hope the **findings** will be useful.

4. The verb *conduct* means _____.

5. The noun *findings* means _____.

A: Did you hear that Professor Albright has lost her job?
B: Yeah, and I'm upset about it. She's worked here for over 25 years apparently. I think the college should have shown more **loyalty** to her.

6. The noun *loyalty* means _____.

A: How was your weekend, David?
B: Not so good. I went to the mall on a **mission** to buy a gift for my sister. I was there for hours, but I couldn't find the right gift. It was pretty **frustrating**.

7. The noun *mission* means _____.

8. The adjective *frustrating* means _____.

A: Excuse me. Where could I find *Marketing Basics*?
B: Sorry to tell you this, but that book's **out of stock** just now. We thought we had ordered **sufficient** copies, but more students purchased it than we expected.

9. The phrase *out of stock* means _____.

10. The adjective *sufficient* means _____.

B Work with a partner. Discuss these questions. Provide reasons and examples to support your opinions.

PERSONALIZING

1. Are you familiar with loyalty cards? In your view, do loyalty cards really make people more loyal to a particular store or restaurant?
2. In your experience, what do you find to be the most frustrating thing about shopping?
3. What are some tasks that children generally consider to be chores, but which people often enjoy as they get older?

VOCABULARY SKILL Participial Adjectives

Participial adjectives are formed from the past (usually *–ed*) or present (*–ing*) participle of a verb. These two forms have different meanings and can be confused.

Typically, past participial adjectives describe an emotion or feeling that somebody has:

> He felt **frustrated** that the item was out of stock.
> Many people were **bored** during the discussion.

Present participial adjectives describe something that causes an emotion or feeling:

> He said that the item being out of stock was **frustrating**.
> The discussion was **boring** to many people.

C Choose the correct word to complete each question. Then interview people in your class and discuss your answers.

1. Which makes you more (frustrated / frustrating): when an item you want is out of stock or when it is too expensive to buy? Why?
2. Which sounds more (excited / exciting): interacting with older people from another country or with people your age from your country? Why?
3. Which would you find more (bored / boring): a documentary about loyalty or one about gender? Why?
4. Which option would make you more (relaxed / relaxing) after working all day: taking a bath or going for a walk? Why?
5. Which would you be more (interested / interesting) in doing: watching a movie or going to a party? Why?

B Listening A Lecture about Gender and Shopping

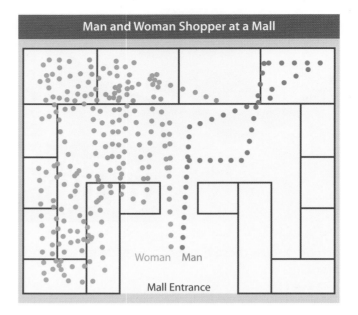

Man and Woman Shopper at a Mall

Woman Man

Mall Entrance

BEFORE LISTENING

CRITICAL THINKING:
MAKING INFERENCES

A Discuss the questions with a partner. Then share your ideas and reasons with the class.

1. Look at the image. Do you think it is intended to be serious or humorous? Why? Do you think it makes a real point about the difference in how men and women shop?

2. The professor discusses a research study titled "Men Buy, Women Shop." What do you think this title most likely means?

WHILE LISTENING

LISTENING FOR
MAIN IDEAS

B 🎧 1.10 ▶ 1.2 Listen to the lecture. Take notes as you listen. Then answer the questions. When you have finished, compare answers with a partner.

1. What subject do you think this professor is teaching?

   a. marketing: the study of how businesses interact with customers
   b. psychology: the study of how and why people think and behave
   c. sociology: the study of how people generally behave in society

2. What do the speakers suggest "Men Buy, Women Shop" most likely means?

   a. Both men and women like shopping, but only men enjoy purchasing items.
   b. For women, the goal of shopping is to shop; for men, it is to buy something.
   c. Men enjoy spending money, but women prefer searching for items to buy.

3. What point does the professor make about shopping behaviors?
   a. There are a number of differences in how the typical man shops compared with the typical woman.
   b. Men usually shop in the same way every time; women may shop differently on different days.
   c. Both male and female shoppers are influenced by the gender of the shop assistants who help them.

C 🎧 1.11 Listen to part of the lecture. Take notes as you listen, dividing them for men and women. Then answer the question below. When you have finished, compare answers with a partner.

LISTENING FOR
DETAILS

According to the instructor, which statements apply to men shoppers, and which ones apply to women shoppers? Put a check (✓) in the correct column.

	Men	Women
1. Become frustrated if store employees are inefficient		
2. Dislike having to wait in a long line to pay for an item		
3. Get upset when sales assistants are not easy to find		
4. May be concerned about the availability of parking		
5. Want store clerks to be polite and knowledgeable		

AFTER LISTENING

D Work with a partner. Discuss these questions.

CRITICAL THINKING:
REFLECTING

1. Do any of the differences in how men and women shop mentioned in the lecture surprise you? Which?
2. At the end of the lecture, the professor asks "*Why* do men and women behave in different ways when shopping?" What reasons can you think of?

E Work in a small group to complete the steps. Then share your ideas with the class.

CRITICAL THINKING:
SYNTHESIZING

1. Think of a group of people who are different from you. For example, you might choose people who are a different gender, a different age, or a different nationality.
2. Come up with a list of things that stores could do to make shoppers of this group happy without upsetting or annoying you and others in the same group as you.

▼ **A customer looks at smartphones in Stockholm, Sweden.**

B Speaking

SPEAKING SKILL Quoting Statistics

Statistics or other numerical data can make your arguments easier to understand and believe. There are three common ways to quote statistics:

1. As a percentage or proportion of something
    *According to the survey, only **30 percent of shoppers** were female.*
    *The findings show that just **three in ten consumers** were satisfied.*

2. As a multiple of some other number
    *After 2015, sales increased **three times** as much as the year before.*
    *The number of customers **tripled** after the company lowered prices.*

3. As a number
    *The company announced that it would open **three** new locations.*
    *There are over **220 million** online shoppers in the United States.*

A 🎧 1.12 Work in a small group. Guess which statistic from the box best completes the infographic and fill in the circles. Then listen to a conversation and check your answers.

| 20 | 46% | 60% | 68% | 80% |

Statistics about Consumer Behavior

1. Percentage of consumers who have not completed a purchase because of poor service

2. Shoppers are this many times more likely to share a bad experience than keep quiet about it

3. Percentage of people worldwide who say they prefer to spend as little time grocery shopping as possible

4. Percentage of people in North America who enjoy finding a bargain

5. Approximate percentage of Americans who research a product online before buying it

PERSONALIZING **B** Work with a partner. Which situations in exercise A have you experienced?

C Work with a partner. Interview each other and make a note of your answers.

1. Do you prefer shopping alone? ☐ Yes ☐ No
2. Do you shop in stores more often than online? ☐ Yes ☐ No
3. Have you written an online review? ☐ Yes ☐ No
4. Do you do research online before buying an expensive item? ☐ Yes ☐ No

D As a class, tally the answers for each of the questions in exercise C. Then use that information to answer the questions below. Are you surprised by any of the results?

QUOTING STATISTICS

1. _____ percent of the people in our class prefer shopping alone.

2. _____ percent of us shop in stores instead of online.

3. _____ students have written at least one online review.

4. In our class, _____ percent do online research before making an expensive purchase.

FINAL TASK Giving a Persuasive Presentation

> You are going to deliver an "elevator pitch." This is a short talk designed to persuade somebody to buy or invest in something. The name comes from the idea that if you were to meet a potential investor in an elevator, you should be able to deliver your whole talk before the elevator completes its journey. This is typically 60 seconds or less.

A Work with a partner. Brainstorm a smartphone app (a software application) that would help shoppers in some way, such as by solving a problem that many shoppers have. Discuss your app's benefits, features, price, and name.

BRAINSTORMING

As part of a class assignment, a marketing student practices giving a pitch to a bank executive in an elevator.

PRESENTATION SKILL Asking Rhetorical Questions

A rhetorical question is one that does not require an answer. When giving a presentation, rhetorical questions can be useful in several ways:

1. They can help you create a connection with the audience.
   We've all wanted an app like this, haven't we?

2. They can persuade the audience to agree with your view.
   Don't you think this new app sounds amazing?

3. They can introduce a point that you will then discuss.
   Why is the app going to be popular? Let me tell you.

B Complete the steps.

1. Create a plan for a 60-second elevator pitch to persuade others that your app would be useful. Think about statistics you could mention and rhetorical questions you could ask.
2. Practice giving your elevator pitch until you are confident that you can deliver your talk in 60 seconds or less.

PRESENTING **C** In a small group, deliver your pitch and answer any questions. Then listen to the other pitches. **Which of the apps do you think would be the most useful to shoppers and why?**

REFLECTION

1. What skill from this unit will help you present more effectively in the future?

   _____

   _____

2. What is the most interesting thing about how shoppers behave that you learned in this unit?

   _____

   _____

3. Here are the vocabulary words from the unit. Check (✓) the ones you can use.

   ☐ addictive   ☐ complex AWL   ☐ loyalty
   ☐ alter AWL   ☐ conduct AWL   ☐ mission
   ☐ assume AWL   ☐ consumer AWL   ☐ out of stock
   ☐ bargain   ☐ findings   ☐ purchase AWL
   ☐ bump   ☐ frustrating   ☐ retail
   ☐ chore   ☐ gender AWL   ☐ sufficient AWL
   ☐ commercial   ☐ interact AWL

MOTHER NATURE 2

A two-toed sloth mother hangs from a tree with her baby at the Aviarios Sloth Sanctuary, Costa Rica.

THINK AND DISCUSS

1 Look at the photo. How would you describe a sloth?

2 As the title "Mother Nature" shows, nature is seen as female in English. Does the word for nature have a gender in your language? What is it?

Look at the photos and read the information. Then discuss the questions.

1. How do bees help flowers reproduce?

2. The baby kangaroo is protected in its mother's pouch for about 10 months. In what other ways do animals protect their young?

3. The life cycle of a salmon is several years. What other animals have short life cycles? What animals have long life cycles?

4. What information was the most surprising to you?

CYCLE OF LIFE

▶ Newborn kangaroos, or joeys, are one inch (2.5 centimeters) long at birth and spend their first four months living in the protection of the mother's pouch. Then the joey begins to leave the pouch for short trips to eat grass. At 10 months, the joey is mature enough to leave the mother's pouch for good.

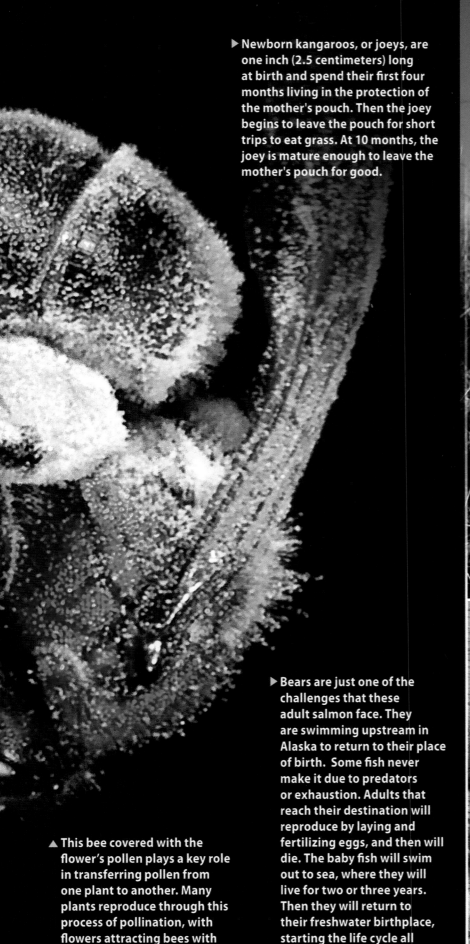

▲ This bee covered with the flower's pollen plays a key role in transferring pollen from one plant to another. Many plants reproduce through this process of pollination, with flowers attracting bees with colors and smells.

▶ Bears are just one of the challenges that these adult salmon face. They are swimming upstream in Alaska to return to their place of birth. Some fish never make it due to predators or exhaustion. Adults that reach their destination will reproduce by laying and fertilizing eggs, and then will die. The baby fish will swim out to sea, where they will live for two or three years. Then they will return to their freshwater birthplace, starting the life cycle all over again.

A Vocabulary

A 🎧 1.13 Look at the photo and read the caption. Then read and listen to the information. Notice each word in **blue** and think about its meaning.

King penguins in tall snowy grass in the spring in the Antarctic

THE KING PENGUIN: Challenges to Reproduction

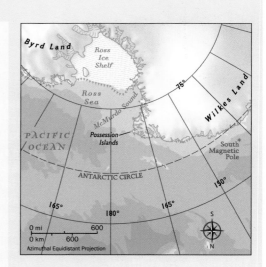

Many islands in the Antarctic such as the Possession Islands have huge **colonies** of king penguins. These birds come to the islands to **reproduce**. Although scientists believe the worldwide population is increasing and king penguins are not in danger of **extinction**, individual birds often have to **struggle** to stay alive.

Weather is one **challenge** that the birds face. This far south, cold temperatures make it hard to keep eggs warm. Female birds share this **responsibility** with their mate. Perhaps surprisingly, climate change can also **threaten** the birds. After eggs hatch, parents feed their chicks. Warmer oceans mean less food nearby. As a result, chicks are left unprotected for longer periods while their parents hunt.

Another **factor** is space. Some colonies have 100,000 or more birds, each of which must find and defend a **territory** of less than three feet (one meter) across. **Predators** are another challenge. Adults must protect young penguins from seals and other sea mammals, and sometimes even from other birds.

B Write each word in **blue** from exercise A next to its definition.

1. _____ (n) a duty that a person or animal has

2. _____ (n) when a species of animal or plant is no longer alive

3. _____ (n) an area of land that belongs to a certain animal

4. _____ (n) animals that eat other animals

5. _____ (n) groups of animals living together in one area

6. _____ (n) something difficult that requires great effort

7. _____ (n) something that partly causes or contributes to a situation

8. _____ (v) to cause danger to

9. _____ (v) to fight or work hard to achieve something

10. _____ (v) to have babies

C Read the statements. Write T for *True* or F for *False*. Then use a dictionary to confirm your answers and correct the false statements.

1. _____ *Extinct* is the adjective form of *extinction*.

2. _____ *Challenge* and *struggle* can be either nouns or verbs.

3. _____ *Colony*, *territory*, and *factor* do not have plural forms.

4. _____ *Threaten* does not have a noun form.

5. _____ *Responsible* is the adjective form of *responsibility*.

D Complete these sentences with the correct form of one of the words in the box. More than one answer may be possible.

challenge	factor	responsibility	struggle	threaten

1. Most people _____ to manage their time.

2. People must always be fully _____ for their actions.

3. Having close friends is a _____ in whether people are happy.

4. People face fewer _____ in life now than in the past.

5. Technology _____ people's relationships with others.

E Work with a partner. Discuss the questions.

1. Do you agree or disagree with each statement in exercise D? Explain.
2. Is there a statement that you and your partner disagree on? Change the sentence so that you both agree with it.

CRITICAL THINKING: EVALUATING

Listening A Panel about a Film Contest

National Geographic filmmaker Bertie Gregory films a baby goat at a farm in Uttarakhand, India.

BEFORE LISTENING

CRITICAL THINKING:
EVALUATING

A Before you listen to the discussion, answer these questions with a partner.

1. In what ways do documentaries differ from other films?
2. Nature is one common subject for documentaries. What other subjects are common?
3. In general, documentaries are less popular than typical Hollywood movies. Why do you think this is?

WHILE LISTENING

LISTENING FOR
MAIN IDEAS

B 🎧 1.14 ▶ 1.3 Listen to the discussion. Then choose the statement that best summarizes what you heard.

a. Some film students are comparing two nature documentaries.
b. Some filmmakers are talking about the best subject for a nature documentary.
c. Some people are discussing a winning nature documentary.

C 🎧 1.14 Listen again. Take notes about each speaker's opinions. Use abbreviations to note who says what. Then use your notes to decide who expressed the opinions below. Write the speaker's initial: *A* for Abdul, *M* for Martha, or *S* for Shannon.

NOTE TAKING

a. _____ There was some effective camerawork and filmmaking.

b. _____ The director did a good job showing the island's climate.

c. _____ The film had moments of danger, humor, and seriousness.

d. _____ The scenes of predators' attacks were hard to watch but necessary to include.

e. _____ The film's music did not match the images on screen.

f. _____ The scenes showing the size of the colony were impressive.

AFTER LISTENING

D Form a small group. Discuss these questions.

PERSONALIZING

1. Would you be interested in watching *The Penguins of Possession Island*? Explain.
2. What documentaries have you watched that you would recommend? Why would you recommend them?
3. In general, do you prefer watching documentaries or other types of movies? Why?

> **CRITICAL THINKING** Deciding on Criteria
>
> When evaluating or deciding something, it is helpful to consider the most important aspects. These are called *criteria* (singular: *criterion*). For example, to choose the winning documentary, the speakers' three criteria were the quality of the camerawork, filmmaking, and music.

E Work with a partner. Follow the steps below. Take notes in your notebook.

CRITICAL THINKING: DECIDING ON CRITERIA

1. Think of a situation you might need to make a decision about. It could be a major or minor decision such as choosing which movie to see with friends, where to attend college, or whom to marry.
2. Brainstorm some criteria you would use to make a decision about it.
3. Decide on the top five criteria, and rank them from most to least important.

F With your partner, present your criteria to the class, but do not mention what situation you are making a decision about. Your classmates will try to infer the situation from your criteria.

A Speaking

PRONUNCIATION Syllable Stress before Suffixes

🎧 **1.15** When suffixes *–ic*, *–ity*, and *–tion* are added to words, the syllable stress changes. The primary stress is on the syllable before the suffix.

romance + –ic → ro**man**tic

possible + –ity → possi**bil**ity

educate + –tion → edu**ca**tion

A 🎧 **1.16** For each word, mark the syllable that you think will have the strongest stress. Then listen to check your answers.

1. academic
2. reproduction
3. responsibility
4. complexity
5. frustration
6. interaction

B Work with a partner. Mark the stressed syllable in each word. Then practice saying each word with the correct syllable stress pattern.

Suffix: *–ic*	Suffix: *–ity*	Suffix: *–tion*
automatic	capacity	construction
domestic	community	information
dynamic	flexibility	motivation
specific	priority	reaction
genetic	electricity	extinction

CRITICAL THINKING: INTERPRETING A FLOWCHART

C 🎧 **1.17** Work in a small group. Study the flowchart on the next page about cloning, which is a technology-assisted form of reproduction. Discuss where the following statements should be added to the chart. Write the statements in the chart. Then check your answers by listening to an instructor explain cloning.

The resulting baby is a clone of the first animal.
A body cell is removed from an adult animal.
Scientists remove the nucleus from that cell.
Chemicals or electricity make the egg divide.

CLONING AN ANIMAL FROM AN ADULT CELL

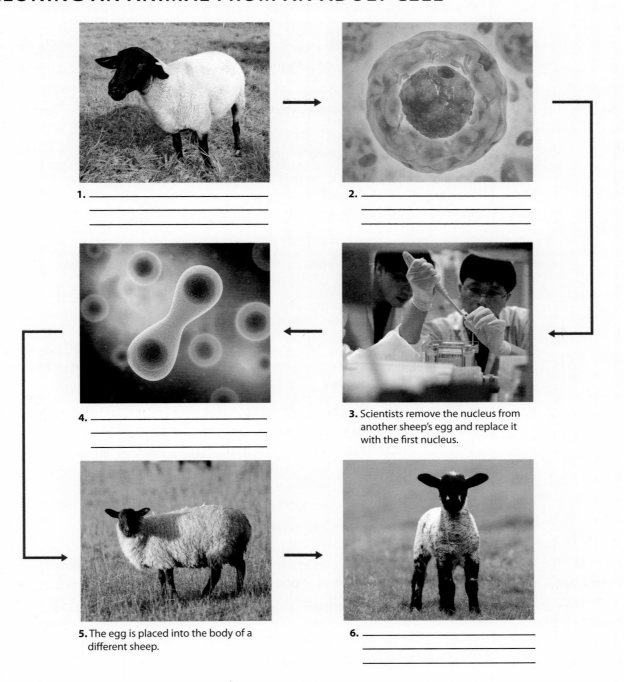

1. _____

2. _____

4. _____

3. Scientists remove the nucleus from another sheep's egg and replace it with the first nucleus.

5. The egg is placed into the body of a different sheep.

6. _____

D Form a small group and discuss the questions.

CRITICAL THINKING: EVALUATING

1. Which of these, if any, do you feel are good reasons for cloning animals? Why?
   • to bring back particular dead animals such as much-loved pets
   • to bring back extinct species such as *Tyrannosaurus Rex* or other dinosaurs
   • to copy animals with certain characteristics such as fast racehorses
   • to produce animals with characteristics that benefit humans
   • to save endangered species such as some types of sea turtles

2. If it were possible for scientists to bring back just one extinct species through cloning, what criteria would you use to decide which species to bring back?

GRAMMAR FOR SPEAKING Adjective Clauses

An adjective clause (also called a relative clause) describes or modifies a noun. We can join two simple sentences together by using an adjective clause.

> I saw a documentary. _It was about king penguins._ →
> I saw a documentary **which/that** _was about king penguins._

If the relative pronoun is the subject of the clause, use _who_ or _that_ for people. Use _that_ or _which_ for animals or things.

> The film showed predators. _They attacked young penguins._ →
> The film showed predators **that/which** _attacked young penguins._

Sometimes, the relative pronoun is the object of the clause. Object relative pronouns are _whom_ (or _who_ in informal language), _that_, and _which_.

> I watched the documentary. You mentioned _it_ to me. →
> I watched the documentary **that/which** _you mentioned to me._

Note: When the relative pronoun is an object, it is often omitted, especially in informal use.

> I watched the documentary you mentioned to me.

E With a partner, take turns forming adjective clauses from these sentences. More than one answer may be possible.

1. King penguins live in large colonies. These may contain 100,000 birds.
2. These penguins have many predators. These include birds and seals.
3. Cloning is a technique. It allows scientists to produce copies of animals.
4. To clone, scientists use a cell. The cell has been taken from an adult animal.
5. Ken Burns is a filmmaker. He is best known for his history documentaries.
6. Many of his films are about important events. These events changed history.
7. I went to the documentary film festival. You told me about it.

CRITICAL THINKING: EVALUATING

F Discuss the following question in a small group. What criteria must a film or person meet in order to win an award in one of these categories?

- Criteria for best documentary: _____

_____

- Criteria for best director: _____

_____

A: _I think best documentary should be a film that tells an interesting true story._
B: _Right, but it also needs to be a film that has amazing camerawork, don't you think?_
C: _Sure. But for me, the most important criterion is that it should challenge my thinking._

LESSON TASK Discussing Conservation and Extinction

The number of giant pandas in the wild has been rising in China. The population has grown due to increased protection from hunters and expansion of protected habitat.

EVERYDAY LANGUAGE   Asking for Repetition

More Formal: *Could you say that again?*   Less Formal: *Come again?*
                   I missed that, I'm afraid.   *What's that?*
                   Sorry. I didn't catch that.   *Sorry?*

A   Work in a small group. Discuss what factors can lead to the extinction of a species. Use different ways to ask for repetition if necessary.

A: *I think that some species go extinct because of climate change.*
B: *Sorry. I didn't catch that.*
A: *I said climate change can cause some species to go extinct.*

B   In your group, rank these ideas in order from most important (1) to least important (4) as reasons in favor of species conservation.

CRITICAL THINKING: RANKING

_____ Some endangered species provide economic benefits (e.g., ecotourism).
_____ The extinction of one plant or animal can affect other plants and animals.
_____ Some endangered species could be a source of medicine for humans.
_____ Humans share Earth with other species; every species deserves to live.

C   In your group, complete these steps. Make notes about your ideas.

PRESENTING

1. Decide on a plant or animal species to discuss.
2. Discuss how life would be affected if this species suddenly went extinct.
3. Discuss what humans could do to make sure this species does not become extinct.

D   Select one group member to present your ideas to the class. Say which species you chose and why it is important, what might happen if it went extinct, and how humans could conserve it.

A rare Kemp's ridley sea turtle swims near Cocos Island off the coast of Costa Rica.

Costa Rica

Turtles under Threat

BEFORE VIEWING

A In Lesson A, you explored challenges to a species' survival. In this video, you will learn about a low-tech way to save one species of sea turtle. Before you watch, discuss the questions below with a partner.

1. The Kemp's ridley sea turtle is the most endangered of all sea turtles. What human activities do you think threaten it?
2. In addition to the threats posed by humans, what other challenges do these turtles probably face?

B Complete these sentences to define words from the video. Then mark the adjective clause in each sentence.

biologists	exclude	population	species
device	marine		

1. A group of animals that can reproduce with one another is called a(n) _____.
2. The _____ of a species is all the individuals that are members of that species.
3. _____ creatures such as sharks and shrimp are animals that live in the sea.
4. Scientists who study life and living organisms are called _____.
5. People usually _____ something that they neither want nor need.
6. A machine or tool that has a special function is called a(n) _____.

WHILE VIEWING

C ▶ **1.4** Watch the video. Then answer each question.

UNDERSTANDING MAIN IDEAS

1. What is the Turtle Excluder Device?
   a. a new type of fishing net
   b. an improved fishing boat

2. Why is the device needed?
   a. to help marine species reproduce
   b. to protect one kind of sea turtle

3. How does the device work?
   a. It separates large animals from small ones.
   b. It lets fishermen see what they have caught.

4. In the United States, who must use the device?
   a. biologists who study sharks and turtles
   b. fishermen who mostly catch shrimp

D ▶ **1.4** Watch the video again and take notes in the T-chart about the advantages and disadvantages of the Turtle Excluder Device.

NOTE TAKING

Disadvantage(s) to Fishermen (according to some fishermen)	Advantage(s) to Fishermen (according to biologists)

AFTER VIEWING

E Work in a small group. Complete these steps.

CRITICAL THINKING: SYNTHESIZING

1. Predict some questions and concerns that fishermen might have about using the Turtle Excluder Device.
2. Come up with answers to these questions and concerns that would make fishermen feel positive about using the device.
3. Join with another group. Share the questions and concerns you predicted and the answers you came up with.

B Vocabulary

A 🎧 1.18 Look at the photo and read the caption. Then read and listen to the interview.
Notice each word in **blue** and think about its meaning.

ALL ABOUT ORCHIDS

Host: Joining me today is Dr. Sam Darrow, a botanist[1] who **specializes** in the study of orchids. Welcome, Dr. Darrow. So, tell me: what factors led to your interest in orchids?

Dr. Darrow: When I was a child, my father grew orchids at home. At first, I loved them for their beauty. But over time, I noticed how amazing they are.

Host: Amazing? How?

Dr. Darrow: Well, like every living **organism**, orchids need to reproduce. Their **primary** way to do this is to **manufacture** nectar, which insects love. When insects visit orchids and **consume** this sweet liquid, they get covered in pollen. This is a **substance** that contains DNA. The insects **transfer** this DNA to other orchids, and reproduction can take place.

Host: So, that's an interesting **method**: use something sweet to attract insects in order to reproduce. What other ways do they attract insects?

Dr. Darrow: One species of orchids smells like dirty diapers[2]. To us, this scent is unpleasant, but it's attractive to some insects. And *Epidendrum* orchids **resemble** milkweed, a favorite food of butterflies, but actually aren't food at all.

Host: So it's a trick.

Dr. Darrow: Right! Butterflies visit expecting food, but get only pollen. Other orchids play different tricks. Some look like typical places where insects make homes or find **shelter** during bad weather. Insects visit, get covered with pollen, but soon leave when they find out the flowers are not good places to live.

Host: Thank you, Dr. Darrow. I've learned a lot.

An *Epidendrum* orchid is
pollinated by a butterfly.

[1] **botanist** (n): a scientist who specializes in the study of plants
[2] **diaper** (n): a type of underwear for babies

Context clues can help you understand the meaning of words and phrases as well as their part of speech. Context clues can be found in the words and phrases around a particular word.

> One species of orchids smells like dirty diapers. To us, this **scent** is unpleasant, but it's attractive to some insects.

The context clues *smells, dirty diapers, unpleasant,* and *attractive* help us understand that *scent* probably means a smell. The word *this* before *scent* tells us that *scent* is a noun.

B With a partner, use context clues to decide whether each word in **blue** in exercise A is a noun, verb, or adjective.

C Read the descriptions. Use context clues to write a definition of each bold word. Then check your definitions in a dictionary.

In nature, some predators **specialize** in hunting a particular species. To protect themselves from these attacks, some species **resemble** something else. For example, stick insects look like small sticks. This **method** of protection works because predators think they are part of a tree, not something to eat.

1. To specialize means to _____.

2. To resemble means to _____.

3. A method is a(n) _____.

Some species of penguins **consume** a lot of krill, which are tiny sea **organisms** that look like shrimp. Krill are among the most abundant species in the world. The **primary** foods consumed by king penguins, however, are fish and squid.

4. To consume means to _____.

5. An organism is a(n) _____.

6. Primary means _____.

Crabs use a **substance** called calcium carbonate to **manufacture** a hard shell. This shell covers and protects their body. Hermit crabs, in contrast, cannot produce their own shell and must use one produced by another organism for **shelter**. As a hermit crab grows and its borrowed shell becomes too small, it simply **transfers** itself to a larger one.

7. A substance is a(n) _____.

8. To manufacture means to _____.

9. Shelter is _____.

10. To transfer means to _____.

Listening A Conversation on Campus

This red air plant is an epiphyte.

BEFORE LISTENING

LISTENING SKILL Listening for Content Words

🎧 1.19 Content words, which are usually nouns and verbs, carry most of the meaning in a sentence. Speakers usually emphasize content words slightly more than other words.

> When I was a **child**, my **father** grew **orchids** at **home**. At first, I **loved** them for their **beauty**. But over **time**, I **noticed** how **amazing** they are.

Because content words are stressed more, you can concentrate on listening for them. This is helpful because if you understand the content words, you will generally have a good idea of what a speaker is talking about.

A 🎧 1.20 Read the beginning of a conversation between two people. Mark the words that you think are the content words. Then listen to see which words are stressed.

Leo: Excuse me? Sorry to bother you, but do you know the way to the conservatory greenhouse? This map isn't helping me much.

Elena: Yeah, the map isn't great and the campus does resemble a maze, doesn't it? Anyway, you're in luck. I'm actually on my way to the conservatory greenhouse right now. We can walk together.

WHILE LISTENING

B 🎧 1.21 Listen to the whole conversation. Then answer the questions.

LISTENING FOR
MAIN IDEAS

1. Who are the two speakers?
   a. professors
   b. scientists
   c. students
2. What do they mainly discuss?
   a. how to get somewhere
   b. what a lecture may cover
   c. what somebody is like
3. What kind of organisms do they mostly discuss?
   a. insects
   b. epiphytes
   c. trees

C 🎧 1.22 Listen again to part of the conversation. Then answer the questions. Mark T for *True*, F for *False*, or NG if the information is *Not Given*.

LISTENING FOR
DETAILS

	T	F	NG
1. Leo, the male student, is new to the campus.	T	F	NG
2. Elena, the female student, knows a lot about epiphytes.	T	F	NG
3. Elena is in her second year of college.	T	F	NG
4. Epiphytes are plants that get water from the air.	T	F	NG
5. Epiphytes usually grow in places with a humid climate.	T	F	NG
6. Many varieties of epiphytes grow in Florida.	T	F	NG
7. Professor Darrow rarely studies orchids or epiphytes.	T	F	NG

AFTER LISTENING

D Work in a small group. Discuss the questions.

CRITICAL THINKING:
REFLECTING

1. When you are lost, are you comfortable asking a stranger for directions? Why or why not?
2. In general, are you comfortable talking to people you don't know? Why or why not?
3. What are some situations in which you might need to begin a conversation with a stranger? What strategies could you use to start talking to that person?
4. Would you be interested in taking a class that focuses on plant life? Why or why not?
5. Why is it important to study how plants survive in a variety of conditions? What useful information can we learn?

B Speaking

College students in Jeddah, Saudi Arabia

BRAINSTORMING **A** Work with a partner. Look at the idea map and add one more common challenge. Then brainstorm at least two possible solutions for each one and add them to the map.

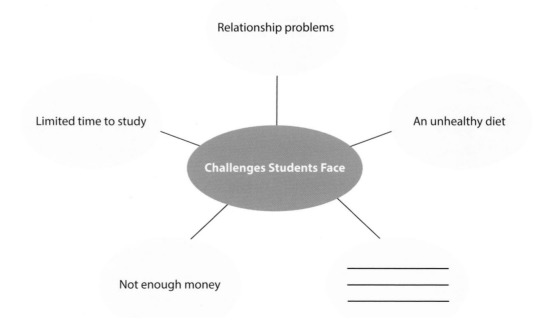

Relationship problems

Limited time to study

An unhealthy diet

Challenges Students Face

Not enough money

_____
_____
_____

SPEAKING SKILL Making Suggestions

There are several expressions you can use to make a suggestion to someone.

Why don't you go …?   *You should make …*

Have you considered doing …?   *I recommend talking …*

You could take …   *I suggest that you get …*

To make a suggestion less strong, use an adverb like *maybe* or *perhaps*. To make a suggestion stronger, use an adverb like *strongly* or *really*.

Maybe you could leave …   I **really** recommend doing …

Perhaps you should go …   I **strongly** suggest that you plan …

B Interview several students in your class. Take turns asking which of the problems from exercise A they have experienced and make suggestions.

C Work with a partner you did not interview in exercise B. Take turns sharing some of the best suggestions you were given.

FINAL TASK Creating and Presenting a Proposal

> You are going to create and present a short proposal for a 10-minute nature documentary.

A Work with two or three students. Brainstorm answers to the following questions. When making your decisions, you may find it helpful to discuss key criteria first.

BRAINSTORMING

- What species will our documentary be about? Why?
- What aspect of this species' life will we focus on? Why?
- What will be the main scenes in our documentary? Why?
- Which country or countries will we need to travel to? Why?
- What will be unique or special about our documentary?

B In your group, make a presentation plan by answering the following questions.

ORGANIZING
INFORMATION

- In what order will we present information about our documentary? Why?
- Who will present which information? (Everyone in your group should speak.)
- How will we present the information? For example, will we use visuals, create slides, or write anything on the board? Why or why not?

PRESENTATION SKILL Presenting with Others

Before your group presentation, select a member to be a time-keeper. This will help you keep to your time limit and not go off topic. Decide on a signal that the time-keeper can give.

When you introduce your group presentation, let your audience know who will say what and when:

> *First, Ahmed will talk about . . .*
>
> *Then Maria will discuss . . .*
>
> *And finally, I'll cover . . .*

It also helps your audience if you give clear transitions between each speaker:

> *Now I'm going to hand this over to Maria, who'll give more information about . . .*
>
> *Next Alex is going to discuss some important points about . . .*

C After you have made your plan, practice your presentation. Make sure you include an introduction of your group members and transitions between speakers.

PRESENTING **D** As a group, present information about your proposed documentary to the class. After your presentation, invite the class to ask questions or make suggestions about how your documentary could be improved.

E As a class, talk about what you liked about the documentary proposals, and why. Then vote on which were the best three documentary ideas.

REFLECTION

1. What specific skill that you learned in this unit is the most useful one for you? Why?

   _____

   _____

2. Has your attitude toward wild animals changed in any way after studying this unit? Explain.

   _____

   _____

3. Here are the vocabulary words from the unit. Check (✓) the ones you can use.

   ☐ challenge AWL   ☐ organism   ☐ specialize

   ☐ colony   ☐ predator   ☐ struggle

   ☐ consume AWL   ☐ primary AWL   ☐ substance

   ☐ extinction   ☐ reproduce   ☐ territory

   ☐ factor AWL   ☐ resemble   ☐ threaten

   ☐ manufacture   ☐ responsibility   ☐ transfer AWL

   ☐ method AWL   ☐ shelter

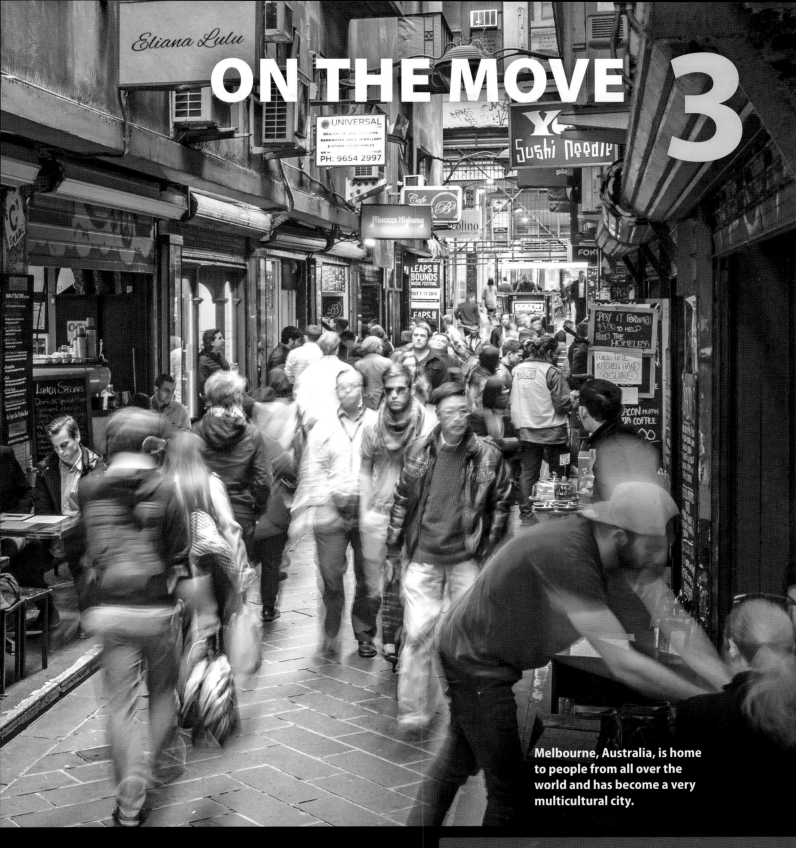

Eliana Lulu

ON THE MOVE 3

Melbourne, Australia, is home to people from all over the world and has become a very multicultural city.

ACADEMIC SKILLS

LISTENING   Listening for the Order of Events
           Noting Contrasting Ideas
SPEAKING   Expressing Probability
           Linking
CRITICAL THINKING   Categorizing Information

THINK AND DISCUSS

1   Why do you think people might have moved to Melbourne, Australia? What may have attracted them to the city?

2   Multicultural means representing many nationalities or ethnic groups. Describe a multicultural area in a city that you are familiar with.

EXPLORE THE THEME

Look at the map and key and read the captions. Then answer the questions.

1. What do the arrows and circles show?
2. Which two cities receive the greatest number of immigrants?
3. Which two cities have the largest proportion of residents who are immigrants?
4. Why do you think the cities on the map are called gateway cities?

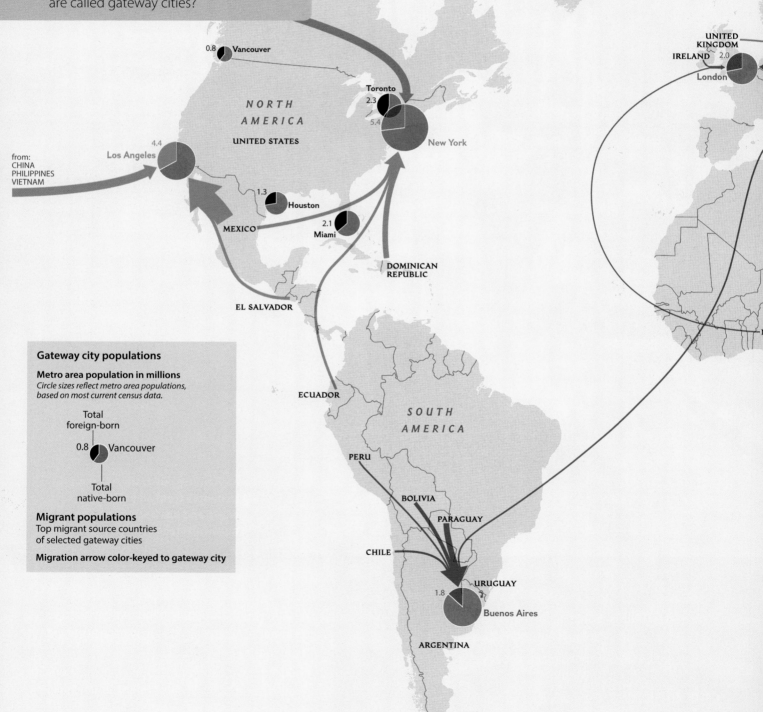

0.8 Vancouver

UNITED KINGDOM
IRELAND 2.0
London

NORTH AMERICA

Toronto
2.3
5.4

UNITED STATES

New York

from:
CHINA
PHILIPPINES
VIETNAM

Los Angeles 4.4

1.3
Houston

MEXICO

2.1
Miami

DOMINICAN REPUBLIC

EL SALVADOR

NI

Gateway city populations

Metro area population in millions
Circle sizes reflect metro area populations, based on most current census data.

Total foreign-born

0.8 Vancouver

Total native-born

ECUADOR

SOUTH AMERICA

PERU

Migrant populations
Top migrant source countries of selected gateway cities

BOLIVIA

PARAGUAY

Migration arrow color-keyed to gateway city

CHILE

URUGUAY

1.8

Buenos Aires

ARGENTINA

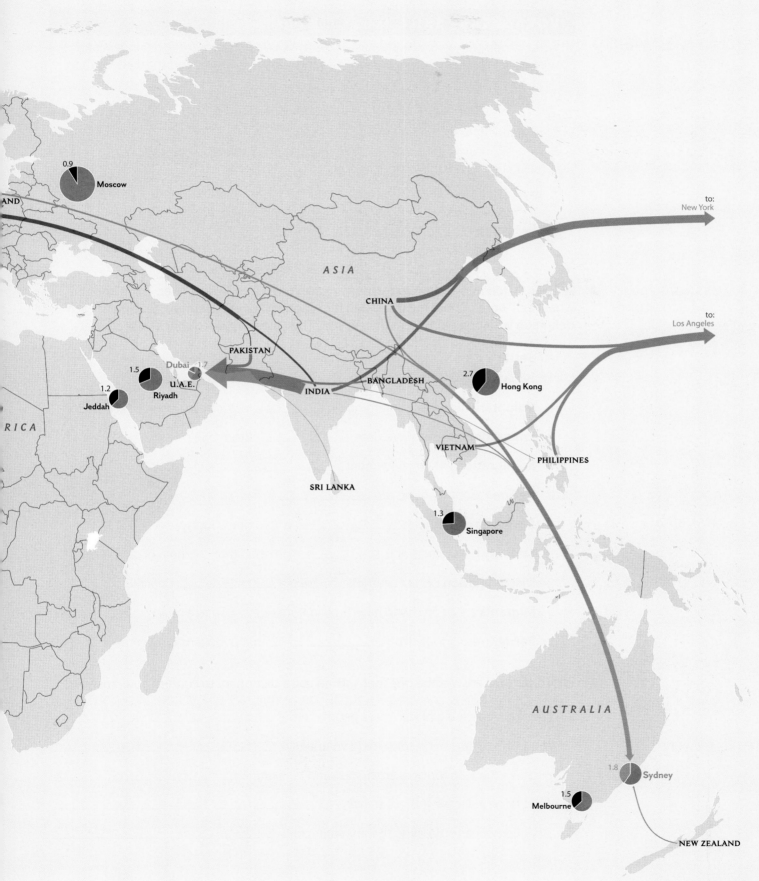

0.9 Moscow

ASIA

to:
New York

CHINA

to:
Los Angeles

PAKISTAN

1.5 Dubai 1.7
U.A.E.
Riyadh

1.2
Jeddah

2.7 Hong Kong

BANGLADESH

INDIA

AFRICA

VIETNAM

PHILIPPINES

SRI LANKA

1.3
Singapore

AUSTRALIA

1.8 Sydney

1.5
Melbourne

NEW ZEALAND

A Vocabulary

MEANING FROM CONTEXT

A 🎧 1.23 Listen to five short excerpts from a lecture you will hear later. Think about what each word in **blue** means. Listen for synonyms or explanations. Complete each definition with one word from the excerpt. Then listen again to check your answers.

1. a. **Settle** means to move to a new country or _____ and make a home there.

   b. **Voluntary** describes something that _____ have freely chosen to do.

2. a. **Emigration** means movement _____ from one place.

   b. **Immigration** means movement _____ somewhere.

3. a. **Nation** is another word for _____.

   b. **Domestic** migration is _____, within one country.

4. a. **Stability** is a political or _____ situation that is certain or safe.

   b. **Discrimination** occurs when people treat a _____ unfairly.

5. a. **Migrants** are people who have moved from one region to a new _____.

   b. **Barrier** means some kind of _____ that people must overcome.

B With a partner, answer the questions. Then use a dictionary to confirm your answers.

1. What noun means a place where people settle? _____

2. What verb means to do something voluntarily? _____

3. What are the verb forms of _emigration_ and _immigration_? _____

4. What is the adjective form of _stability_? _____

5. What verb means the thing that migrants do? _____

Workers from Romania at an apple orchard in Spain.

ROMANIA

C Read the article and fill in the blanks with the correct word from exercise A. Two of the words from exercise A will not be used.

MIGRATION IN ROMANIA

Romania is the largest _____ in southeastern Europe. It has a population
1

of around 20 million people. At the end of the last century, Romania saw a lot of

_____ migration. People moved from the countryside to large cities such
2

as Bucharest. Since joining the European Union in 2007, migration out of the country

has become more common. Studies show that up to 2.5 million Romanians have

made a(n) _____ choice to leave the country in recent years. Some of these
3

people have chosen to _____ in Spain and Italy. Because Romanian is a
4

Romance language like Spanish and Italian, the language _____ in these
5

countries may be easier for Romanian _____ to overcome. In addition
6

to _____ from Romania, over a quarter of a million people have moved
7

into the country recently. Most of this _____ comes from the Republic
8

of Moldova, a small country that borders Romania and has Romanian as its official

language.

D Discuss these questions in a small group.

1. If you could settle in any nation in the world, where would you choose?
2. Are you more interested in domestic news or international news?
3. What is one barrier to learning English that you are working to overcome?

A Listening A Lecture about Migration

BEFORE LISTENING

PREDICTING **A** Work in a small group. You will hear a lecture in which a professor discusses some reasons why people migrate. Look at the photos and discuss what reasons they represent. Then predict some other reasons the professor might mention.

The effects of drought in East Kenya

An unemployed man looking for work

WHILE LISTENING

LISTENING FOR MAIN IDEAS **B** 🎧 1.24 ▶ 1.5 Listen to the lecture. Check (✓) the statements that match points the professor makes.

1. _____ There are two kinds of migration: domestic and international.

2. _____ Push factors give people a reason to emigrate from a country.

3. _____ Pull factors make a country attractive to potential immigrants.

4. _____ Countries with strong economies rarely experience emigration.

5. _____ Push and pull factors can be divided into several categories.

6. _____ The majority of people who migrate can speak two languages.

NOTE-TAKING SKILL Noting Contrasting Ideas

During lectures or presentations, it is common for speakers to contrast one idea with one or more other ideas. In some cases, the ideas may be different such as economic stability and political stability; in other cases, they may be opposite ideas such as immigration and emigration. When you hear speakers mention contrasting ideas, make a note of what they say. You can use a slash (/) to mark a contrast.

C 🎧 1.24 Listen again to the lecture. As you listen, complete these notes with words from the lecture. Write one word only in each blank.

Migration can be:

- forced or _____
  1

- domestic or _____
  2

Emigration = out of a country

Immigration = into a country

Push factors – cause emigration

- economic / societal / _____
  3

_____ factors – attract immigration:
  4

- also economic / societal / environmental

Exact reason(s) for migration typically _____ of push and pull factors;
  5

(for both: _____ factors usually most important)
  6

New migrants may face _____ barrier; discrimination
  7

AFTER LISTENING

D Work with a partner. Think of a city, area, or country you would both be interested in migrating to. Which factors might influence your decision? Fill in the chart. Then share your ideas with the class. Which factors seem to be strongest?

Where we would migrate to: _____		
	Push Factors	Pull Factors
Economic		
Societal		
Environmental		

A Speaking

GRAMMAR FOR SPEAKING *Enough* and *Too*

To say that there is the right amount of something, use adjective + *enough* or *enough* + noun.

> Their income is **high enough** to live in a great neighborhood.
> They have **enough money** to live wherever they want.

To say that you need more of something, use *not* + adjective + *enough* or the negative form of a verb + *enough* + noun.

> His grades are **not good enough** to get into Harvard, unfortunately.
> He **did not spend enough time** on his college applications.

To say that something is negative because it is more than necessary or more than you want, use *too* + adjective.

> She didn't buy it because she felt the price was **too high**.

To say that something is negative because it is more/less than necessary, use *too* + *much/little* + uncountable noun or *too* + *many/few* + plural noun.

> That restaurant uses **too much salt** in many of its dishes.
> The restaurant closed down because **too few people** ate there.

A Interview two of your classmates. Write their answers in the blanks. When it is your turn to be interviewed, speak in full sentences.

1. What is a book you have read that was good enough to read at least twice?

   _____   _____

2. What is something you want that you don't have enough money to buy?

   _____   _____

3. What is one kind of food you love but think is too unhealthy to eat often?

   _____   _____

4. What is something you enjoy that you have too little time to do these days?

   _____   _____

5. What is one annoying thing you think too many people are doing these days?

   _____   _____

B Work with a partner you didn't interview in exercise A. Share what you learned about one of the people you interviewed.

> *One of the people I interviewed was Jung Ho. He said that …*

The Hundertwasser House, an apartment building in Vienna, Austria

C Work in a small group. Think about what makes a city a great place to live. Complete the sentences with different ideas. Then compare your answers with another group.

1. A city needs to have enough _Hospital_.

2. There should be enough _____.

3. There shouldn't be too much _Ghetto Gun Violence_

4. _Hospital and Education_ shouldn't be too expensive.

5. The city shouldn't have too many _Homeless_.

PRONUNCIATION Linking

🎧 1.25 In natural, fluent speech, speakers typically link certain sounds.

1. A consonant sound with a vowel sound:

    The magazine publishes a list of the most livable cities.

2. A consonant sound with the same consonant sound:

    This neighborhood has some cheap places to live.

3. A vowel sound with a vowel sound:

    High housing costs are often a barrier to owning a home.

The Peace Bridge, for pedestrians and bicyclists, crosses the Bow River in Calgary, Canada.

D 🎧 1.26 Read the information about livable cities. How do you think each sentence would be spoken with linked sounds? Mark the links between sounds. Then listen to confirm your answers. Practice saying the sentences.

> *The Economist* magazine publishes an annual list of cities with the best living conditions. These "World's Most Livable Cities" have many of the things that people want in a city. These things include access to health care, good or great transportation, and relatively cheap places to live. In recent years, Melbourne in Australia, Vienna in Austria, and Vancouver, Toronto, and Calgary in Canada have all been in the top five.

E Think about a city you know well. Make notes in answer to these questions.

- What is the city called and where is it?
- What does the city have enough of?
- What does the city have too much of?
- How livable do you think the city is?

CRITICAL THINKING: EVALUATING

F Work in a small group. Summarize your ideas from exercise E. Then discuss what specific features make a city attractive and livable.

< *I like San Jose because it's big enough to have a good variety of things to do.*

LESSON TASK Discussing a Case Study

CRITICAL THINKING   Categorizing Information

An important part of critical thinking is being able to put ideas or information into categories or groups. You might categorize cities according to how livable they are, to their size, or to their geographical location.

A Work with a partner. Read the case study. Then add notes to complete the chart.

CRITICAL THINKING: CATEGORIZING INFORMATION

Case Study

Lana, who is 30 years old, lives in Zagreb, the capital of Croatia. She studied architecture at university. However, there are too few jobs for architects in her country, which makes it hard for her to find work in her field. As a result, she currently works as a retail assistant in a store. She can only work part-time because she also has to spend time taking care of her parents, both of whom are in poor health. Lana has heard that there are not enough architects and other professionals in New Zealand. Lana's husband, who is a nurse, argues that he and Lana should emigrate there even though neither of them speaks English well.

Reasons to Stay	Reasons to Move	
	Push Factors	Pull Factors

EVERYDAY LANGUAGE   Asking for or Giving Reasons

Asking for reasons	Giving reasons
Why do you say/think that?	*Why do I say/think this? Well, …*
What's your reason for saying that?	*My main reason is that ….*

B Your teacher will assign you to one of the groups below. Work with your group members to follow the steps.

CRITICAL THINKING: APPLYING

Group A – Lana should stay in Croatia
Group B – Lana should move to New Zealand

1. In your group, discuss the reasons that support your position.
2. Groups A and B debate whether Lana should stay or leave by taking turns to give their reasons.
3. Have a class vote to decide which team had the stronger argument.

A photo of immigrants on a wall of the abandoned Ellis Island Hospital is part of an art installation by French artist JR.

What Ellis Island Means Today

BEFORE VIEWING

A Work with a partner. Match these words from the video to their definitions. Then use a dictionary to check your answers.

Word	Meaning
1. _____ ancestors (n)	a. (informal) brave or showing courage
2. _____ faith (n)	b. a person who lives in a particular place
3. _____ generation (n)	c. a strong belief that something is good or true
4. _____ gutsy (adj)	d. people who are about the same age
5. _____ liberty (n)	e. freedom to live the way you want
6. _____ resident (n)	f. family members who lived a long time ago

B In a small group, read this short history of Ellis Island. Then discuss the questions.

> Between 1892 and 1954, more than 12 million immigrants entered the United States through Ellis Island. After arrival, they were checked for health issues. They were also asked 29 interview questions, including some about the United States such as: What is the national anthem called? What are the three branches of government? Who was the first president? Who is the current president? What are the names of the 13 original colonies?

1. How many of the five questions can you answer? Where could you find the answers to the questions you don't know?
2. Do you think immigrants should be asked questions like these? Why or why not?

WHILE VIEWING

C ▶ 1.6 Watch the video. Which statement best summarizes the main message of the video?

UNDERSTANDING
MAIN IDEAS

a. Many citizens of the United States currently live on Ellis Island.
b. Ellis Island is important in the family history of many Americans.
c. The Statue of Liberty is a symbol of the long history of Ellis Island.
d. Most immigrants on Ellis Island were concerned about their bags.

D ▶ 1.6 Watch the video again. Correct these details. You will hear somebody say the correct information and/or see it on the screen.

UNDERSTANDING
DETAILS

1. David Luchsinger is the son of people who came through Ellis Island.

2. Just over 1.8 million bags were lost in the United States in 2012.

3. Judith Leavell's grandmother was 30 when she arrived at Ellis Island.

4. Peter Wong's grandparents emigrated to Ellis Island from Hong Kong.

5. Raea Hillebrant says her ancestors emigrated from Lithuania in 1940.

6. The maximum number of daily visitors to Ellis Island during the summer is about 18,000.

AFTER VIEWING

E In the video, we learned that immigrants to Ellis Island only brought one or two bags. If you were emigrating to another country and could only bring one suitcase, what would you put in it? Make a list, and then share your ideas with a partner.

PERSONALIZING

F Work in a small group. Complete the steps.

CRITICAL THINKING:
CATEGORIZING

1. Brainstorm some of the emotions that immigrants to Ellis Island might have felt.
2. Sort your list of emotions into two categories: positive and negative.
3. Join with another group and share your lists.

Vocabulary

A 🎧 1.27 Read and listen to the reports. Then work with a partner and discuss the likely meaning of each word in **blue**.

1. The professor began her lecture with an **overview** of migration within the United States in the middle of the nineteenth century. She said that for much of that period, the midwest and western regions were seen as the **frontier**.

2. The speaker explained that these days, more and more people are choosing to **relocate** from rural to urban areas. These people believe they have the **prospect** of a better life in a city.

3. The architect described a new high-tech **habitat** designed for areas with dangerous climates. Its most important **aspect** is its weight. Although designed for two dozen people to live in comfortably, it weighs less than a car.

4. The presenter argued that in the future, humans might live elsewhere in the **solar** system such as on Mars or even Mercury, the closest planet to the sun. He said that humans might **colonize** other planets within the next few decades.

5. The engineer gave a talk on some of the dangers people would **encounter** if they were to move to another planet. Despite the risks, she was optimistic that new technologies would soon allow humans to **survive** on other planets.

B Complete each definition with one of the words in **blue** from exercise A.

1. _____ (n) the edge of explored and civilized land

2. _____ (v) to send people to another place to gain control of it

3. _____ (n) a general review or summary of a subject or topic

4. _____ (v) to move somewhere new

5. _____ (v) to unexpectedly find or experience something

6. _____ (v) to continue to live, especially under difficult conditions

7. _____ (n) a place in which an animal or plant usually lives; a home

8. _____ (n) the possibility of some future event happening

9. _____ (adj) relating to the sun

10. _____ (n) a specific feature or part of something

C Work with a different partner. Take turns answering these questions.

1. What is one movie that you enjoyed watching? Give a short overview of it.
2. Where would you like to relocate to? Why?
3. Think about one of your dreams for the future. What is the prospect that it will come true?
4. What is your favorite subject at school? Which aspect of it do you like most?
5. Think about a difficult situation you have encountered. How did you deal with it?

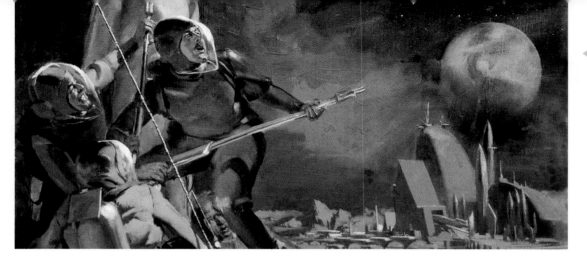

D Fill in this chart with as many nouns as you know. Then use a dictionary to fill in words you don't know and to check the meanings of each word.

Verb	Noun(s)
colonize	(3)
encounter	(1)
relocate	(1)
survive	(2)

E ∩ 1.28 Complete this description with the correct form of words from exercise A. You will need to use three different forms of one word. Then listen to check your answers.

In his classic science fiction novel *Red Mars*, Kim Stanley Robinson tells the

tale of a human _____ on Mars. The story describes the initial

1

struggle for _____ of a small number of people in an artificial

2

_____ on the surface of Mars. The other two books in the trilogy, *Green*

3

Mars and *Blue Mars*, focus on the challenges—physical, emotional, and even social—

that these people _____ as they live on the _____

4   5

of human civilization. They also tell how the _____ turn Mars into

6

a planet suitable for human life and then _____ other places in our

7

_____ system.

8

F Work in a small group. Discuss how you feel about science fiction movies and books. Use some of the adjectives below, and give examples to support your views.

appealing	dramatic	fascinating	uninteresting
childish	entertaining	realistic	unlikely

A: *I'm not a fan of science fiction, to be honest. For me, it's … because …*
B: *I'm the opposite. I really find sci-fi to be … The reason is that …*

Listening A Study Group Discussion

BEFORE LISTENING

A Work in a small group. You are going to listen to three students discussing a presentation assignment. Based on what you've studied so far in Lesson B, what do you think their presentation will be about? Which aspects of giving a presentation might they discuss?

WHILE LISTENING

> **LISTENING SKILL** Listening for the Order of Events
>
> The specific order of actions or events is often important. The order in which speakers discuss information is often the same as the order of actions or events. However, sometimes speakers may discuss information out of order. Speakers can give the order by using:
>
> 1. Sequence words
>   *First, … / Then …, / After that, … / Finally, …*
>
> 2. Time adverbs and adverbial phrases
>   *Initially, … / At the same time, … / Until … / Eventually, … / At the end, …*
>
> 3. Time prepositions or conjunctions
>   *Before … / After … / During … / While … / When …*
>
> 4. Verbal phrases
>   *To start off with, … / Now moving on, … / To conclude, …*

LISTENING FOR
ORDER OF EVENTS

B 🎧 **1.29** Listen to three students discussing a presentation they are going to give. Number these topics in the order students discuss them.

a. _____ what information their talk should include

b. _____ what their presentation should be titled

c. _____ when and where they should next meet

d. _____ which of them should discuss which points

LISTENING FOR
DETAILS

C 🎧 **1.29** Listen again to the conversation. Take notes on the decisions that the students make.

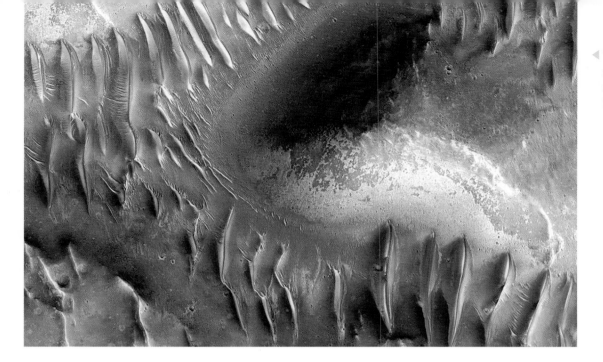

▶ **This image of the surface of Mars shows dunes that have formed.**

D 🎧 1.30 Complete this summary, using your notes from exercise C. Write no more than three words in each blank. Then listen to check your answers.

The students discuss a presentation they are going to give. First, they decide on "Human Migration: _____ 1 " as the title of their presentation. After that, they agree that their talk should include information about the various _____ 2 factors that might cause people to leave Earth. They also discuss the types of _____ 3 that humans will need if they are going to live on other worlds and when emigration to such places might happen. After that, the students decide that their talk should mention which _____ 4 are likely to want to leave Earth. Finally, they agree that their presentation should include information about which other places in the _____ 5 such as the moon or Mars humans might emigrate to.

AFTER LISTENING

E Work in a small group. Discuss these questions.

CRITICAL THINKING: EVALUATING

1. Look back at your ideas for exercise A. Which of your predictions were true about the discussion?
2. Choose one of the ideas below that you think the three students should also include in their presentation. Explain the reasons for your choice.

   a. how much human colonization of other worlds is expected to cost
   b. what issues humans who emigrate to other worlds are likely to face
   c. which countries, groups, or organizations should colonize space first

B Speaking

There are several ways you can express how probable or improbable a future event is.

probable

I am sure that I will graduate this year.
I will definitely graduate this year.
It's possible that I will graduate.
I may graduate.
It seems unlikely I will graduate.
I probably won't graduate.
There's no chance I will graduate.
I definitely won't graduate.

improbable

A For each question below, ask a student and record the answer. Then share what you learned with somebody you did not interview.

1. What is something that you think is certain to happen in the future?

_____ thinks _____.

2. What is something that you imagine will probably happen in the future?

_____ imagines _____.

3. What is something that you believe is unlikely to happen in the future?

_____ believes _____.

4. What is something that you feel will definitely not happen in the future?

_____ feels _____.

CRITICAL THINKING: CATEGORIZING

B Work with a partner. Brainstorm some reasons why people might want to emigrate from Earth to another planet. Fill in the T-chart to categorize each idea as either a push factor or a pull factor.

Push factors from Earth	Pull factors to a planet

C 🎧 1.31 Look at the infographic on the next page about SpaceX, a company that designs space transport. Add a phrase from the list below to complete each caption. Then listen to check your answers.

- 115 days
- $10 billion
- $100,000
- 75 pounds
- 200 people
- −80 degrees
- the year 2024
- 8 billion people

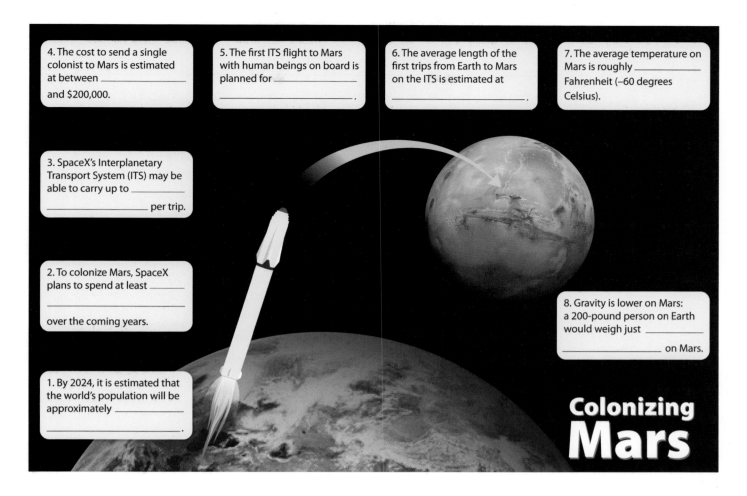

4. The cost to send a single colonist to Mars is estimated at between _____ and $200,000.

5. The first ITS flight to Mars with human beings on board is planned for _____.

6. The average length of the first trips from Earth to Mars on the ITS is estimated at _____.

7. The average temperature on Mars is roughly _____ Fahrenheit (–60 degrees Celsius).

3. SpaceX's Interplanetary Transport System (ITS) may be able to carry up to _____ per trip.

2. To colonize Mars, SpaceX plans to spend at least _____ over the coming years.

8. Gravity is lower on Mars: a 200-pound person on Earth would weigh just _____ on Mars.

1. By 2024, it is estimated that the world's population will be approximately _____.

Colonizing Mars

D How likely is it that each of these things will happen? Discuss in a small group. Support your ideas with reasons and details.

- SpaceX will achieve its goal of colonizing Mars for less than the estimated budget.
- SpaceX will achieve its goal of sending a crewed mission to Mars before 2030.

E Work in a small group. What skills or knowledge will the first colonists on Mars need? Note your ideas under the correct category. Then share your ideas with another group.

CRITICAL THINKING: EVALUATING

A: *So, what do you think? What technical skills would colonists need?*
B: *I think being able to program computers would be vital, don't you?*
C: *Yeah, that's a good idea. And perhaps they'd need to be good at …*

Technical Skills	Personal Skills	Other Skills

FINAL TASK Presenting a Viewpoint

> You and a partner are going to give a five-minute presentation about the colonization of Mars. Choose one of these viewpoints, or use your own. Then find a partner who has the same point of view:
>
> • Humans should focus on colonizing Mars as soon as possible.
> • Humans should fix the problems on Earth before colonizing Mars.
> • Humans are meant to live on Earth; we should not colonize Mars.

PRESENTATION SKILL Expressing Your Opinion Strongly

If you want to express a strong opinion about something, you can use certain adverbs and adjectives to emphasize your words. Here are some examples of natural collocations:

I **really** think . . .	It is our **firm** belief that . . .
We **strongly** believe . . .	It is my **honest** feeling that . . .
I **definitely** feel . . .	It is our **strong** opinion that . . .

ORGANIZING IDEAS **A** **Work with your partner. Complete these steps.**

1. Decide what ideas, reasons, details, and examples you will use to support your point of view. Do some research if necessary.
2. Find images or visuals you could use to support your point of view.
3. Decide how to organize your talk and who will say what. Write an outline and notes.
4. Practice giving your presentation and finishing within the time limit.

PRESENTING **B** **Work with another pair of students. Give your presentation. Listen to feedback from the other pair about how you could improve your talk. Then watch their presentation and give feedback to them.**

REFLECTION

1. What is the most useful skill you learned in this unit? Explain.

   _____

   _____

2. What was the most interesting thing that you learned about human migration? Explain.

   _____

   _____

3. Here are the vocabulary words from the unit. Check (✓) the ones you can use.

☐ aspect AWL	☐ frontier	☐ relocate AWL
☐ barrier	☐ habitat	☐ settle
☐ colonize	☐ immigration AWL	☐ solar
☐ discrimination AWL	☐ migrant AWL	☐ stability AWL
☐ domestic AWL	☐ nation	☐ survive AWL
☐ emigration	☐ overview	☐ voluntary AWL
☐ encounter AWL	☐ prospect AWL	

OUR CHANGING PLANET 4

The Snake River flows through a valley in Grand Teton National Park, Wyoming, USA.

ACADEMIC SKILLS

LISTENING	Recognizing Digressions
	Noting Supporting Information
SPEAKING	Answering Questions Effectively
	Word Stress for Emphasis
CRITICAL THINKING	Being Creative

THINK AND DISCUSS

1 Look at the photo. How would you describe this place?

2 How might this landscape be different 1, 000 years from now?

Look at the photo and read the information. Then discuss the questions.

1. Which of the statistics about Yellowstone National Park do you find most surprising? Why?

2. Why do you think so many people visit Yellowstone National Park each year?

3. What park in your country is most similar to Yellowstone National Park? Explain.

Almost like clockwork, every 60 to 110 minutes, the geyser Old Faithful shoots up a jet of steam and hot water at Yellowstone National Park in Wyoming, USA.

YELLOWSTONE NATIONAL PARK

VISITORS
On average, there are more than 4 million visitors each year.

WILDLIFE
There are 67 species of mammals, 16 species of fish, and 285 species of birds.

WATER
There are over 290 waterfalls, 300 active geysers, and 10,000 hydrothermal features.

LAND
With 2.2 million acres, it is the second largest national park in the United States.

TRAFFIC
There are 310 miles of paved roads in the park, though many are closed during the winter months.

HUMAN IMPACT
In 2015, over 1,117 tons of waste were generated. At least 337 animals were killed in traffic accidents.

A Vocabulary

A Look at the photographs. Tell a partner about similar landforms in your country. Explain where they are and what they are called.

A: *Do you have any famous caves in your country?*
B: *I don't think so, but there's a large canyon called . . .*

mountain peak

cave

canyon

volcano

MEANING FROM
CONTEXT

B 🎧 **1.32** Read and listen to these statements. Think about the meaning of each word in **blue**. Then complete each definition with one of the words in **blue**.

a. The **landscape** consisted of grass-covered hills with rocky peaks.
b. Over very long periods, heat and **pressure** can turn mud into solid rock.
c. Years of wind and rain caused the rocks to **erode** into unusual shapes.
d. This particular beach is often **exposed** to strong winds.
e. During an extended period without rain, a **crack** formed in the ground.
f. Photographs of the gas clouds rising from the volcano were very **dramatic**.
g. It is important to wear **appropriate** shoes when hiking in the canyon.
h. The textbook gave a step-by-step explanation of the **formation** of valleys.
i. The earthquake was so strong it caused the roof of the cave to **collapse**.
j. According to the guide, the area has many **unique** geological features.

1. _____ (adj) correct or suitable for the situation

2. _____ (adj) different from everything else; one of a kind

3. _____ (adj) impressive or sudden and surprising

4. _____ (adj) unprotected, such as from the weather

5. _____ (n) a narrow space or line on the surface of a damaged thing

6. _____ (n) force or power that presses against or down

7. _____ (n) the creation of something

8. _____ (n) the way an area of land looks, especially in the countryside

9. _____ (v) to gradually reduce or damage something through the natural action of wind or water

10. _____ (v) to fall down suddenly because of a lack of strength or support

C Write short answers to these questions. Then ask others in your class the same questions. How many people gave the same answers as you?

1. Do you prefer taking photos of people or dramatic landscapes? Why?
2. In addition to water and wind, what else might cause a landscape to erode?
3. Which type of weather do you least enjoy being exposed to?
4. Give an example of a situation when water is under pressure. What happens if the pressure is released?
5. What is one thing people might continue to use even if it has a crack in it?
6. What do you think is the most unique thing about you?

D Choose the answer for each question. Then use a dictionary to check your answers.

1. What is the noun form of *erode*?

   a. erasure   b. erosion   c. eruption

2. Which prefix can you add to *appropriate* to make its antonym, or opposite?

   a. *in-*   b. *dis-*   c. *un-*

3. Which preposition is commonly used with *formation*?

   a. formation at   b. formation of   c. formation to

4. What is the meaning of the word root *uni-* in the word *unique*?

   a. huge   b. new   c. one

5. Which phrase is the best antonym of *exposed to*?

   a. protected on   b. protected from   c. protected with

6. What is the noun form of *exposed*?

   a. exposure   b. expulsion   c. explosion

Listening   An Earth Sciences Lecture

BEFORE LISTENING

A Work in a small group. You will hear a lecture about a national park in Madagascar. What national parks are important in your country? Explain.

WHILE LISTENING

LISTENING FOR
MAIN IDEAS

B 🎧 1.33 ▶ 1.7 Listen to the lecture and take notes. Then use your notes to complete a sentence summarizing what you heard.

A geology professor described _____

_____

C 🎧 1.34 Listen again to part of the lecture and take notes. Then use your notes to complete the diagram by writing the correct letter in each space. One answer has been done for you.

Formation of the Tsingy de Bemaraha

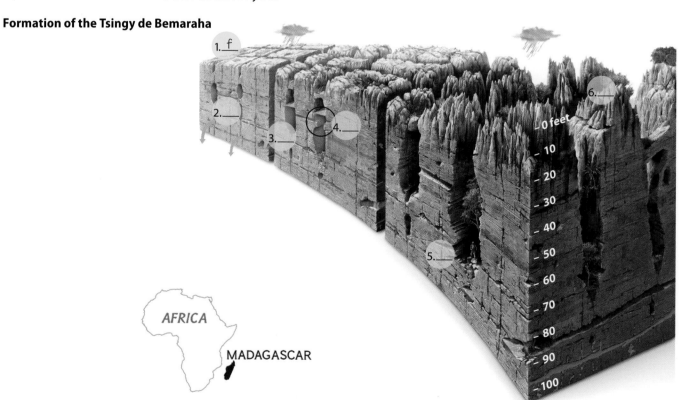

a. More cave roofs collapse, leaving deep canyons and rock pillars.
b. Over time, the holes become larger and form small caves.
c. Rain dissolves the top of these pillars to form sharp points.
d. The action of water enlarges existing weak points and holes.
e. The tops of some caves collapse, creating bigger caves.
f. Water begins to erode the limestone, causing holes and weaknesses.

Sometimes a lecturer or speaker may say something that is not directly relevant to his or her main points. During these temporary digressions, or sidetracks, the speaker may tell a story or add information that is interesting or amusing but only indirectly related to the topic. Recognizing a digression can help you focus on the more important points a speaker is making. A speaker will often, but not always, use a specific phrase when starting or ending a digression.

Starting a digression:

Interestingly, …   *As an aside, …*   *This is off the topic, but …*

Returning to the main topic:

Anyway, …   *As I was saying, …*   *Getting back to the topic, …*

D 🎧 1.35 **Read and listen to an extract from the lecture. Mark the two sentences in which the speaker digresses from her main point. Also mark the words that signal a return to the main point.**

Today we'll begin by discussing some limestone landscapes. As you probably know, this rock is formed when sea creatures die and fall to the ocean floor. Over time, layers of skeletons build up, and the bottom layers are pressed down. Eventually, the pressure turns them into limestone. Interestingly, the term *limestone* doesn't come from the color of the rock, which is typically white or gray, not green, but from *lime*, an important industrial product made from limestone. Anyway, limestone is a relatively hard rock, but water can wash it away, especially water that is slightly acidic. Uh, we usually think of acid rain as being caused by human industry, but sometimes acid rain can be caused by gases from volcanoes. Now as I was saying, water can erode limestone.

E 🎧 1.36 **Mark each statement as either a key point (*KP*) or a digression (*D*). Then listen again to part of the lecture and check your answers.**

LISTENING FOR
DETAILS

1. _____ It takes a very long time for water to shape limestone landscapes.

2. _____ The name for karst landscapes originally comes from German.

3. _____ An alternative name for the Tsingy area is the "Forest of Knives."

4. _____ Water is the main factor in the formation of the Tsingy landscape.

5. _____ Tourism in parks in Madagascar has been affected by political events.

AFTER LISTENING

F **Work in a small group. Discuss these questions.**

CRITICAL THINKING:
EVALUATING

1. What are some things that you learned from the lecture that you did not know before?
2. The speaker makes a number of digressions during the lecture. For a speaker, what are some advantages and disadvantages of making digressions?

A Speaking

We use the passive voice to focus attention on the person or thing that is affected by the action of a verb. Passives are commonly used in writing, but we also use them in speech. This is especially true when we are describing a process or explaining scientific or technical information. The passive is formed by using a form of *be* plus the past participle of a verb.

> This rock **was formed** millions of years ago.

When it is important to include the person or thing doing the action, we use a *by* phrase to indicate the agent.

> This geological study was conducted **by graduate students**.

However, the agent can be omitted if it is obvious, unimportant, or unknown.

> This rock is formed when sea creatures die and fall to the ocean floor.

A 🎧 1.37 **Work with a partner. Discuss how to rephrase the underlined parts of the text so they are in the passive voice. Then listen to check your answers.**

The eruption[1] of Mount Vesuvius in AD 79 is one of the most famous in history. <u>It destroyed two Roman towns and killed numerous citizens</u>. <u>The writer Pliny the Younger observed the eruption</u>. He described the eruption in two letters to Tacitus, another famous Roman. His description was so detailed and accurate that <u>modern geologists call similar eruptions Plinian</u>. These days <u>tourists often visit the sites of the destroyed towns</u>. However, this may not be a safe thing to do as <u>many experts consider Vesuvius to be an extremely dangerous volcano.</u>

[1]**eruption** (n): an explosion, for example of a volcano

Ruins of Pompeii, Italy, with Mount Vesuvius in the background

B With a partner, discuss what questions you would like to ask about Vesuvius. Then share one of your questions with the class.

C Interview two students in your class. Take turns asking and answering these questions. When it is your turn to speak, answer in full sentences and use the passive voice.

1. When and where were you born?
2. What were you often told by your teachers at school?
3. When you were a child, what is one thing you were rarely allowed to do?
4. What is your favorite movie called, and who was it directed by?
5. Who are you most influenced by in your personal or professional life?

SPEAKING SKILL Answering Questions Effectively

Although answering people's questions is often straightforward, you may need to ask for clarification.

1. Ask for clarification or repetition if you don't understand all or part of a question:
   Sorry. What does … mean?
   Could you repeat the second thing you said?

2. You can confirm that you have understood the question by repeating some or all of the questioner's words when you respond. This also gives you time to think about your response and shows that your answer is relevant.
   So, what you're asking is …
   You asked about …

D Work with a partner. Decide who is student A (this page) and who is student B (next page). Then take turns following these steps. Ask for clarification when needed.

1. Read the notes on this page (if you are student A) or on the next page (student B).
2. Use the notes to answer your partner's questions. Speak in full sentences and use the passive voice when it is appropriate. Answer questions effectively by asking for clarification or confirming what you have heard.
3. Ask your questions and take notes on your partner's answers.

Student A

Hoodoos
- sometimes called tent rocks or earth pyramids
- have hard rock on top of a thick layer of softer rock
- formed when softer rock is eroded by weather
- more are found at Bryce Canyon National Park than anywhere in world
- park is located in Utah

Questions to ask Student B about the Legend of Red Painted Faces
1. Who are the Southern Paiute (pie-yute)?
2. Who originally lived at Bryce Canyon National Park?
3. Why were these people turned to stone by Coyote (kai-oh-di)?
4. What is Bryce Canyon National Park called by some of the Southern Paiute?

Student B

The Legend of Red Painted Faces
- Southern Paiute (pie-yute) = Native American tribe
- Tribe has story about how hoodoos were formed:
    - "Legend People" originally lived at Bryce Canyon
    - They were bad → were turned to stone by Coyote (kai-oh-di) spirit
- Park is called "Red Painted Faces" by some tribe members

Questions to ask Student A about Hoodoos

1. What other names can hoodoos be called?
2. What rock layers do hoodoos usually have?
3. How are hoodoos typically formed?
4. In which state is Bryce Canyon National Park located, and why is the park special?

E Work in a small group. Share a traditional legend or story from your country.

LESSON TASK Creating a Legend

CRITICAL THINKING Being Creative

Being creative is an important 21st-century skill. Research shows that one way to develop creativity is to think of as many possible solutions for a problem or answers to a question as possible. Brainstorming, writing a journal, and using a mind map are effective methods for thinking creatively.

Bryce Canyon National Park in the USA has many tall, thin rock pillars called hoodoos.

Fingal's Cave on the island of Staffa, Scotland

A split rock in Tasman Bay, New Zealand

A Work in a small group. Choose one of the landforms above. Brainstorm a funny or interesting legend that explains how it was formed. Fill in the mind map with your ideas. Then practice telling your group's legend, making sure each person speaks.

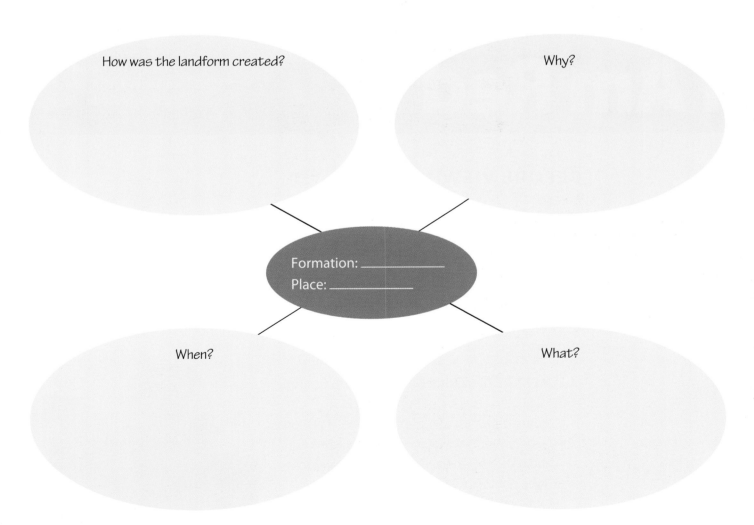

How was the landform created?

Why?

Formation: _____
Place: _____

When?

What?

B With your group, tell your legend to the rest of the class. Make sure each person speaks. Then vote on which groups came up with the most creative legend(s).

I Am Red

An aerial view of the Colorado River winding through the Grand Canyon in Arizona, USA, in a photo by Pete McBride

BEFORE VIEWING

A Read the information about Pete McBride, writer and director of "I Am Red," a video about the Colorado River. Why do you think the filmmaker might have chosen this title? Choose from the reasons below.

a. Because the name of the river is related to the color red
b. Because the water flowing in the river is sometimes red
c. Because the filmmaker wants to imply the river is angry

MEET PETE McBRIDE. A native of Colorado, McBride is a self-taught photographer, filmmaker, writer, and public speaker. A National Geographic Freshwater Hero, he paddled and hiked the entire length of the Colorado River, photographing and filming this endangered river.

B Work with a partner. What do you know or what can you guess about the Colorado River? Circle T for *True* or F for *False*. You will check the answers when you watch the video.

1. The Colorado River has existed for five million years.   T   F
2. It flows through seven states and two countries.   T   F
3. It is the strongest and largest river in the United States.   T   F
4. It is the most endangered river in the United States.   T   F

C Work with a partner. Match these words from the video with the correct definition.

1. _____ scorching (adj)   a. extremely dry, without rain
2. _____ arid (adj)   b. sense of fun
3. _____ playfulness (n)   c. the heart of somebody or something
4. _____ tapped (adj)   d. to control something such as a natural resource
5. _____ harness (v)   e. to support or care for somebody or something
6. _____ soul (n)   f. used or used up, especially of a natural resource
7. _____ sustain (v)   g. very hot

WHILE VIEWING

D ▶ 1.8 Watch the video. Answer the questions. Then discuss your answers with a partner.

UNDERSTANDING MAIN IDEAS

1. What main idea(s) does the video express?

    a. The Colorado River is important but endangered.
    b. The Colorado River should have a different name.
    c. both a and b

2. How did the director express the main idea(s)?

    a. through the words spoken by the narrators
    b. through the images shown in the video
    c. both a and b

E ▶ 1.8 Watch the video again. Check your answers to the questions in exercise B. Correct any answers that are false.

UNDERSTANDING DETAILS

AFTER VIEWING

F Work in a small group. Discuss these questions.

CRITICAL THINKING: EVALUATING

1. Which of the answers to exercise A best matches what you saw in the video? Explain.
2. The film you just watched has been described as a "visual poem." What do you think this means? Do you agree that the film is like a visual poem? Why or why not?
3. Think of an important river in your country. In what ways is it similar to the Colorado River? In what ways is it different? What is unique about it?

B Vocabulary

A 🎧 1.38 Listen to excerpts from academic lectures. As you listen, focus on understanding the meaning of the word or phrase in **blue**. Then write the word or phrase to complete each definition.

1. To **preserve** means to keep something _____.

   a. calm   b. free   c. safe

2. **Balance** means the act of giving _____ importance to things.

   a. equal   b. legal   c. normal

3. **Impact** means _____.

   a. contact   b. change   c. advice

4. **Compromise** means an _____ that does not completely satisfy anybody.

   a. account   b. agreement   c. alternative

5. **Harm** means _____ to something or somebody.

   a. an explanation   b. benefits   c. damage

6. **In theory** means something that is _____ but may not happen.

   a. educational   b. possible   c. useful

7. **Fragile** means _____.

   a. easily damaged   b. poorly designed   c. quickly confused

8. **Consultant** means a person who provides _____.

   a. expert advice   b. great patience   c. new equipment

9. **Analysis** means a _____ something.

   a. careful examination of   b. detailed education for   c. strong emotion about

10. **Infrastructure** means the basic _____ that a city, state, or country needs to run effectively.

    a. information   b. responsibilities   c. structures

VOCABULARY SKILL Using Digital Tools

Here are some online tools that can help you use vocabulary more naturally and effectively.

- A **thesaurus** shows you the synonyms and antonyms of a word. Some online visual thesauruses show a web of similar and related words and are designed for visual learners (search for "online thesaurus" or "free visual thesaurus").
- A **collocations dictionary** shows words that are commonly used with other words, such as "good weather" or "make progress" (search for "collocations dictionary").
- A **concordancer** is a tool that lets you see how words are typically used in a sentence. This can help you find examples of collocations and see what grammar patterns are common (search for "web concordancer").

B Work with a partner. Use these sample lines from a concordancer to answer the questions.

```
of modern life is finding a  balance between work and other parts o
argued about how to get the  balance between the positive things sh
challenge to find the right  balance, but most would accept that it
```

1. What two verbs are collocations with *balance*? _____
2. What preposition is common after *balance*? _____

```
was saying, this had a major  impact on the situation.  What kind o
unsurprisingly, the regional  impact was much greater than the nati
stated it would have a major  impact on how many tourists could vis
```

3. What adjective is a strong collocation with *impact*? _____
4. What preposition is common after *impact*? _____

```
it was necessary to reach a  compromise, and both sides reduced the
shocked that they came to a  compromise more quickly than people ha
asked about reaching a fair  compromise, she stated that she was no
```

5. Is *compromise* a countable or uncountable noun? _____
6. What two verbs are collocations with *compromise*? _____

```
that the new park would cause  harm to local wildlife. They were co
despite this, she suffered no  harm to her reputation as a result o
said the policies caused more  harm than good, although that was no
```

7. What two verbs are collocations with the noun *harm*? _____
8. What preposition is common after *harm*? _____

```
researchers carried out a careful  analysis of the data that took a
she said she would perform a full  analysis of the sales results by
they were unable to carry out the  analysis because the data was no
```

9. What preposition is common after *analysis*? _____
10. What verb and verb phrase are collocations with *analysis*? _____

C Work with a partner. Say whether each statement is true for you or not, and why.

1. I often think about how humans can preserve the environment.
2. I have a large number of items in my home that are fragile.
3. It would be interesting to work as a consultant in the future.
4. I only make decisions after I have done an analysis of the situation.
5. The infrastructure in the region where I grew up is good.

B Listening A Conversation about Selecting a College

BEFORE LISTENING

A Work in a small group. What factors do people generally consider when deciding where to attend college? Write down at least five ideas.

_____

WHILE LISTENING

LISTENING FOR
MAIN IDEAS

B 🎧 1.39 Listen to two students discuss where one of them might go to college. Which factors do they discuss? How many of these factors did you predict in exercise A?

Factors discussed: _____

NOTE-TAKING SKILL Noting Supporting Information

It is common for speakers to support their opinions with reasons, details, and examples. In many cases, a speaker will give the supporting information *after* giving his or her view. In other cases, a speaker may give supporting information *before* summarizing his or her view. In both cases, it is a good idea to take notes of any supporting points that a speaker makes.

Some of the most common types of supporting information include:

- reasons
- statistics or other people's opinions
- examples or stories
- names of people, places, and so on
- numbers, including dates, percentages, and so on

LISTENING FOR
DETAILS

C 🎧 1.39 Listen again to the conversation. Take notes as you listen. Write no more than three words or a number for each answer.

1. How many colleges is Liam currently considering? _____

2. What subject does Liam say he wants to major in? _____

3. What does Serena say is bad for the environment? _____

4. Which place does Serena think must be Liam's top choice? _____

5. How many countries does Liam say he is a citizen of? _____

6. Where would be the cheapest place for Liam to study? _____

AFTER LISTENING

D Work in a small group. Discuss these questions.

CRITICAL THINKING: REFLECTING

1. After listening to the conversation, how would you explain what ecotourism is to somebody who has never heard of it?
2. What information would you need to understand the concept of ecotourism better?
3. How could you find out the information you discussed in question 2?

E Work in a different small group. Look at the descriptions of the two package vacations. Then discuss the questions.

CRITICAL THINKING: EVALUATING

VACATION PACKAGES

Imagine yourself on the island of Maui, Hawaii, at Secret Beach at sunset.

ACTIVE HAWAII

Explore beautiful Hawaii with our expert guides. Available activities include hiking, mountain biking, diving, and whale watching (December through May). Guests will stay in a modern five-star hotel with excellent restaurants and stunning views. The hotel is close to several fashionable shopping areas. This is the perfect vacation for active families! **Click here** for more information and prices.

NATURAL HAWAII

Experience all Hawaii has to offer without worrying. This vacation has been carefully designed to minimize the impact of all activities. Guests will stay in a modern, environmentally-friendly lodge and eat delicious meals prepared with seasonal local ingredients. This is your chance to visit Hawaii without changing it! **Click here** for more information and prices.

1. Which description sounds like an ecotourism vacation? Why do you think so?
2. Which of the two vacations do you think would be more expensive? Why?
3. Which of the two vacations would you most like to take? Why?

B | Speaking

A Work in a small group. Discuss what you think each of the sayings below means. Then discuss whether you agree fully, partially, or not at all with each saying, and why. Use appropriate stress.

- If you get lost in nature, you will find yourself.
- Nature is not a place to visit; it is home.
- Earth does not belong to us. We belong to Earth.
- We change nature, but nature also changes us.

Fairy chimneys in the rugged landscape of Honey Valley, Cappadocia, Turkey

1. Do people in your country have any common sayings about nature or the planet like the ones in exercise A? Share them with your group.
2. As a group, come up with a new saying about nature or the world. Your saying should be one that you all fully agree with. When you have decided, share your saying with the class.

FINAL TASK Presenting a Business Report

> You and a partner are going to do some Internet research about ecotourism and then use what you learned to present a short business report.

A Work with a partner. The Internet has many possible sources of information. Add your own ideas and examples to this list. When you have finished, share your ideas with another pair of students.

- Online encyclopedia (e.g., _Wikipedia_ ⎯⎯⎯⎯⎯⎯⎯)

- Newspaper website (e.g., ⎯⎯⎯⎯⎯⎯⎯)

- Personal blog post (e.g., ⎯⎯⎯⎯⎯⎯⎯)

- ⎯⎯⎯⎯⎯⎯⎯ (e.g., ⎯⎯⎯⎯⎯⎯⎯)

- ⎯⎯⎯⎯⎯⎯⎯ (e.g., ⎯⎯⎯⎯⎯⎯⎯)

- ⎯⎯⎯⎯⎯⎯⎯ (e.g., ⎯⎯⎯⎯⎯⎯⎯)

B With your partner, decide which of the online sources you brainstormed in exercise A match each of these categories. Some sources may match several categories.

CRITICAL THINKING: CATEGORIZING

Neutral[1]	Up-to-Date	Accurate

Biased[2]	Out-of-Date	Inaccurate

[1]**neutral** (adj): not supporting any side; unprejudiced

[2]**biased** (adj): supporting one side; prejudiced

C **With your partner, read the situation and then complete the steps.**

> You are an intern at a large travel company that is interested in offering ecotourism vacations in your country. Your manager has asked pairs of interns to present a two-minute researched report. The report should answer these questions:
>
> - What are some of the advantages and disadvantages of ecotourism holidays?
> - What kinds of ecotourism package holidays are currently popular?
> - Which destinations in your country are most suitable for ecotourism vacations?

1. Decide which kinds of sources you will use for your research, and why.
2. Decide who will do the research for which aspect of the report.
3. Do the research and share what you learned with your partner.
4. Decide which information to include in your report. Prepare an outline and decide who will say what.
5. Practice giving your report within the time limit and using natural stress.

PRESENTATION SKILL Making Eye Contact

When you deliver a presentation, make sure you make eye contact with the audience from time to time. Doing this has a number of benefits, including the following:

- It can give you feedback about how listeners are reacting to your talk.
- It helps listeners feel more engaged and interested in your talk.
- Your speech will be more natural.

PRESENTING **D** **With your partner, deliver your report. Remember to make eye contact. After your report, answer any questions that your classmates may have. Then listen to the other reports and, as a class, select the best one.**

REFLECTION

1. Think of a situation in which it is important to use English well. Which skills that you have learned in this unit will help you in that situation?

   _____

   _____

2. What was the most interesting information you learned in this unit?

   _____

   _____

3. Here are the vocabulary words from the unit. Check (✔) the ones you can use.

☐ analysis AWL	☐ dramatic AWL	☐ in theory
☐ appropriate AWL	☐ erode AWL	☐ infrastructure AWL
☐ balance	☐ exposed AWL	☐ landscape
☐ collapse AWL	☐ formation	☐ preserve
☐ compromise	☐ fragile	☐ pressure
☐ consultant AWL	☐ harm	☐ unique AWL
☐ crack	☐ impact AWL	

MAKING A LIVING, MAKING A DIFFERENCE

5

games
photos
videos
television
favorites
news
profile

National Geographic Explorer Tan Le wears a special headset that reads brainwaves, making it possible to control virtual and physical objects with thoughts.

ACADEMIC SKILLS

LISTENING	Listening for Similarities and Contrasts
	Using Abbreviations
SPEAKING	Using Numbers and Statistics
	Indirect Questions
CRITICAL THINKING	Personalizing

THINK AND DISCUSS

1 How can Tan Le's invention make a difference in people's lives?

2 Think about the unit title. How can a person make a difference in the lives of others while making a living?

WAYS OF WORKING

Three entrepreneurs work in a start-up company in Amman, Jordan.

A factory worker assembles electronic switches in Shanghai, China.

A bakery owner stands in front of his shop in Bodrum, Turkey.

A nurse checks a boy before surgery in Bharatpur, Nepal.

A Vocabulary

A Mark the words you already know. Then use a dictionary to look up the others.

conventional (adj)   cooperate (v)   diverse (adj)   models (n)   profits (n)

MEANING FROM
CONTEXT

B 🎧 2.2 Fill in each blank with a word from exercise A. Then listen and check your answers.

COOPERATIVES

Cooperatives, or co-ops, are different from corporations or other

_____Cm_____ business __Coor__₂_____. The main difference is

that the employees are also the owners of the cooperative. They agree to

_____diverse_____ by selling their products or services together rather than

separately. If the co-op makes money, the members share the __Profits__₄___.

This allows all co-op members to earn a good living.

Cooperative businesses are quite _____models_____. They provide every

imaginable kind of goods and services and can range from quite large to very

small. For example, in Boston, computer experts decided to work for themselves

and formed TechCollective. At TechCollective, customers can simply walk in and

have their computer problems solved by the same people who own the business.

CRITICAL THINKING:
EVALUATING

C With a partner, discuss the questions below.

1. According to the article, what are the benefits of cooperatives to members?
2. Do you think a cooperative would earn higher or lower profits than a conventional business? Why?
3. As a customer, would you like to get products or services from a co-op? Why or why not?

D Mark the words you already know. Then use a dictionary to look up the others.

assess (v)   effective (adj)   entrepreneurs (n)   generate (v)   poverty (n)

E 🎧 **2.3** Fill in each blank with a word from exercise D. Then listen and check your answers.

MEANING FROM
CONTEXT

**PERUVIAN WEAVERS:
A PROFITABLE ARTISAN¹ COOPERATIVE**

In the Andes Mountains of Peru, people in the village of Chinchero were living in ___poverty___ during much of the 20th century. Their agricultural products— potatoes, barley, and sheep—were bringing in very little income. In 1996, the women of Chinchero became ___entrepreneurs___ and started the Chinchero Weaving Cooperative. They began selling their traditional handmade fabrics to tourists. Now, the women ___assess___ more income for their work, and their earnings stay within the community. Starting a co-op was a(n) ___effective___ way for villagers in Chinchero to bring in more money. However, before deciding to start a cooperative, owners of small, home-based businesses need to ___generate___ their situation carefully.

A weaver in the Chinchero community, Sacred Valley of the Incas, Peru

¹**artisan** (n): a person who is skilled at making something by hand

F Work in a small group. Discuss these questions.

CRITICAL THINKING:
EVALUATING

1. How did forming the cooperative help families generate more income in Chinchero?
2. Why is it important to have diverse kinds of businesses in a community; for example, large department stores, small family-owned businesses, and entrepreneurs?

VOCABULARY SKILL Suffix *–ive*

We can add the suffix *–ive* to some verbs to form adjectives. The adjective form means tending to or having the quality of. Notice the spelling changes.

addict	→	addic**tive**	effect	→	effec**tive**	compete	→	competi**tive**
create	→	crea**tive**	decide	→	deci**sive**	persuade	→	persua**sive**

G With a partner, change each verb into an adjective with the *-ive* suffix. Then write a sentence with each adjective in your notebook. Use a dictionary as needed.

cooperate _____   interact _____   attract _____

communicate _____   express _____   protect _____

Listening A Talk about a Cooperative Business

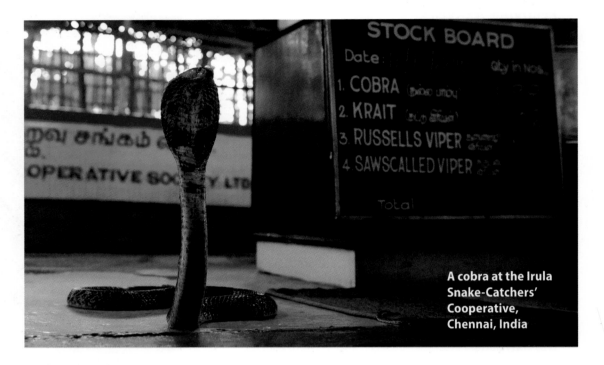

A cobra at the Irula Snake-Catchers' Cooperative, Chennai, India

BEFORE LISTENING

CRITICAL THINKING: **A** **2.4** Read and listen to the information. Then discuss the questions with a partner.
ANALYZING

> **SNAKE HUNTERS FIND CURE FOR JOBLESSNESS**
>
> Most people run away when they see a poisonous snake—but not the Irulas of India. For generations, the Irulas made their living by catching wild snakes, including deadly poisonous cobras. In the past, the snakes' skins were sold and made into luxury goods such as handbags and boots. But that changed in 1972, when the Indian Parliament adopted the Wildlife Protection Act, making the Irulas' main income source suddenly illegal.

1. Why do you think the 1972 law was passed?
2. What other situations might force people to change the way they make a living?

NOTE-TAKING SKILL Using Abbreviations

You can take notes more quickly by using abbreviations, or shortened forms of words. An abbreviation can be just part of a word, or it might be only a few letters. Here are some common abbreviations, but any system that makes sense to you will help make your note taking faster.

corp. = corporation	*info.* = information	*org.* = organization	*w/* = with
hosp. = hospital	*mktg.* = marketing	*vs.* = versus	*w/o* = without

WHILE LISTENING

B 🎧 **2.5** ▶ **1.9** Read the notes outlining the main ideas. Then listen and complete the notes using abbreviations.

Spkr: Marsha Nolan, _Director_ of Worldwide Co-op
1

Topic today: _information_ about co-op in India
2

Irula tribe: - Pre-1972, caught snakes such as _India_ cobra; sold skins for $
3

(but lived in _unknown_)
4

- After 1972, became _illegal_ (started a co-op); now milk snakes
5

for venom (used for anti-venom, cures snakebites)

Benefits: - Snakes not killed; 1000s of _human_ lives saved; Irulas earn more
6

C 🎧 **2.5** Listen again and choose the correct answer.

1. According to the speaker, what does Worldwide Co-op offer to cooperatives?
   a. bank loans
   b. online information
   c. health insurance

2. Each year, how many people in India die from snakebites?
   a. 26,000
   b. 36,000
   c. 46,000

3. How many members does the Irula co-op have?
   a. 200
   b. 300
   c. 400

4. What kind of organizations do the people in the audience belong to?
   a. wildlife organizations
   b. medical organizations
   c. youth organizations

AFTER LISTENING

D In a small group, discuss the three co-ops. How has each co-op directly benefited its members? What other positive effects do you think each co-op might have on the community or on the world? Compare your notes with another group.

	Benefits to Members	Other Positive Effects
TechCollective		
Chinchero Weaving Cooperative		
Irula Snake-Catchers' Cooperative		

A Speaking

A Work with a partner. Practice saying the numbers.

1. 250   two fifty / two hundred and fifty
2. 4,900   forty-nine hundred / four thousand nine hundred
3. 728,000   seven hundred and twenty-eight thousand
4. 1,000,000   one million
5. 1.5 million   one point five million
6. 7,000,000,000 seven billion

B 🎧 2.6 Work with a partner. In your notebook, write out how you would say each number. Then listen and check your answers.

1. 50,000   *fifty thousand*   3. 9,600 *night thousand on Hundred*   5. 8,000,000,000 *eight billion*

2. 3,200,000 *tree million and two thousand*   4. 740,000 *seven thousand forty Hundred*   6. 1,297,300 *one million two Hundred nigty seven Hundred and tree Hundred*

C 🎧 2.7 With a partner, discuss where you think each number below should go in the paragraph. Then listen and check your answers.

7.4	18	60	85	2,500

Kudzu, originally brought to the United States from Japan in 1876, is an invasive plant species. During the 1930s, the U.S. government provided farmers with _____ million kudzu seedlings

1

to hold dry soil in place. That may have been a mistake because kudzu can grow very quickly—up to _____ feet, or

2

_____ meters, in one growing season. It can cover as many

3

as _____ acres of land each year. Currently, kudzu covers

4

around _____ million acres of land in the United States.

5

D In a small group, read about an entrepreneur who is making a profit from kudzu. Then discuss the questions below.

NANCY BASKET'S KUDZU MAGIC

Nancy Basket is a Native American artist who runs a small business, Kudzu Kabin Designs, from her home in South Carolina, in the United States. She is one of a few people who sees the benefits of the vine that most Americans hate. "It's very invasive. It grows 12 inches (30 centimeters) every single day, and people haven't been able to use it. But I use it for everything, and people can buy it (from me) in a form that's guaranteed to never grow again," Basket said.

In addition to her baskets, she sells lamp shades made from kudzu vines, and cards and posters made from kudzu paper. Even her artist's studio is made out of kudzu bales[1]—the only such structure of its kind. From an invasive and destructive plant, Basket has created a successful business.

[1] **bales** (n): large cubes of material such as hay, paper, or kudzu tied together tightly

1. Would you be interested in buying Basket's products? If so, which ones?
2. How is her business similar to and different from the Irula Snake-Catchers' Cooperative?
3. Do you think that kudzu entrepreneurs can effectively reduce the amount of kudzu in the United States? Why or why not?
4. Making a product is only part of what Basket does. Discuss in what ways each activity listed below is important to a small business owner. What other responsibilities does an owner have?

   - marketing and advertising a product
   - maintaining a website
   - managing employees
   - getting supplies
   - selling and shipping products
   - doing accounting and paying taxes

PRONUNCIATION Pronouncing Large Numbers

🎧 **2.8** When saying large numbers, we use thought groups and intonation to make them easier for listeners to understand. Each numerical group in a large number ends with a rising intonation and slight pause except for the last group, which ends with falling intonation.

67,400 *sixty-seven thousand, four hundred*

3,011,382 *three million, eleven thousand, three hundred (and) eighty-two*

CRITICAL THINKING:
INTERPRETING
STATISTICS

E Work with a partner. Read the data below. Then ask and answer the questions. Remember to pronounce large numbers correctly.

2014 U.S. BUSINESS STATISTICS

- There were 5,825,458 businesses with paid employees.
- Small companies with under 500 employees represented 99.7 percent of employers.
- There were 19,076 large businesses.
- Small businesses employed almost half of the 121,069,944 workers.
- Small firms accounted for 63.3 percent of new jobs created between 1992 and 2013.

U.S. SMALL BUSINESS STATISTICS, 2009–2013

Category	2009	2010	2011	2012	2013
Start-ups	409,065	387,976	401,156	411,252	406,353
Closures	493,994	424,610	413,882	375,192	400,687
Bankruptcy[1]	58,721	58,322	49,895	44,435	36,061

Sources: Small Business Administration; U.S. Census Bureau

[1]**bankruptcy** (n): the legal state of being unable to pay bills

1. How many businesses with paid employees were there in the United States in 2014?
2. How many large businesses were there in 2014?
3. About how many workers were employed by small businesses in 2014?
4. Did the number of new business start-ups increase or decrease between 2009 and 2013? Why do you think this happened?
5. How many businesses in the United States closed in 2013? How does that number compare with 2009?
6. Did the number of bankruptcies increase or decrease between 2009 and 2013? How might you explain this?
7. What surprises or interests you about the statistics in the table? Why?

LESSON TASK Discussing Small Businesses

A Work with a partner. Discuss how each type of small business can benefit a community. For example, can they provide employment, convenience, or a social benefit? Think of examples in your own community.

CRITICAL THINKING: EVALUATING

- Restaurants and coffee shops
- Retail shops (clothing, shoes, electronics, etc.)
- Manufacturers (windows, equipment, etc.)
- Service providers (auto repair, accountants, etc.)

B Discuss these questions with your partner and take notes on your ideas. Then together organize and prepare a one-minute presentation.

ORGANIZING IDEAS

1. What kind of small business would you like to see open in your community? Why?
2. How many employees does this kind of business have? Do employees receive any job benefits, such as health insurance, employee discounts, or free meals?
3. Besides employment, what other benefits does the business provide to the community?
4. What statistics from page 90 can you use to support your ideas?

> *We would like to see a new grocery store open in our community. It would make food shopping more convenient, and it could employ around 25 people. In fact, small businesses created 63.3 percent of new jobs in the United States between 1992 and 2013.*

C With your partner, present your ideas from exercise B to another pair of students. As a group, discuss the questions below.

PRESENTING

1. Which small business might bring the most benefits to the community?
2. Did numbers and statistics strengthen the presentations? What other numbers or statistics would have been useful to include?
3. If only one of the small businesses could open, which one would you choose? Why?

Second Shot Coffee in East London, U.K., founded by Julius Ibrahim (left), employs people who are homeless. Customers can purchase coffee or food for a person in need.

Video

A man and child sit under a light powered by a solar microgrid in a village near Jehanabad, Bihar, India.

Light for India's Villages

BEFORE VIEWING

A Work with a partner. Discuss the meanings of the terms you already know. Then fill in each blank with one of the words or phrases. You may use a dictionary to help you.

> extend   infrastructure   kerosene   lack   working conditions

1. When you __lhran__ something, you don't have enough of it.

2. The __lack__ of a place includes its physical structures such as buildings and roads.

3. When you __extend__ something, you make it bigger or make it include more.

4. You can burn __kerosene__ as a fuel.

5. Good __working condition__ make it easier and healthier for people to do their jobs.

B The video is about a small power company that is bringing power to villages that are "off-grid"—without access to electricity. With a partner, list the daily challenges that are faced by people who live "off-grid."

WHILE VIEWING

C ▶ `1.10` **Watch the video and write T for *True* or F for *False*. Correct the false statements.**

UNDERSTANDING MAIN IDEAS

1. __T__ The Terra Watt prize money is being used to supply electric power to rural villages.

2. __T__ Some women's groups can now make products at night to sell in the market.

3. __X__ People in rural villages used to spend very little money for kerosene or for cell-phone charging.

4. __F__ A new microgrid from Mera Gao Power requires villages to give up some land.

D **Which daily challenges that you listed in exercise B were mentioned in the video?**

E ▶ `1.10` **Watch the video again and fill in each blank with the number that you hear.**

UNDERSTANDING DETAILS

1. Uttar Pradesh is a state of __200 million__ people just to the east of New Delhi, with more than __60%__ percent off-grid.

2. In order to provide services to __20 million__ homes, our technology is very simple.

3. Each one of our microgrids costs us about __$1000__ dollars to provide service to a typical off-grid hamlet[1].

4. When Mera Gao Power completes the project under the Terra Watt Prize, we'll have connected __3500__ households in __140__ villages.

[1]**hamlet** (n): a small village

AFTER VIEWING

> **CRITICAL THINKING**   Personalizing
>
> When you personalize information, you consider it in relation to your own life and experiences. Doing this can make the information more interesting to you and can help you to understand topics on a deeper level.

F **Work in a small group. Complete these tasks.**

CRITICAL THINKING: PERSONALIZING

1. Brainstorm a list of six or more ways you use electricity in your home. Then check the three things you would miss the most if you didn't have access to electricity.

2. Compare your list with the challenges you listed in exercise B. How is your use of electricity similar or different from that of the rural villagers in the video?

3. Mera Gao Power has received money from National Geographic and from investors, and in time, it will likely be a profitable company. If you were one of the owners, would you care more about the company's financial success or about its positive contributions to village life? Explain your answer.

Vocabulary

A 🎧 2.9 Listen and check (✓) the words you already know. Then discuss their meaning with a partner. Check the dictionary for any words you are not sure about.

☐ **accessible** (adj)	☐ **corporation** (n)	☐ **outcome** (n)
☐ **affordable** (adj)	☐ **demonstrate** (v)	☐ **response** (n)
☐ **charity** (n)	☐ **donate** (v)	
☐ **concept** (n)	☐ **fundamental** (adj)	

B Complete each statement with the correct form of a word from exercise A.

1. The _____ of keeping costs low and profits high is a(n) _____ idea for many businesses. They can't imagine doing business any other way.

2. The public _____ to the idea of space-tourism business has been mixed. Some people are eager to travel to space while others have no desire to go.

3. A(n) _____ is a large company such as Microsoft or BNP Paribas that meets a certain legal definition.

4. The hardware store plans to _____ part of its profits to a local _____ that helps people in need.

5. Many hospitals and clinics in India now have anti-venom so that lifesaving medicine is _____ to any person who lives near enough to those places.

6. The employees clearly _____ their community spirit by actively volunteering in a wide variety of community events.

7. For companies that want to make the world a better place, looking at profits is not the only way to measure a successful _____. It's also important to look at the difference the company has made in people's lives.

8. A product or service usually needs to be _____ in order to be successful. If it is too expensive, many people will not buy it.

▶ **Shivani Siroya, shown with her California team, founded InVenture to help people in developing countries establish credit and get loans. They provide personal data about people who want to start a small business.**

C 🎧 2.10 Read the information and fill in each blank with a word from exercise A. Then listen and check your answers.

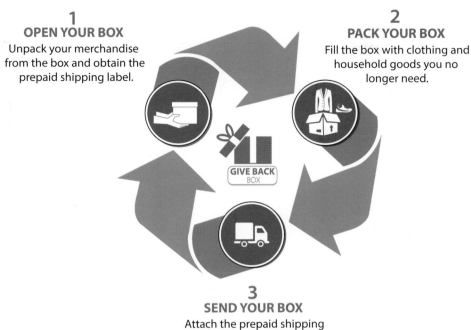

1
OPEN YOUR BOX
Unpack your merchandise from the box and obtain the prepaid shipping label.

2
PACK YOUR BOX
Fill the box with clothing and household goods you no longer need.

3
SEND YOUR BOX
Attach the prepaid shipping label provided to the box and ship as usual.

GIVE BACK BOX

THE GIVE BACK BOX

The _____ behind the Give Back Box is pretty simple. When someone
1
receives a box from an online retailer such as Amazon or Overstock, they can fill

it with clothing or household goods they want to _____. Using a free
2

shipping label, the box is shipped to a local _____ where the goods are
3

sold at very _____ prices or given away for free to people who need them.
4

Give Back Box itself is not a charitable organization. They're a for-profit company,

but one of their _____ goals is to do more than make money. Founder
5

Monika Wiela sees the company as a way to help people in need and, at the same

time, help online companies _____ their social responsibility[1]. So far, the
6

_____ from customers has been good. They're eager to help others by
7

donating goods, and they're happy to reuse their cardboard boxes as well.

[1]**social responsibility** (n ph.) the concept of businesses making positive contributions to society

---

D Discuss these questions with a partner.   PERSONALIZING

1. Would you use a service such as the Give Back Box? Why or why not?

2. Many people have more clothing, furniture, and other goods than they need. What are some ways to make these goods accessible to people who really need them?

B Listening   A Meeting about Social Responsibility

BEFORE LISTENING

PERSONALIZING **A** Work with a partner. Look at the statistics. Then discuss the questions below.

> **Consumers' Attitudes about Corporate Social Responsibility (CSR)**
>
> 93% have a more positive opinion of companies that demonstrate CSR
> 90% would decide to purchase or not based on companies' CSR practices
> 88% are more loyal to companies that practice CSR
> 80% would tell friends and family about a company's CSR efforts
> 72% believe their purchases have some impact on social or environmental issues

1. Which of these statements are true for you? Explain.
2. Which statistic is the most surprising to you? Why?

WHILE LISTENING

LISTENING FOR
MAIN IDEAS **B** 🎧 2.11 Listen to the meeting and take notes to complete the chart.

	Type of Company	How Are They Socially Responsible?
1.	GSK Glaxxo smith klient	provide medical training to places needed reduce energy used Martin medicot on cheaper
2.	Stale bag	buy are give are mostly to child that goes to school

---

LISTENING SKILL Listening for Similarities and Contrasts

Listening for expressions such as the ones below will help you understand whether two ideas, things, or people are similar in some way or are different.

Similarity: *also*   *too*   *both*   *as well*   *the same*

> *Jason and I had **the same** idea. We were **both** thinking about opening a cafe.*

Contrast: *although*   *though*   *even though*   *but*   *yet*

> ***Although** it is a small company, it makes a big difference in the community. How could our company do some good, **yet** still make a profit?*

C 🎧 2.12 Listen to excerpts from the meeting and fill in each blank with the word(s) you hear. Then with a partner, discuss whether each excerpt shows a similarity or contrast.

1. One is a huge drug manufacturer, and this one looks like a small company that makes handbags and backpacks. They _____both_____ seem to be very different from our company.

2. That's interesting, _____though_____ surprising as well. I thought they were just interested in making a profit.

3. Their customers like the idea of doing something to help kids, and State Bags is doing well as a business, especially for a young company. That's the kind of outcome we're looking for, _____too_____.

4. _____even though_____ we're a small company, we can still make a difference. Why don't we do some brainstorming?

AFTER LISTENING

D Discuss the questions with a partner.

1. The two companies mentioned in the meeting are doing very different things. How much social good do you think their different actions accomplish? Explain.

2. At the end of the meeting, you hear a suggestion for a brainstorm session to think of ways the software engineering firm could become more socially responsible and still make a profit. Which of the actions below might have the most impact? Explain.

   a. reducing the company's use of paper in its daily operations
   b. providing free software to help local charities manage their operations
   c. offering a free after-school software development class for high school students

Volunteers help prepare backpacks for school children in New York City, USA.

Speaking

GRAMMAR FOR SPEAKING Indirect Questions

An indirect question is a question inside another question or statement. We use indirect questions because they are often more polite than direct questions.

What are these companies doing?   (direct question)

Can you please explain <u>what</u> *these companies are doing?*   (indirect question)

Indirect questions begin with a polite phrase and use the word order for statements, not questions. Here are some other phrases we use for indirect questions.

Do you know <u>whether/if</u> *the company is socially responsible?*
Can you tell me <u>how</u> *the box recycling program works?*
Could you explain <u>why</u> *you chose these particular companies?*

Indirect questions can also be in the form of statements. These are less polite but common.

I'm wondering <u>why</u> *you chose these two companies.*
I'd like to know <u>how</u> *people make a living selling snake venom.*

A Work with a partner. Change the questions to indirect questions. Then practice asking and answering them.

1. What time is it?

   _____

2. Why are you taking this class?
   Can you tell me

3. How old were you when you took your first English class?
   Do you know

4. What kind of career do you hope to have in the future?
   I'm wondering

5. How do you make decisions about the clothing you buy?
   I'd like to know

6. Where should I go for a day trip this weekend?

   _____

EVERYDAY LANGUAGE   Showing Interest

More formal: *How interesting. Is that right? I didn't know that.*

Less formal: *Wow! Really? That's amazing. That's great.*

Hotlin Ompusunggu, dental surgeon, conservationist, and National Geographic Explorer, combines conservation and healthcare through community-based projects such as this tree-planting effort in Indonesia.

B Change each question to an indirect question. Then ask and answer the questions with a partner, continuing each conversation as long as possible. Remember to show interest in what your partner says.

1. What is the most influential technology company?
2. How do people get jobs with good companies?
3. Would you want to be a member of a cooperative?
4. What kind of small business would you like to start?

C Read each statement. Choose if it is true for you or not. Then change the false statements to be true for you.

1. I would like to start my own business someday.	T	F
2. If I had my own business, I would donate some of my profits to charity.	T	F
3. I would like to work for a large corporation.	T	F
4. I would prefer to work for a small business.	T	F
5. I would like to raise children and be a homemaker.	T	F
6. I already have some work experience.	T	F
7. I'd rather have an affordable lifestyle and not work long hours.	T	F
8. I'd prefer to work longer hours and have more money to spend.	T	F

D Work with a partner. Share and explain your answers from exercise C. Then discuss these questions about your work-related dreams for the future. Ask indirect questions to get more information and use expressions to show interest.

1. What do you think is the most appropriate kind of career for you? Why do you think so?
2. What is your dream job?

A: *Can you tell me why you think a new bakery would be successful in your hometown?*

B: *Sure. It's because two bakeries have closed in recent years. Now there is no place to buy fresh bread and cakes, and most people don't have time to bake those things themselves.*

FINAL TASK Presenting a Socially Responsible Business

> You are going to research a business that is socially responsible and give a presentation about it.

A For the topic of your presentation, choose a business that you know or that you want to learn more about. Locate the business's website and follow these steps.

1. Read general information about the company on the "About Us" page. Take notes.
2. Look for information about its corporate social responsibility. This may be under "Social Responsibility," "Mission," or "Values."
3. Write down three interesting facts about the company, and three interesting facts about its social responsibility efforts.

> **PRESENTATION SKILL** Looking Up While Speaking
>
> When speaking in front of a large group, it is important to connect with your audience. One way to do this is by looking up and making eye contact. Try to look down at your notes only occasionally, and then look up and speak. When you look at the audience, look at different members of the audience, including those close to you and those in the back of the room.

B Practice your presentation. Use the notes you took in exercise A and your own words to talk about the business you researched. Practice looking up while speaking.

PRESENTING **C** Give your presentation to a small group of students. Remember to look up from your notes while you are speaking. Answer any questions your classmates might have.

REFLECTION

1. What did you learn about using numbers and statistics in this unit?

_____

_____

2. What topics from the unit were the most interesting to you? Why?

_____

_____

3. Here are the vocabulary words from the unit. Check (✓) the ones you can use.

☐ accessible AWL	☐ corporation AWL	☐ generate AWL
☐ affordable	☐ demonstrate AWL	☐ model
☐ assess AWL	☐ diverse AWL	☐ outcome AWL
☐ charity	☐ donate	☐ poverty
☐ concept AWL	☐ effective	☐ profit
☐ conventional AWL	☐ entrepreneur	☐ response AWL
☐ cooperate AWL	☐ fundamental AWL	

DESIGN WITH PURPOSE 6

A moose sculpture hangs on the wall while an employee works in a quiet common area of a Google office in Waterloo, Ontario, Canada.

THINK AND DISCUSS

1 Look at the photo. Why do you think the company has a space like this for employees?

2 What is your opinion about the design of the room? What would you change?

Look at the photo and read the information. Then discuss the questions.

1. Do you visit museums or art galleries often? Why or why not?
2. What do you personally think about Pei's design for the Louvre?
3. Why do you think the initial reaction to his design was so negative?

AN ELEGANT SOLUTION

In 1983, architect I.M. Pei was commissioned by French president François Mitterrand to design a new grand entrance for the world-famous Louvre Museum and to reorganize the museum's interior. The project presented many challenges. The historic buildings were in disrepair; the entrance could not handle the large number of visitors; art galleries were not connected; and people got lost in the corridors.

A visitor admires the Louvre Museum at night as he stands in front of Pei's pyramid.

Pei came up with a grand plan. His solution was to place a new entrance in the exterior courtyard. He would build new areas underground that would welcome visitors, provide public spaces, and give easy access to the art galleries. The new entrance would be marked by a glass-and-metal pyramid, mirroring the Great Pyramid of Giza in Egypt. When Pei unveiled his design, the international response was extremely negative, and Pei received criticism from all sides. However, he completed his plan, and the updated Louvre was opened in 1989. Today the glass pyramid at the Louvre is a beloved jewel of the Paris landscape, admired by both Parisians and tourists.

A Vocabulary

A 🎧 **2.13** Read while you listen to the texts and think about the meaning of the words in **blue**. Then work with a partner to choose the correct definition for each word.

Wainwright Building, 1892, St. Louis, Missouri, USA

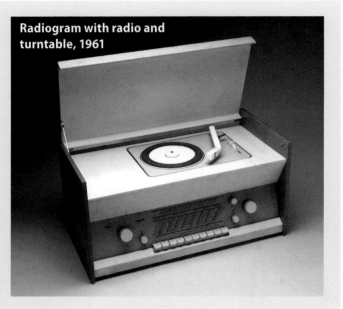

Radiogram with radio and turntable, 1961

Louis Sullivan was an American architect who died in 1924. He worked for clients in many U.S. cities including Chicago, Illinois, and Buffalo, New York, and was one of the first architects to design and build tall skyscrapers using **materials** such as steel and concrete. His ideas have had a major **influence** on design and architecture. He is best known for stating the **principle** that "form follows **function**." This means that the way a building or product looks must depend on how people will use it, not on how it was designed in the past.

Dieter Rams, born in 1932, is a German industrial designer. Many of the products he designed in the 60s and 70s are still stylish and **appealing**. Rams is deeply **committed** to good design, and this led him to come up with 10 principles of good design. One key **element** of his **philosophy** is that "less is better," meaning that good design should be as simple as possible. He also believed good designs should be **innovative** rather than old-fashioned, and made from **sustainable** materials that are good for the planet. His approach has generated many designs with a timeless quality.

1. Materials are substances _____.
   a. such as metal and stone
   b. that are made by hand

2. To influence means to __*b*__.
   a. spend other people's money
   b. have an effect on somebody

3. A principle is a __*rule*__.
   a. way of learning
   b. rule or belief

4. The function of something is _____.

   a. its purpose   b. its value

5. Something that is appealing is _____.

   a. careful   b. attractive

6. A person who is committed to an idea _____.

   a. came up with the idea   b. believes strongly in it

7. An element is an _____.

   a. important part of something   b. effective way of doing something

8. A person's philosophy is his or her _____.

   a. belief about others   b. attitude toward life

9. Something that is innovative is _____.

   a. cheap and useful   b. new and modern

10. Something that is sustainable _____.

   a. can be made from any type of material   b. does little harm to the environment

B Work in a small group. Discuss the questions and explain your answers.

1. What kinds of vacation destinations do you find appealing?
2. What design element is most important for you in selecting a chair?
3. Think of something you own that has more than one function. What is its main function? What other functions can it have?
4. Who has had the biggest influence on your life: a relative, a friend, or somebody else?
5. Why are you committed to learning English?
6. What are some principles, such as "treat others with respect," that parents should teach their children?
7. Which of these materials do you find the most attractive: glass, steel, stone, or wood?
8. Which do you feel is a better philosophy for being successful in life: learn from your mistakes or avoid making mistakes?
9. Designers are often described as innovative. What are some other jobs that require people to be innovative?
10. When you go shopping, are you usually willing to pay more for goods that are labeled as "sustainable"?

C Use a dictionary to complete the chart with different word forms. Then write four sentences in your notebook, using four words that you added to the chart.

Noun	Verb	Adjective
		appealing
		committed
influence		
		innovative

An industrial designer works on a light.

A Listening A Guest Lecture about Design

BEFORE LISTENING

A Work in a small group. Match these different types of design to the correct definition. Then discuss which you would be most interested in learning more about and why.

1. _____ automotive design
2. _____ graphic design
3. _____ interior design
4. _____ industrial design
5. _____ landscape architecture
6. _____ video game design

a. communicating with diagrams, photos, and so on
b. creating outdoor areas that are appealing
c. designing cars, trucks, motorcycles, and so on
d. designing goods that are mass produced
e. making interesting, interactive entertainment
f. making the inside of a building look good

B Work with a partner. Read this excerpt from the lecture and discuss the most likely meaning of the word *prototype*. Then share your idea with another pair of students.

"When I was at design college, my professor gave me an assignment. The task was to design and make a chair using any materials I wanted. Well, I spent several weeks coming up with a design and then making a **prototype**."

WHILE LISTENING

LISTENING FOR
MAIN IDEAS

C 🎧 2.14 Listen to the lecture. What does the guest speaker mainly discuss? Check (✓) three answers.

- ☑ An influential experience she had as a design student
- ☑ Examples of the designs that she finds most appealing
- ☑ People who have had a major impact on her philosophy
- ☑ Reasons why she enjoys designing things for her clients
- ☑ Some principles she thinks are important for good design
- ☐ Why different people have different ideas about design

D 🎧 2.15 Listen again to part of the lecture. The speaker discusses a student project. Number the steps she mentions in the order she did them. When you have finished, compare answers with a partner.

_3_ She built a prototype.

_4_ She felt pleased with her hard work.

_6_ She tested her prototype.

_8_ She learned from the experience.

_7_ She realized that her design was poor.

_5_ She showed her professor her design.

_2_ She spent time thinking up a design.

_1_ She was given an assignment to do.

LISTENING SKILL Listening for Inferences

Speakers will usually say what they mean directly. In some cases, though, a speaker may imply something by saying it in an indirect way. To infer a speaker's meaning, ask yourself "Why is he saying this?" or "What point is she trying to make?" as you listen.

In conversation, a speaker may imply something by saying the opposite of what he or she actually means. A speaker will often do this in order to be funny.

The weather was great: three whole days of rain!
(We can infer that the weather was terrible.)

E 🎧 2.16 Listen to three excerpts from the lecture. Write the inference you can make about each excerpt. Then compare and discuss your answers with a partner.

1. _____

_____

2. _____

_____

3. _____

_____

AFTER LISTENING

F Work in a small group. Complete the tasks.

1. The guest speaker, Ana Fuentes, describes learning from her mistakes. Think about when you learned from a mistake that you or somebody else made. Explain the situation and what you learned.

2. Some people say, "The biggest mistake in life is to be afraid of making mistakes." Discuss whether you agree or disagree with this idea and why.

A Speaking

GRAMMAR FOR SPEAKING Making Comparisons

To make comparisons, use either a comparative, superlative, or *as … as* with adjectives and adverbs.

We use comparatives to compare one thing with another:

> *His suggestion was* **better / more useful / worse / less clear** *than I had expected.*
> *She spoke* **more / more quickly / less / less often** *than others.*

We use superlatives to compare one thing with many things:

> *Among all the suggestions, his was* **the best / the most useful / the worst / the least clear**.
> *Everyone helped, but she helped* **the most / the most willingly / the least / the least often**.

We use *as … as* to say that two things are equal (or different) in some way:

> *His suggestion is* **as useful as / not as clear as** *hers.*
> *I needed her help* **as much as** *his. / I didn't need her help* **as often as** *his.*

A   Read these quotes from the lecture. Mark the comparisons in each quote.

1. For me, good design must meet certain criteria, certain principles. The most important of these is that a product must serve a useful function.
2. It has to help people do something better, or more easily, or less expensively.
3. If I had to name the person who's had the biggest influence on my design philosophy, it would be Dieter Rams.
4. Sometimes I work with clients who feel form is just as important as function.

PERSONALIZING   **B**   Complete these sentences in your own words. Then share and explain your ideas in a small group.

1. The person who has had the biggest influence on my sense of fashion is _Nobody I get most of my stuff online_.

2. For me, the most important principle when buying clothes is that _It got a good quality_.

3. An example of a clothing brand that has good design but is less expensive than designer brands is _____.

4. I usually wear _Sneaker_ more often than other types of shoes.

5. When I buy _Clothes_, price is not as important as quality.

SPEAKING SKILL Using Descriptive Language

We often use common adjectives when we give an opinion about something. For example, we might say something is *great, fantastic, horrible,* or *beautiful.* Adjectives like these are acceptable in casual conversations, but it is better to use more descriptive words to be more persuasive and clear.

1. Use specific adjectives.

   In my opinion, this chair has a <u>creative</u> design.

2. Use comparisons to expand on descriptions.
   For me, this chair is made from <u>better</u> quality materials <u>than</u> the other chairs.

3. Use figurative language such as similes or metaphors.
   In my view, this chair looks <u>as</u> beautiful and natural <u>as</u> a tree.

C Write answers to the questions in your notebook, using descriptive language to explain your answers. Then discuss with a partner and take notes on your partner's answers.

1. What are your three favorite foods?
2. Which kinds of activities do you do less often: indoor ones or outdoor ones?
3. Of all the countries in the world, which one would you most like to visit?
4. Thinking of all the activities you have ever done, which one would you least like to do again?
5. Do you think watching a movie alone is as good as watching one with friends?

CRITICAL THINKING Making Inferences

When you infer, you notice specific evidence or clues and come to a conclusion. Clues can be facts or ideas that help you understand or recognize something. For example, a speaker's tone of voice can be a clue that helps you understand his or her feelings, or the clothes that people in a photo are wearing can be a clue as to when the photo was taken. Noticing clues allows you to make inferences based on informed ideas rather than guesswork.

EVERYDAY LANGUAGE Expressing Inferences

Informal	Formal
It seems likely that …	*This suggests that …*
This probably means that …	*This implies that …*

D Work with a different partner. Using your notes from exercise C, take turns summarizing your other partner's answers. Make sure you use comparative language correctly. Then make an inference based on your partner's answer.

> *My partner said that he likes pizza, hamburgers, and tacos, but likes pizza the best. It seems likely that he probably eats a lot of fast food.*

CRITICAL THINKING:
MAKING INFERENCES

E Work in a small group. Look at the photos and read the information. Then discuss the questions.

The word *chindogu* translates as "weird tools." The International Chindogu Society was founded by Japanese designer and inventor Kenji Kawakami and U.S. journalist Dan Papia. Kawakami, who came up with the name *chindogu*, has invented hundreds of strange and unusual objects. *Chindogu* inventions are impractical solutions to everyday problems. Every invention is somewhat useless, but always fun.

1. Have you ever heard of *chindogu* or anything similar before?
2. What do you think of the idea of *chindogu*? Why?
3. Would you ever use either of the *chindogu* inventions? Explain.
4. What other *chindogu*-style alarm clocks or helmets can you imagine?

A: *I've never heard of chindogu before. Have you?*
B: *No, but I think the inventions are really …*
C: *I agree, but don't you think they're also … ?*

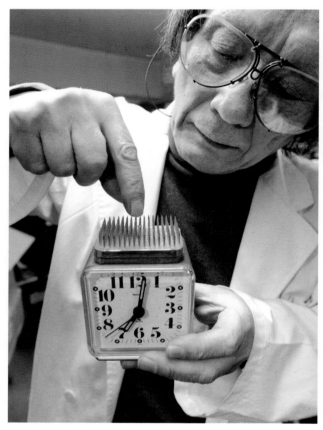

▲ **Kawakami demonstrates his alarm clock. It has a snooze button under a bed of sharp pins to make sure you don't go back to sleep.**

▲ **This *chindogu* is the perfect bike helmet for those who like to wear their hair in braids or ponytails.**

F Work with a partner. Discuss what two or three principles describe *chindogu* inventions. Then mark which of the principles below summarize the opinions of Dieter Rams (DR) about design and which describe *chindogu* inventions (C).

1. _____ It cannot have a very useful function.
2. _____ It has to look visually appealing to users.
3. _____ It must be designed to last for a long time.
4. _____ It should be funny.
5. _____ It must have a practical, useful function.

LESSON TASK Presenting a Design

A Work in a small group. Come up with your own idea for a *chindogu* invention. Make sure your idea meets the principles of *chindogu* in exercise F.

B In your group, work together to draw or create a picture of your design. Then use the outline below to plan a three-minute talk.

1. Introduction with a question to the audience. (*Have you ever… ?*)

   _____

   _____

2. Explanation of what your invention is called and how it works.

   _____

   _____

3. Explanation of who might use it.

   _____

   _____

C Practice your presentation. Keep these points in mind.

Make sure:
- you display the picture of the design that you created
- that everyone in your group has the chance to say something
- you can deliver your talk in three minutes or less

D As a group, deliver your talk and answer any questions from other students. Then listen to the other groups present their ideas, and ask questions.

E Work with a partner. Discuss these questions.

1. Did all of the presented ideas meet the *chindogu* principles?
2. Which of the ideas did you think was the most interesting? Why?
3. What part of your presentation were you most pleased with? Why?
4. What will you try to do better next time you give a presentation? Why?

Skylar Tibbits, National Geographic Explorer and founder of the Self-Assembly Lab at MIT in Cambridge, MA, USA

Designing the Future

BEFORE VIEWING

A Work with a partner. Use clues to complete the definitions (listed in the order the words are used in the video).

1. To **transform** means to change from _____.
2. **Components** are a part of something _____.
3. To **trigger** something is to cause it to _____.
4. **Assembly** is the action of joining _____.
5. **Morph** is very similar in meaning _____.
6. **Fluctuations** are irregular changes _____.
7. **Collaboration** means to work with _____.
8. **Precision** means either being accurate _____.

a. components to make something
b. happen, to start, or to exist
c. in the level of something
d. larger, such as a machine
e. to the word *transform*
f. one thing or shape into another
g. or paying attention to detail
h. others to produce something

B Read about Skylar Tibbits. As a class, discuss what types of things he may be designing in his laboratory.

> **MEET SKYLAR TIBBITS.** He's a National Geographic Explorer, designer, computer science researcher, and a professor at the Massachusetts Institute of Technology. His invention of 4D printing has led to a unique area of design research.

WHILE VIEWING

C ▶ 1.11 Watch the video with the sound off. Number these statements in the order you see them on the screen. Then compare your answers with a partner.

a. _____ Self-assembling materials could be used in airplanes.

b. _____ Self-assembling materials could be used in cars, medicine, even clothing and sporting goods.

c. _____ Skylar Tibbits creates materials that help various objects transform themselves.

d. _____ These high-tech materials are triggered by temperature, water, time, and the slightest touch.

e. _____ They respond to the same triggers that nature does.

f. _____ Would you want furniture that can build itself?

D ▶ 1.11 Watch the video again, this time with sound. What is the main message of the video? Discuss in a small group.

UNDERSTANDING MAIN IDEAS

a. Machines like airplanes must be made of strong materials.

b. Nature has produced materials that humans cannot copy.

c. Robots are becoming better at assembling components.

d. Self-assembling materials offer many benefits to humans.

E ▶ 1.11 Complete each sentence with a phrase from the box. Two of the phrases will not be used. Then watch the video once more to confirm your answers.

UNDERSTANDING DETAILS

build some furniture	the future of robotics
remove components, complexity	pairs of shoes
the creativity of humans	put things together
environments and users	temperature, moisture, pressure

1. Skylar Tibbits says he and his team aim to _remove components_.

2. He wants to make smart products that respond to _environments and user_.

3. He says that in nature, there is just a single way to _put things together_.

4. He mentions carbon fiber sheets that are affected by _temperature_.

5. He says that for different tasks, people have different _pairs of shoes_.

6. Tibbits says that his group believes materials are _the future of robotic_.

AFTER VIEWING

F Discuss these questions with a partner.

CRITICAL THINKING: EVALUATING

1. Which of the ideas mentioned in the video is most interesting for you personally? Why?
   - furniture that can assemble itself
   - smart products that can respond to users
   - shoes that can change to perform better
   - high-tech materials that respond to touch

2. Do you think the work of Skylar Tibbits is more closely related to design, to engineering, or to some other field?

B Vocabulary

MEANING FROM
CONTEXT

A 🎧 2.17 Read and listen to the information and think about the meaning of the words in **blue**. Then choose the best definition for each word in **blue**. When you have finished, compare answers with a partner.

> **Course Description UXDN 364 – User Experience Design**
>
> Digital technology is becoming increasingly **sophisticated** and important, but often such technologies are poorly designed and hard to use. User experience (UX) design is the process of increasing the **satisfaction** level of users by making digital products such as websites or computer applications more appealing and easier to use. The main **objective** of the course is to help students **identify** and apply the key principles of UX design. The course describes the typical ways that users **browse** websites and use applications; it explains and **illustrates** how poor design choices can be frustrating to users; and it **explores** how better, more user-friendly UX design can solve these problems and **enhance** overall user experience. This course is delivered through lectures and online sessions, and is graded through a **combination** of continuous **assessment** and final exam.

1. The adjective *sophisticated* means _____ .

    a. advanced or experienced   b. valuable but hard to find

2. The noun *satisfaction* means the feeling of _____ .

    a. pleasure from a good experience   b. relaxation after a difficult job

3. The noun *objective* means a _____ .

    a. desire or wish   b. goal or purpose

4. The verb *identify* means to _____ .

    a. decide how to design something   b. recognize a person or thing

5. The verb *browse* is closest in meaning to _____ .

    a. look at information online   b. read information in detail

6. The verb *illustrate* means to make something _____ .

    a. available to people online   b. clear by giving examples

7. The verb *explore* is closest in meaning to _____ .

    a. study a subject in detail   b. spend time visiting a place

8. The verb *enhance* means to _____ .

    a. enjoy for the first time   b. improve the quality of something

9. The noun *combination* means _____ .

    a. joining two or more things   b. thinking about several possibilities

10. The noun *assessment* likely means measurement of _____ .

    a. academic progress   b. financial value

B 🎧 **2.18** Listen to a short conversation between two students. Complete each statement with one word from the conversation. The missing words are from the blue words in exercise A.

CRITICAL THINKING: ANALYZING

1. She says Professor Selkirk helped her _identified_ what she wanted.
2. She says she understood what her _objectives_ for the class should be.
3. She got an excellent grade through a _combination_ of hard work and reading.
4. She felt a lot of _satisfaction_ after getting an A on her final exam.

VOCABULARY SKILL Multiple Meanings

Some words in English have more than one meaning. Many academic words have two or more meanings. For instance, the word *academic* itself has several meanings:

a. related to education: *The student had an excellent academic record.*
b. not real, practical, or relevant: *His argument was interesting but academic.*
c. a professor: *She worked as an academic for 40 years until her retirement.*

When you learn new vocabulary, check whether a word has more than one meaning and decide which meaning is most useful to you.

C Work with a partner. Decide who is A and who is B. Then write the correct words with multiple meanings in each space. You can use a dictionary to help you. Then share and discuss your answers.

Student A – Blue words from page 104

- _objective_ ₁ : a large or formal social event, or the purpose of something
- _identify_ ₂ : a person who affects others or the power to affect someone or something
- _assessment_ ₃ : an academic subject or a person's way of thinking
- _objectives_ ₄ : a rule or law or a specific way of thinking

Student B – Blue words from page 114

- _browse_ ₅ : to look at goods in a store in a casual way or to view information online
- _identify_ ₆ : to say or prove who a person is or to recognize someone or something
- _illustrates_ ₇ : to draw a picture or to give clear examples
- _explore_ ₈ : to travel in an unfamiliar country or to discuss or study a subject in detail

---

D Interview your classmates by asking these survey questions. Note their answers. What was the most interesting answer?

PERSONALIZING

1. What kinds of websites do you like to browse?
2. What is one thing that would enhance your life?
3. What kind of assessment is the most difficult for you in school?
4. What is one objective you want to achieve soon?
5. What is something that gives you satisfaction?

Listening A Conversation with a Teaching Assistant

BEFORE LISTENING

www.PHDCOMICS.com

CRITICAL THINKING:
MAKING INFERENCES

A 🎧 **2.19** Read and listen to the comic strip about a university student and a teaching assistant (TA). Then discuss the questions in a small group. Be prepared to explain your answers.

1. Read the comic strip. What does it tell you about what TAs do?
2. What clues in the comic strip tell you that the TA feels frustrated?
3. The TA says, "Yes, please! My life is at your disposal!" meaning "I'm ready to do whatever you would like me to do." What can you infer from this?
4. Would you be interested in working as a TA in the future? Explain.

WHILE LISTENING

LISTENING FOR
MAIN IDEAS

B 🎧 **2.20** Listen to the conversation. Then answer the questions.

1. Why does the student go to see the teaching assistant?
   a. to ask about the design process
   b. to get feedback on a new design
   c. to get help with an assigned task
   d. to submit a finished assignment

2. What do the speakers mainly discuss?
   a. the steps and benefits of the design process
   b. what information the professor expects
   c. typical user-experience design problems
   d. how many stages the design process has

3. What is the student most likely to do next?
   a. choose a design process to use
   b. follow the woman's suggestions
   c. begin working on a new assignment
   d. enhance and redesign his original idea

NOTE-TAKING SKILL Noting Steps in a Process

When you hear a speaker describe a process, use these strategies to take more effective notes:

1. Listen for sequence words and phrases such as *first, after that,* or *the next step is to.* These will help you recognize all the steps in the process and organize your notes clearly. Numbering each stage in your notes—even if the speaker does not use numbers to introduce each step—is also helpful.

2. Use abbreviations to note key points about each stage in the process more quickly. For example, instead of writing *ask for feedback from users,* your notes could be *ask 4 fdbck.*

3. For complex processes, it can be helpful to draw arrows or simple diagrams to help you understand the order of the steps.

C 🎧 2.20 Listen to the conversation again and take notes. Then complete this diagram of the design process by writing one word from the conversation in each space.

LISTENING FOR DETAILS

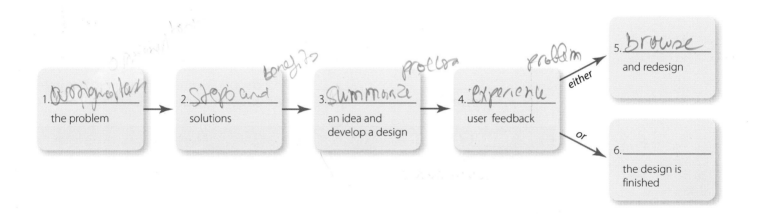

1. _____ the problem
2. _____ solutions
3. _____ an idea and develop a design
4. _____ user feedback
5. browse and redesign *(either)*
6. _____ the design is finished *(or)*

AFTER LISTENING

D Work in a small group. Discuss the questions and support your opinions with reasons and examples.

CRITICAL THINKING: APPLYING

1. Instead of asking the TA for help, what else could the student have done about his problem? What would you have done in this situation?

2. Would the design process discussed in the conversation be useful in the following situations? If so, describe how it would be useful. If not, explain why not.
   - choosing where to go on vacation
   - deciding what to wear for a special event
   - writing an essay for English class

Speaking

A Work in a small group. Write phrases from the list that best complete the information about UX principles. One of the phrases will not be used.

Be for non-experts	Help save time	Offer a valuable service
Cost very little	Look attractive	Work and look the same

KEY PRINCIPLES OF GOOD UX DESIGN

Good user experience design should:

1. _____. A good user experience allows users to work quickly, efficiently, and without mistakes; UX should never waste users' time.

2. _____. Users want sites and applications with a design that is clean, simple, beautiful to look at, and without unnecessary elements.

3. _____. It is not enough for sites or applications to look nice; they also need to provide an experience that users find useful.

4. _____. Sites should have a standard appearance and be usable in a consistent way; one way to achieve this is by reusing icons and colors.

5. _____. Most people are not computer programmers or designers; they want a user experience that is easy to understand.

PRONUNCIATION Effective Pausing

In general, speakers who pause effectively are easier to understand. Here are some strategies for when and how long to pause.

- Short pause—after each thought group; after each sentence; after each item in a list; before and after words or phrases that you want to emphasize
- Longer pause—before you move on to a new point to give listeners time to understand what you have just said; to give the audience time to look at a slide; to build interest in what you are going to say next

---

▶ **These control buttons illustrate key principles of good UX design. The design is clear and attractive, and the icons are easy to understand.**

B With a partner, mark where you would pause when reading aloud the information about good UX design in exercise A. Mark / for a short pause and // for a longer pause. After you have finished, practice reading it aloud with effective pauses.

C Think of a website or software application you know well. Make notes about how well it matches the five principles of good UX design outlined in exercise A.

CRITICAL THINKING: EVALUATING

Principles	Notes
1. Help save time	
2.	
3.	
4.	
5.	

D Work in a small group. Share information about your site or app from exercise C.

FINAL TASK Presenting a Process

In this unit you have learned about the design process. This same process can be followed any time you create something. You will give a presentation about the process you followed when you designed, created, made, changed, improved, or developed something.

PRESENTATION SKILL Body Language

When you give a presentation, your body language is an important part of your message. Positive body language can make your message clearer and give your audience a better feeling about your presentation. There are four elements of good body language:

1. Gestures—move your hand up or down to show that something is increasing or decreasing, or hold up one, then two, then three fingers to show steps in a process.

2. Posture—standing up straight can help you look more confident and speak more loudly and clearly; sitting down can make you seem more relaxed and friendly.

3. Position—when you are presenting, make sure you face your audience rather than turning your back to them; if you have slides, do not stand in front of them.

4. Facial expressions—use your eyes and mouth effectively by smiling often and making eye contact with individual people in your audience.

A Follow these stages as you prepare your talk.

- Identify the process you will describe in your talk.
- Brainstorm the steps in the process.
- Create an outline for your talk with ideas about what to say.

B Work with a partner. Complete the steps.

1. Review the information in the Presentation Skill box. Think about how you can use positive body language when you deliver your presentation.

2. Take turns practicing your talk. Give each other feedback about how to improve especially in terms of body language.

3. Make changes to your presentation based on your partner's feedback. Then practice giving your presentation again.

PRESENTING **C** Present your talk. After your presentation, answer questions from other students. Then watch their presentations and ask questions.

CRITICAL THINKING: **D** Work in a small group. Discuss these questions.
REFLECTING

1. What did you like most about your talk? What will you try to do better next time?
2. Did you think your body language was as good as usual or better than usual? Why?
3. Which talk did you think was the most interesting? Why?

REFLECTION

1. Which of the skills or language that you learned is most likely to be useful to you during the next week? Why?

_____

_____

2. What did you learn about design or UX (or anything else) that you would like to share with somebody? Who would you tell and why?

_____

_____

3. Here are the vocabulary words from the unit. Check (✓) the ones you can use.

☐ appealing	☐ explore	☐ objective AWL
☐ assessment AWL	☐ function AWL	☐ philosophy AWL
☐ browse	☐ identify AWL	☐ principle AWL
☐ combination	☐ illustrate AWL	☐ satisfaction
☐ committed AWL	☐ influence	☐ sophisticated
☐ element AWL	☐ innovative AWL	☐ sustainable AWL
☐ enhance AWL	☐ materials	

INSPIRED TO PROTECT

7

Students learn about the outdoors from young rangers and graduate students at North Cascades National Park in Washington, USA.

THINK AND DISCUSS

1 Look at the unit title. What do you think it means? How does it relate to the photo?

2 What can children learn about the environment by exploring the outdoors?

3 Are you interested in the topic of the environment?

Look at the photos and read the quotes by three National Geographic Explorers. Then discuss the questions.

1. How has each person helped get others involved in environmental issues?
2. Which approach do you think is most effective? Why?
3. What environmental issue are you most concerned about? Least concerned about? Why?

INSPIRING OTHERS

"There is always a solution. People sometimes are desperate, even myself—I'm desperate about all the destruction happening in Sumatra—but then, do something, even a small [thing]. When you see a problem and you see things not happening and you feel that someone else will fix it, then that is the start of destruction. I created a volunteer opportunity for local people, young people that have now become dedicated staff to help the forest and the orangutans. People are now thinking, wow, you do something and there's progress."

Panut Hadisiswoyo, conservationist at the Orangutan Information Centre, Sumatra, Indonesia

"I have worked for a long time with the [native] people in my country and I'm going to be focusing a lot more on their wisdom. With Ösel Foundation, a lot of our projects and trips [with schoolgirls] will be about taking care of Mother Earth and really reflecting on how much our time on Earth affects it negatively. It's just mindful awareness on walking this planet."

Wasfia Nazreen, mountain climber, activist, and writer from Bangladesh

"I wanted to . . . find new things and learn about them and share them with other people. It had never occurred to me that you could do that as a photographer. . . . The way I define science is just a careful observation of your surroundings. . . . If people value that systematic process of careful observation, I think it could solve a lot of the problems and I think it would help people enjoy their lives and enjoy their planet. . . . I want to get people to revisit their assumptions about parasites, bees, bugs, hummingbirds, and natural history overall."

Anand Varma, science photographer from the United States

A Vocabulary

MEANING FROM
CONTEXT

A 🎧 **2.21** **Read these definitions. Complete each sentence with one of the words in blue. Then listen to check your answers.**

a. **capacity** (n) – the ability to do, experience, or hold something
b. **conservation** (n) – the protection of something, especially nature
c. **fatigue** (n) – a strong feeling of physical or mental tiredness
d. **passion** (n) – a strong enthusiasm for some activity or thing
e. **resources** (n) – things that are useful

1. Even as a child, Lina loved caring for other people, and this _**passion**_ for helping was the main reason she accepted a job working for a charity.

2. According to a report, the world has a limited supply of important _**resources**_ called rare earth metals that are needed to make smartphones.

3. The newspaper article about _**conservation**_ was interesting, but Melissa wasn't in the mood to read about more problems with the environment.

4. Nico's intelligence and _**capacity**_ for hard work were the main reasons he was awarded an academic scholarship.

5. After his baby was born, Ben experienced a sleep deficit[1], and his constant _**fatigue**_ made it hard for him to concentrate at work.

[1]**deficit** (n): a lack of something

VOCABULARY SKILL Using Word Maps

A word map is a visual way to organize key information about new words to help you learn vocabulary. This key information could include:

- the definition
- the part of speech (e.g., noun)
- different forms of the word

- synonyms or antonyms
- common collocations
- an example sentence

Here is a word map model you could use in your vocabulary notebook:

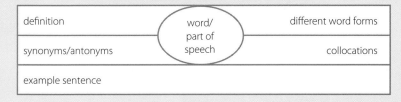

definition	word/ part of speech	different word forms
synonyms/antonyms		collocations
example sentence		

B 🎧 2.22 Listen to the words in **blue**. In your notebook, create a word map for each word. *Apathetic* is done as an example. Use a dictionary if necessary. Then compare your maps with a partner.

apathetic	inspire	motivation	perceive	sacrifice

showing no enthusiasm or concern for something	apathetic adj	apathy (uncountable n) apathetically (adv)
uninterested; unconcerned/ enthusiastic		is apathetic about an <u>apathetic person</u>
People must stop being apathetic about the environment.		

C Complete this survey by checking (✓) the boxes that best describe you.

	Usually	Sometimes	Rarely
1. I feel fatigue because my life is so busy.	☐	☐	☐
2. I have a lot of passion for studying English.	☐	☐	☐
3. I use natural resources such as water and gas carefully.	☐	☐	☐
4. I am willing to sacrifice my time to help friends.	☐	☐	☐

D Interview classmates to find the person whose survey answers are closest to yours.

A: *Reza, is your life so busy that you feel a lot of fatigue?*
B: *Sometimes. I bet you answered the same way, didn't you?*
A: *Yeah, I did!*

E Work in a small group. Discuss the questions.

1. How can energy conservation help the environment?

2. At what age do you think a person has the greatest capacity for learning?

3. What kind of music do you have a passion for?

4. What environmental issue do you feel apathetic about?

5. What person has inspired you the most in your life?

6. How do you keep your motivation when you feel like quitting a task or an activity?

7. Why do some people perceive environmentalists as being against big businesses?

Listening A Podcast about the Environment

BEFORE LISTENING

CRITICAL THINKING:
PREDICTING

A You will hear a podcast with two National Geographic Explorers, both of whom are interested in ocean conservation. Work with a partner to list four possible topics that they may discuss.

Kenny Broad

Tierney Thys

WHILE LISTENING

LISTENING FOR
MAIN IDEAS

B 🎧 2.23 Take notes as you listen to the podcast. What do the speakers mainly discuss? Check (✓) three answers. Then compare your answers with a partner.

a. ☑ how environmental fatigue affects people's emotions
b. ☑ what environmental fatigue is and why it occurs
c. ☑ what people can do to reduce environmental fatigue
d. ☐ when environmental fatigue usually affects people
e. ☐ who is most likely to suffer environmental fatigue
f. ☑ why environmental fatigue is a serious problem

LISTENING FOR
DETAILS

C 🎧 2.23 Take notes as you listen again to the podcast. Which speaker expresses which idea? Write *KB* for Kenny Broad, or *TT* for Tierney Thys.

1. _____TT_____ One effective way to inspire people is by sharing positive stories.
2. _____KB_____ People generally worry less about distant or long-term issues.
3. _____TT_____ Although the environment has issues, these problems can be solved.
4. _____KB_____ Children understand environmental issues more than adults do.
5. _____TT_____ It is important that people not be apathetic about the environment.
6. _____KB_____ Environmental fatigue is a cultural issue, not a scientific one.

D 🎧 2.24 Listen to excerpts from the podcast. After each, choose the correct answer.

LISTENING FOR A
SPEAKER'S PURPOSE

1. Why does Kenny Broad say this?

   a. to give an example of a personal problem that many people experience
   b. to point out that some people do not have enough food to eat at home

2. Why does Kenny Broad say this?

   a. to argue that most scientists should focus on research, not communication
   b. to suggest that scientists should share their ideas better with nonscientists

3. Why does Tierney Thys say this?

   a. to explain why stories are a great way to communicate with people
   b. to emphasize a key way to inspire people to protect the environment

4. Why does Tierney Thys say this?

   a. to give an example of one way that environmental issues can be solved
   b. to imply that people can be trained to fix environmental problems at home

AFTER LISTENING

E Work in a small group. Complete the tasks.

PERSONALIZING

1. Did Broad and Thys discuss any of the topics you listed in exercise A?
2. Look back at exercise C. Which of the ideas expressed by Broad and Thys do you agree with? Explain.

Tierney Thys shows the underside of a fish in California, USA.

A Speaking

GRAMMAR FOR SPEAKING Tag Questions

Tags are words that you can add to a statement to turn it into a question. If the statement is affirmative, the tag is negative. If the statement is negative, the tag is affirmative.

- If the statement has an auxiliary verb or modal verb, use the same auxiliary or modal in the tag:

    We **can** do something about it, **can't** we?   You **aren't** listening, **are** you?

- If there is no auxiliary or modal, use the correct form of *do* in the tag:

    Those stories **affect** us less and less, **don't** they?   She **didn't like** the gift, **did** she?

- Tag questions can be confusing to answer. Answer with a full sentence rather than just giving *yes* or *no* as your answer:

    A: *I'm not late, am I?*
    B: *You're not late. / No, you're not late.*

PRONUNCIATION Intonation with Tag Questions

🎧 2.25 Tag question intonation depends on the meaning you intend.

To ask a real question because you are unsure of some information, use a rising intonation when you say the tag.

    It's not going to be an issue, is it?   (You are unsure if it will be an issue.)

To confirm information you already know, use a falling intonation.

    It's going to be an issue, isn't it?   (You think it is likely to be an issue.)

A 🎧 2.26 Add a tag to each statement. Listen to check your tags and mark each tag as rising or falling with an arrow. Then ask and answer the questions with a partner.

1. You haven't lived here for more than a year, _____

2. You were at the last class, _____

3. Your smartphone is less than a year old, _____

4. You don't come to school by bus or train, _____

5. Your hobbies include reading and running, _____

6. You can't play the guitar, _____

7. You've visited Canada before, _____

8. You aren't going to the party, _____

B With your partner, turn these statements from the podcast into tag questions. Then practice asking and answering them with natural intonation.

1. We are affecting the environment negatively, and we can't just be apathetic.
2. Facts aren't what influence people.
3. You inspire people through their emotions.
4. It's also really important to show people the challenges and the impacts we're having on the natural world.
5. We can train local people, and give them resources.
6. The kids get it, but the adults don't seem to want to sacrifice for the future.

CRITICAL THINKING Considering Other Views

Critical thinking involves having an open mind and the willingness to consider other views. Consider other views to understand, connect with, or persuade others more easily. Notice how the speaker considers other points of view in this example:

As a scientist, I base my beliefs on facts, and facts point to signs of global warming. But I understand that for most people, the facts may be very confusing.

C Complete the steps.

CRITICAL THINKING: CONSIDERING OTHER VIEWS

1. Think of someone who probably feels environmental fatigue and someone who probably does not.
2. Put yourself in these people's shoes and think of reasons why you think they probably do or do not feel environmental fatigue. Add your reasons to the T-chart below.
3. Join a small group. Talk about the two people you identified and the reasons you considered in step 2. Then listen to your classmates' information.

Name: _____	Name: _____
Environmental Fatigue	No Environmental Fatigue
Reasons:	Reasons:

SPEAKING SKILL Using Analogies

An analogy is a way of explaining something by pointing out how it is similar or related to something else. An analogy often uses the phrase *be like*.

> *A successful personal relationship **is like** a beautiful garden: It takes planning, hard work, and a lot of care.*

In some analogies, a speaker relates the scale, or size, of something to a familiar object. This kind of analogy often uses an *if / then* structure.

> ***If** the sun were the same size as a basketball, **then** Earth would be about the size of a pea, approximately 100 feet (30 meters) away from it.*

D Work with a partner to complete each statement to make a logical analogy.

1. Roads and highways are sometimes described as being like the _____.
   a. veins and arteries in a body
   b. rivers and lakes in a country

2. Both bacteria and viruses are small, but the latter are much smaller. If a single bacterium were the size of a basketball, then a single virus _____.
   a. would be roughly as big as a soccer ball
   b. might be the size of a table tennis ball

CRITICAL THINKING: EVALUATING

E Work with a partner. Look at the two illustrations and discuss the questions.

1. In what ways are the structure of Earth and the structure of a baseball similar?
2. In what ways, if any, is the analogy between Earth and a baseball not a good one?
3. It is also common to compare Earth with an onion. Which analogy do you think is better: onion or baseball? Why?

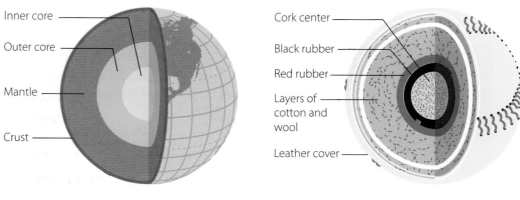

Earth   **Baseball**

F Work in a small group. Choose one of the situations below or your own idea. Then come up with an analogy to explain the situation you chose. You may want to draw a simple diagram to illustrate your analogy. Then share your analogy with other groups.

- Learning a language
- Starting at a new school
- Making a new friend
- Buying a cell phone

LESSON TASK A Group Presentation about the Environment

Trash on a beach in Ireland

A Work in a small group. Make a list of environmental issues that you are familiar with. Then brainstorm an analogy that would help explain one of the issues to others.

BRAINSTORMING

> *Dumping trash in the ocean is like …*

B In your group, read the information below. Then complete the steps.

> You work for a non-profit organization that protects the environment. You have been asked to speak to a group of people who have donated money to your organization in the past but no longer do so. You are worried that these people might have environmental fatigue.

1. Prepare and practice a three-minute talk that encourages people to donate to your non-profit.
2. Make sure that your talk:

- discusses a specific environmental issue
- explains why this is an important issue
- includes at least one analogy explaining the issue
- shows that you have considered other views
- gives everyone in your group a chance to speak

C As a group, deliver your talk. Answer any questions. When all groups have delivered their talks, discuss which analogies were the most effective and why.

PRESENTING

Satellite image of the continent of Africa

BEFORE VIEWING

PERSONALIZING

A Many people think that watching videos is a good way to improve their English. Choose the best word to complete these statements so that they describe you. Then share your statements with a partner and discuss any differences you have.

- I (often / sometimes / occasionally) watch videos in English to improve my English skills.
- I think it's (important / unimportant) to understand every word in a video.
- I (always / sometimes / never) turn on subtitles when watching videos in English.

B Work in a group of three. Each person chooses one of the three lists of words you will hear in the video. Use a dictionary to check the meanings of the words in your list. Then explain those meanings to your two partners.

A	B	C
condense (v)	greedy (adj)	reaction (n)
corporation (n)	miracle (n)	symptom (n)
era (n)	neglect (v)	toxin (n)
existence (n)	oppression (n)	wisdom (n)

WHILE VIEWING

CRITICAL THINKING: MAKING INFERENCES

C ▶ 1.12 Watch the video without sound. Take notes on what you see. With a partner discuss which statement is the main message of the video.

a. Earth has many types of life such as animals, humans, and plants.
b. Humans need to do a much better job caring for the world.
c. It may soon be time for humans to emigrate to other planets.
d. Water is the most important ingredient for life.

D ▶ 1.12 Watch the video with sound. The man speaks quickly, but you don't have to understand every word. Do you still think your answer to exercise C is correct?

UNDERSTANDING MAIN IDEAS

E ▶ 1.12 Complete each statement about the video with a number from the box. Then watch the video again to check your answers.

UNDERSTANDING DETAILS

3	fourth	4.5	33	1,000	140,000

1. The speaker, Prince Ea, says that Earth is __4.5__ billion years old.
2. Prince Ea claims that humans are __140 000__ years old.
3. Humans have been on Earth for the equivalent of __3__ seconds.
4. Species are going extinct __33__ times faster than usual.
5. A billion, trillion, trillion is a one followed by __1000__ zeroes.
6. Prince Ea worries humans may not survive until the __fourth__ second.

AFTER VIEWING

F Rank these quotations from 1 to 5 according to how much you agree with them. Then share your order with a partner and discuss any differences of opinion.

CRITICAL THINKING: RANKING

_____ The real crisis … is us.
_____ It is our duty to protect Mother Nature.
_____ We should have the right to eat food that's safe.
_____ Only together can we make it to the fourth second.
_____ Everything, every species, is connected genetically.

G Work in a small group. Which of these words would you use to summarize the video?

a poem/a rap	doubtful/trustworthy	effective/ineffective
negative/positive	powerful/weak	

Richard Williams, better known by his stage name Prince Ea, is an American spoken word artist, poet, rapper, and filmmaker.

B Vocabulary

MEANING FROM CONTEXT

A 🎧 2.27 Read and listen to the sentences. Think about the meaning of each word in **blue**. Mark the words you already know.

1. As a political **activist**, she went to many government meetings and met with government officials.
2. We must first be **aware** of a problem before we can solve it.
3. The snowstorm caused a **crisis** when it forced two power stations to shut down.
4. The politician will certainly **deny** that she has received any illegal gifts.
5. Her small, dark apartment was **depressing**, so she didn't invite friends to visit.
6. He worked hard on the assignment, so he felt **discouraged** when he received a poor grade.
7. Surprisingly, losing his job three times in two years did not change Jon's **optimism**.
8. My friend is a nice guy, but I sometimes get tired of his constant **pessimism**. He always expects the worst.
9. Three examples of **renewable** sources of energy are solar, wind, and water.
10. A government website can be a valuable **source** of statistical information.

B Write the words in **blue** from exercise A next to the correct definitions.

1. _renewable_ (adj) can be replaced
2. _crisis_ (n) a very difficult or dangerous time or situation
3. _optimism_ (n) the expectation that good things will happen in the future
4. _depressing_ (adj) feeling a loss of confidence or hope
5. _activist_ (n) a person who works to cause political or social change
6. _deny_ (v) to say something is untrue
7. _aware_ (adj) conscious of; knowing about something
8. _pessimism_ (n) the expectation that bad things will happen in the future
9. _discouraged_ (adj) making people feel unhappy and without hope
10. _source_ (n) the place, person, or thing from which something originally comes

C Work with a partner. Identify the part of speech for these forms of the words from exercise A. Then write five sentences with five of the words in your notebook.

1. activism _____
2. awareness _____
3. critical _____
4. denial _____
5. depression _____
6. discourage _____
7. optimistic _____
8. pessimist _____
9. renew _____
10. source _____

D Work in a small group. Spend 30 seconds making a list in response to each question. Then compare your answers with another group.

BRAINSTORMING

1. What environmental problems are you aware of?

    _____

2. What social issues do you feel pessimistic about?

    _____

3. What gives you a feeling of optimism?

    _____

4. What sources of news do people use?

    _____

5. What crises have recently been in the news?

    _____

E Work with a partner. Read these headlines. Discuss why the people mentioned in the headlines might feel this way.

CRITICAL THINKING: CONSIDERING OTHER VIEWS

A: *It's obvious why higher prices discourage older people, isn't it?*
B: *Yeah. They discourage everyone. But senior citizens have less income, right?*

> • Senior Citizens Discouraged by Rising Food Prices
>
> • Environmental Activists Say Crisis Can Be Avoided
>
> • Most Office Workers Find Workplace Depressing
>
> • People Want More Investment in Renewable Energy
>
> • Survey: Children Have More Optimism about Future

F Interview other students in your class to find out if they feel the same way as the people mentioned in the newspaper headlines.

A: *Are you discouraged by rising prices, Adira?*
B: *A little. How about you, Kenzo?*
C: *Not really. Prices are always rising.*

◀ **A customer reads a newspaper in a coffee house in Addis Ababa, Ethiopia.**

B Listening A Talk about the Environment

BEFORE LISTENING

CRITICAL THINKING:
RANKING

A Work in a small group. Rank these groups of people in order from most likely to protect the environment (*1*) to least likely (*5*). Then share your order with another group and explain your views.

_____ businesspeople

_____ celebrities

_____ children

_____ politicians

_____ scientists

WHILE LISTENING

LISTENING FOR
MAIN IDEAS

B 🎧 2.28 ▶ 1.13 Listen to the talk. The first speaker says that the lecture was advertised in a library newsletter. Check the title you think the newsletter used for the lecture.

_____ Answers to Environmental Questions

✓ The Future of Environmental Activism

_____ Environmental Issues around the World

NOTE-TAKING SKILL Dividing Your Notes

Sometimes it is obvious that a speaker is moving on to a new point. For example, you might hear a speaker say something like:

> *OK, so let's move on to my next point.*
> *Next I'd like to introduce …*

In such cases, you may want to draw a line across your paper to separate your notes and show a new point. This will help you understand your notes more easily.

At other times, it may not be obvious that a speaker has moved on to a new point until after you have finished listening. In such cases, you can draw lines or boxes around different points when you review your notes.

LISTENING FOR
DETAILS

C 🎧 2.28 Listen again and take notes on a separate piece of paper. Use lines and boxes to divide the points. How many times does the speaker move to a new point?

AFTER LISTENING

D Use your notes to complete the summary. Then compare answers with a partner.

Madhav Rajaram Subrahmanyam and his friends raised funds to help endangered _and to protect tiger_ . They did things like shining shoes, delivering packages, and selling items to raise _1000_ of dollars. They have also made more people in _becoming_ aware of conservation.

Hannah Alper from _Toronto Canada_ started writing blog posts when she was only _13_ years old. Her online blogs focus on the environment. She has been seen on TV and in newspaper articles, and she often gives public talks. Her _big idea_ is that doing small things can have a big impact.

Nikita Rafikov from the United States came up with a great invention when he was just _11_ years old. His invention combined a protein from marine creatures with glass to make _Bioluminate_ that produce their own light. This invention may allow future homes to use less _electricity_ .

Adeline Tiffanie Suwana from _Indonesia_ has been recognized by the UN. When she was 12, she formed a group that educates people, helps coral reefs, cleans up the environment, and plants _trees_ . Her group also manages a project that provides clean power to people in rural _Village at Indonesia_

Hannah Alper

Adeline Tiffanie Suwana

EVERYDAY LANGUAGE Introducing a New Topic

Here are some expressions you can use to introduce a new topic.

In terms of _____ , ...

Thinking about _____ , ...

If we consider _____ , ...

Moving on to talk about _____ , ...

E Work in a small group. Discuss the questions.

1. Why do you think some people don't recycle?
2. Why do you think some politicians might deny that the climate is changing?

CRITICAL THINKING: CONSIDERING OTHER VIEWS

B Speaking

A It is easy to imagine that the children in the listening are proud of their efforts. Think about your own childhood. What is one thing you are proud of having done? Discuss with a partner.

> *When I was 12, I won a big tennis tournament in my city. I was very proud of myself.*

B Work in a small group. Discuss different ways to answer the question below. Then share your ideas with the class.

What can parents do to inspire their children to have the passion and motivation to change the world?

CRITICAL THINKING:
SYNTHESIZING

C Work in a small group. Discuss these questions.

1. In the video "Three Seconds," Prince Ea says that humans must take action to save the planet. How do you think the actions of the children would help us "make it to the fourth second"?
2. In the talk, the speaker describes actions that children have taken to protect the environment. In your view, would he think Prince Ea's video is also a useful action? Explain.

Designers use a storyboard to brainstorm ideas for an advertising brochure.

FINAL TASK Planning a Video

> At the end of the video "Three Seconds," Prince Ea asks whether humans can survive until "the fourth second." You are going to work in a small group to create a plan for a short video of up to 60 seconds. Your video will be titled "The Fourth Second." You can use your phone or tablet to film your video.

A Work in a small group. Decide what you want your video to be about. For example, it could be about one of these ideas or your own idea.

- imagining how the world will look *after* humans have fixed the environment
- describing an idea that you think would help humans reach the fourth second
- summarizing an environmental conservation project that you know about

PRESENTATION SKILL Storyboarding

A storyboard is a sequence of drawings that illustrate, for example, the main scenes in a film, the main steps in a process, or even the key slides in a presentation. The drawings, which are normally all the same size, can be very rough and unfinished. The idea is that the drawings should make it easier to imagine what the final film, process, or presentation will look like. The drawings will often have notes or short explanations underneath them.

B In your group, create a storyboard for your video. The storyboard should show what you will do in each section of your film, who will say what, what visuals you will show, and so on.

ORGANIZING IDEAS

C Complete the appropriate steps.

If you are *not* going to record your video:	If you *are* going to record your video:
1. Discuss how you will present your video plan and storyboard to other groups.	1. Discuss how you will film your video. Consider what problems you might experience such as with sound or lighting, and how you can fix the issues.
2. Rehearse your presentation. Make sure everyone in your group has a chance to speak.	2. Rehearse and then record your video.
3. Present your video plan to other groups. Answer any questions they have.	3. Share your video on a computer or on a device with a large screen.
	4. Let other groups watch your video. Answer any questions they have.

CRITICAL THINKING: REFLECTING **D** Write at least one positive comment about every presentation or video that you saw. As a class, share your positive comments. Say how you could improve your video or presentation.

REFLECTION

1. What information that you learned in this unit is likely to be the most useful for you? Why and how?

_____

_____

2. After studying this unit, will you change your behavior to protect the environment? If yes, how will you change it? If no, why not?

_____

_____

3. Here are the vocabulary words from the unit. Check (✓) the ones you can use.

☐ activist	☐ depressing **AWL**	☐ perceive **AWL**
☐ apathetic	☐ discouraged	☐ pessimism
☐ aware **AWL**	☐ fatigue	☐ renewable
☐ capacity **AWL**	☐ inspire	☐ resource **AWL**
☐ conservation	☐ motivation **AWL**	☐ sacrifice
☐ crisis	☐ optimism	☐ source **AWL**
☐ deny **AWL**	☐ passion	

TRADITIONAL AND MODERN MEDICINE

8

A man undergoes cryotherapy in New York, NY, USA. Cryotherapy, which is the use of very cold temperatures for medical treatment, was used as early as the 17th century.

Look at the photos and read the information. Then discuss the questions.

1. What information on this page surprises you?
2. What experiences have you had with these or other home remedies?
3. What are some differences between traditional medicine and modern medicine?

HOME REMEDIES

Lavender contains an oil that may have calming effects and relax muscles. More research is being done to determine the science behind its effects.

Garlic has long been used as a natural remedy. Garlic may reduce the frequency of colds, and it has possible cardiovascular benefits. Garlic oil has been used as a mosquito repellent.

▶ Chili peppers have been used for health purposes for thousands of years. Chilis can be used as a decongestant. Capsaicin, a compound in chilis, is thought to increase life-span and help cure some kinds of cancer.

▶ Ginger is an effective remedy for nausea and vomiting, according to research. This root contains anti-inflammatory elements that can help relieve a sore throat.

Vocabulary

A 🎧 **3.2** Read and listen to the information. Notice each word in **blue** and think about its meaning.

PLANT-BASED MEDICINES

Using plants as natural **remedies** for health problems is nothing new. In fact, for some people, medicinal plants are the only affordable and available kind of medicine. When these people become ill, they discuss their **symptoms** with a traditional healer rather than a medical doctor. Now some scientists want drug manufacturers to take a new look at the ability of plants to **restore** health and fight diseases such as cancer.

Rosy periwinkle

Root of chicory plant

Nat Quansah, an ethnobotanist in Madagascar, studies plants such as the rosy periwinkle. A **synthetic** version of the chemical from that plant is now made into drugs that **inhibit** cancer growth. These drugs have dramatically increased survival rates for two kinds of childhood cancer.

Jim Duke, retired from the U.S. Department of Agriculture, grows and writes about medicinal plants such as chicory. Chicory contains chicoric acid, which could be useful in fighting a deadly virus[1]. Duke says that **empirical** studies of medicinal plants are **crucial** to developing new medicines.

PROBLEMS WITH PLANT-BASED MEDICINES

The effectiveness of a medicine can be difficult to study scientifically. One reason for this is that sick people who use a medicine and then recover may **associate** their recovery correctly or incorrectly with its effects. In addition, herbal remedies may not be **consistent** because the amounts of natural chemicals in plants can vary significantly. The **variables** include the soil plants are grown in and the time when they are harvested, among other factors.

[1]**virus** (n): a tiny organism that causes diseases such as influenza and the common cold

B Write each word in **blue** from exercise A next to its definition.

1. _____ (n) medicines or things that make us feel better

2. _____ (adj) repeated in the same way

3. _____ (adj) based on scientific observations and experiments

4. _____ (adj) extremely important

5. _____ (v) to connect or relate two things

6. _____ (v) to slow or prevent

7. _____ (v) to return to its original condition

8. _____ (n) factors in a situation

9. _____ (adj) artificial; human-made

10. _____ (n) signs of illness

C Discuss the questions with a partner.

1. When was the last time you were sick? What were your symptoms? What medicines or remedies did you use?

2. Why are empirical studies important when developing medicines based on plants?

3. Name two habits that are crucial to good health. Do you have these habits? Explain.

4. After a natural disaster, communities try to restore medical services as soon as possible. What other services would be important to restore quickly?

5. Do you think your parents were consistent or inconsistent with the way they set rules when you were growing up? Why do you think so?

6. Think of a time you were successful. What feelings do you associate with that time? Explain.

VOCABULARY SKILL Word Families

A word family includes words that share the same root. A root gives a word its meaning. For example, the root *var* (from Latin) means "change." Suffixes added to the root indicate the part of speech. Learning about the members of word families can help you to build your vocabulary.

Verb	Noun	Adjective	Adverb
vary	*variation, variable, variability, variety*	*variable, varied, various*	*variably*

D Use a dictionary to complete the word-family chart. Then with a partner, create sentences with each word.

Verb	Noun	Adjective	Adverb
restore			X
X		consistent	
inhibit			X

A Listening A Lecture about Plant-Based Medicines

BEFORE LISTENING

CRITICAL THINKING:
MAKING INFERENCES

A With a partner, look at the steps in the development of a new medication under the U.S. Food and Drug Administration (FDA). Then discuss the questions.

1. Which steps usually take place in a laboratory? Which seem to focus on a new medication's safety? On its effectiveness?

2. How much time would you guess this process typically takes? Explain.

The Drug Development Process

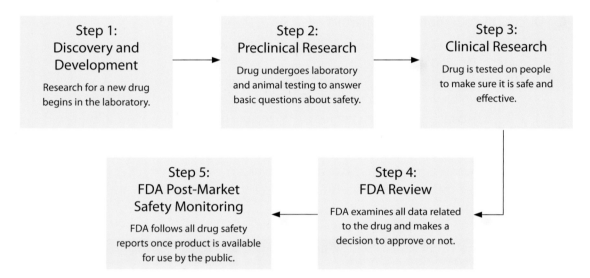

**Step 1:
Discovery and
Development**

Research for a new drug
begins in the laboratory.

**Step 2:
Preclinical Research**

Drug undergoes laboratory
and animal testing to answer
basic questions about safety.

**Step 3:
Clinical Research**

Drug is tested on people
to make sure it is safe and
effective.

**Step 5:
FDA Post-Market
Safety Monitoring**

FDA follows all drug safety
reports once product is available
for use by the public.

**Step 4:
FDA Review**

FDA examines all data related
to the drug and makes a
decision to approve or not.

WHILE LISTENING

LISTENING FOR
MAIN IDEAS

B 🎧 3.3 ▶ 1.14 Listen to the lecture. Check (✓) the points that the professor makes.

☐ a. Many useful older medications were based on plants.

☐ b. A new plant-based drug is being used to treat people with diabetes.

☐ c. Two new drugs are effective at fighting cancer in children.

☐ d. Plant-based medicines are made directly from plants or from synthetic versions of the chemicals found in plants.

☐ e. The path from discovery to government approval is quicker with plant-based medicines than with completely synthetic medicines.

NOTE-TAKING SKILL Indenting Details

When you are taking notes, it's helpful to have a visual way to distinguish main ideas from details. Indenting the details makes your notes easier to read and understand.

> *Main idea 1…*
> > *Detail 1…*
> > *Detail 2…*

C 🎧 3.3 Read through the partial notes. Then listen again and complete the notes. Notice that the details are indented to distinguish them from the main ideas.

LISTENING FOR
DETAILS

Many useful older meds _____

    Aspirin: chem. found in _____

    Digoxin: heart disease med. from _____

Another plant: rosy periwinkle

    Traditional: used for people with _____

    New: _____

Meds. not made directly from plants

    _____ chemical in plant

    Synthesize chemical in _____

New plant-based meds: Devel. is long, $$ process b/c many variables.

    1. Study effect'ness of trad. remedy.

    2. Plant variables: e.g., picked wrong _____ of plant, picked
        at wrong _____, effect of other plants growing nearby.

    3. Scientists need to know _____ is active and what
        _____ to put in each tablet, injection, etc.

Overall, devel. of synthetic drugs is _____

AFTER LISTENING

D Work with a partner. Use your notes from exercise C to explain the ideas from the lecture in your own words to your partner. Then switch roles.

A Speaking

GRAMMAR FOR SPEAKING Adverb Clauses of Reason and Purpose

Adverb clauses of reason and purpose tell us why something happens.

main clause   adverb clause
People use medicinal plants <u>because they are available and affordable</u>.

Scientists study home remedies <u>so that they can identify possible new medications</u>.

We introduce adverb clauses of reason with *because* and *since*. Notice that the adverb clause can come before or after the main clause.

> **<u>Because</u>** <u>the amounts of natural chemicals in plants can vary significantly</u>, *herbal remedies may not be consistent.*

> *Native Americans used to chew the tree bark* **<u>since</u>** <u>it relieved pain</u>.

We introduce adverb clauses of purpose with *so (that)*.

> *Those chemicals are taken from the foxglove plant* **so (that)** *they can be used to make a medication to treat heart patients.*

A Work with a partner. Match each sentence beginning to its ending. Then discuss the relationship between the clauses. Which clause explains why something happens?

1. I eat fruits and vegetables _____.
2. Because plants are affordable, _____.
3. Scientists study a plant _____.
4. Since aspirin is easily available, _____.
5. Plants can be difficult to study _____.

a. many people use it to relieve pain
b. so that they can understand its properties
c. because they're a crucial part of a good diet
d. since there are many variables involved
e. many people use them as remedies

B Complete each statement so that it is true for you. Then share your statements with a partner. Ask and answer follow-up questions about the statements.

1. I (sometimes / rarely) visit the doctor because _____.

2. I (use / don't use) natural remedies because _____

   _____.

3. I (have / don't have) a positive view of plant-based medicines since _____

   _____.

4. Since I am (not) very healthy, I _____.

5. So that I can be as healthy as possible, I _____.

6. Because I learned about plant-based medicines in this unit, I _____

   _____.

A: *I rarely visit the doctor because I am pretty healthy.*
B: *How do you stay healthy? What's your secret?*

◀ **Feliciano dos Santos performs in a concert.**

C 🎧 3.4 Read and listen to information about a National Geographic Explorer. How is he making his country a healthier place?

> **FIGHTING DISEASE WITH A GUITAR**
>
> As a child in Mozambique's Niassa Province, Feliciano dos Santos caught the polio virus from the dirty water in his tiny village. The disease affected his ability to walk. "When I was young," he recalls, "I never believed I would grow up, get married, have children, drive a car, and live such a full life."
>
> These days, dos Santos and his band *Massukos* use music to spread messages of sanitation and hygiene[1] to some of the poorest, most remote villages in Mozambique. Their hit song, "Wash Your Hands," is part of a public health campaign created by dos Santos's non-governmental organization (NGO), Estamos.
>
> Dos Santos's NGO also works on programs to install pumps for clean water, conduct health studies, and fight infectious diseases. Says dos Santos, "Clean water is a basic human right, yet so many don't have it. I'm using my music to be the voice of people who have no voice."

[1]**sanitation; hygiene** (n): cleanliness

D With your partner, use these words and phrases to write statements with adverb clauses of reason and purpose. Use the information from exercise C and your own ideas.

1. Dos Santos / not expect / live a full life / because

   _____

2. Since / Massukos's health message / in a popular song / pay attention

   _____

3. So that / more people / have clean water / dos Santos's NGO

   _____

E Discuss these questions with a partner.

1. Describe public health campaigns you have seen or heard about. For example, what TV commercials or outdoor signs with health messages have you seen?
2. Do you think a popular song would work well in a public health campaign in your country? Give reasons for your opinion using adverb clauses.

We sometimes use a phrase at the beginning of a statement to let our listeners know that we are giving a reason for something.

For this reason, …   *Because of this, …*   *That is why…*   *That's the reason…*

Diseases can spread from person to person through dirty water. ***That is why*** *it's crucially important to use clean water for drinking and cooking.*

F Work with a partner. Follow each statement below with one or more new statements that contain a reason. Try to use all four phrases from the box.

1. The common cold is highly contagious and spreads easily.
2. We associate regular exercise with good health.
3. Some natural remedies are quite effective.
4. A good diet contributes to overall health.

CRITICAL THINKING:
EVALUATING

G Follow these steps with your partner.

1. Look at the list of health issues in the chart below. Which information surprises you the most. Why?
2. Brainstorm some of the public health issues in your country. Examples might include tobacco use, sanitation, diet, air quality, and so on. Which one is the most concerning? Give reasons.
3. Join another pair of students and discuss which issues are the most serious.

Public Health in the United States: The Top Four Concerns	
Diabetes (high blood-sugar levels)	– 8.3 percent of Americans have diabetes
Obesity (being very overweight)	– 38 percent of American adults are obese
Heart disease	– Causes around 25 percent of deaths
Cancer	– Second leading cause of death in the United States

H With a partner, think of a title of a new song that could be used to spread a message about one of the issues you discussed in exercise G. Then share your ideas in a group.

LESSON TASK Discussing Claims about Public Health

> **CRITICAL THINKING** Evaluating Claims
>
> A claim is a statement that is presented as true. It should be logical and be supported with evidence such as research of some kind. A claim may also use tentative language (*suggests*, *may be*, *can*) to show that the claim is not an absolute or undeniable truth.
>
> *A recent study suggests that air quality may be the worst threat to public health in this city.*

A Work in a small group and evaluate the claims below. Discuss these questions to help you decide if each claim is strong.

CRITICAL THINKING:
EVALUATING CLAIMS

1. Does the person provide statistics, research results, expert opinions, or some other evidence that I can trust?
2. Is the claim reasonable and logical based on what I know?
3. Is the claim current, or is it outdated or based on outdated evidence?
4. Does the person have anything to gain by making the claim?
5. How would you rank these claims from 1 (most believable) to 3 (least believable)?

> a. *Our dentists are the best in the region, and good dental care is the basis of good health. Give us a call and let Southwest Dentists take care of your teeth.*
> Andrea Walker, Outreach Director, Southwest Dentists Associated
>
> b. *A 2016 study published in* The New England Journal of Medicine *found that the meningitis B vaccine[1] was only effective in around two-thirds of the college students who received it. However, since the disease can cause death, we strongly recommend the vaccine for all students aged 17–21.*
> Luigi Maglio, chancellor of a large public university
>
> c. *Absent workers cost U.S. companies over $225 billion a year according to the Center for Disease Control's 2015 report. Don't wait for your employees to call in sick. Call us about our employee wellness program. You're in Good Company.*
> Max Rosas, Sales and Marketing Director, Good Company Health Solutions

[1]**vaccine** (n): a medicine that stimulates the body's immune system to protect against a disease

B With your group, discuss how you would support the claims below. Explain your reasons.

> Types of support:
>
> statistics   expert opinions   personal stories   other

1. Fewer children have gotten malaria since the new water wells were installed.
2. Adults are often more afraid of getting injections than children are.
3. Reducing salt intake lessens the likelihood of heart disease.
4. Parents noticed unusual symptoms after their children received the new flu vaccine.

Video

Wildebeests in the Masai Mara National Reserve, Kenya

Wild Health

BEFORE VIEWING

A The video you are going to watch, *Wild Health,* discusses what animals do to self-medicate, or cure themselves, when they are sick or injured. What are some things you think animals might do to self-medicate? List two ideas below.

_____   _____

B Work with a partner. Write each word or phrase from the video next to its definition. You may use a dictionary.

avoidance	curative	groundbreaking	nausea
compounds	fermentation	lactation	preventative

1. _____ (adj) helping to keep disease away

2. _____ (n) a chemical change to a substance

3. _____ (n) substances that consist of two or more elements

4. _____ (adj) able to restore health

5. _____ (n) the condition of feeling sick to your stomach

6. _____ (n) the production of milk by female mammals

7. _____ (n) the act of staying away from something

8. _____ (adj) innovative and important

WHILE VIEWING

C ▶ 1.15 Watch the video and complete the notes.

NOTE TAKING

1. Cindy Engel, animal behaviorist, studies zoopharmacognosy (means "animal

   _____")

2. Acc. to Engel, _____ was based on watching sick animals

   e.g., _____ have shown us 6–7 new compounds to use

3. Engel's book focuses on 3 main areas:

   curative measures (_____ can cure ailments themselves)

   _____ measures (animals do something to protect against illness)

   _____ measures (not eating certain foods)

D ▶ 1.15 Engel uses different animals as examples to support her research. Watch the video again. Match each animal with the correct example.

UNDERSTANDING
DETAILS

1. Chimpanzees _____.

2. Snow leopards _____.

3. Wildebeests _____.

4. Cattle/cows _____.

a. eat grass to avoid nausea

b. migrate to places that have essential minerals for lactation

c. travel to find the right kind of dirt

d. have helped scientists discover several new compounds

AFTER VIEWING

E Discuss the questions below in a group.

CRITICAL THINKING:
EVALUATING

1. Which of your predictions from exercise A were mentioned in the video?
2. Based on what you learned in Lesson A about evaluating claims, what do you think of Engel's claim that observing animal behavior is important to human medicine? Is it a believable claim? Why or why not?

A pair of young chimpanzees in the Republic of the Congo

B Vocabulary

MEANING FROM CONTEXT **A** 🎧 3.5 Read and listen to the information. Notice each word in blue and think about its meaning.

HIGH-TECH MEDICINE

Science fiction writers in the 1960s imagined the "tricorder." The **radical** idea behind the device was its ability to scan the body from the outside and "see" everything from tiny bacteria to **internal** organs such as the heart. This meant patients didn't need to **undergo** surgery or other invasive procedures in order to get a medical diagnosis—in fictional stories, at least. Now, the tricorder idea might soon be a reality, and could be used by patients to monitor their own health or by doctors in places far from hospitals.

In the area of regenerative medicine, researchers are using 3-D printing techniques to create replacement body tissues. This synthetic nose was created by Dr. Anthony Atala at the Wake Forest Institute for Regenerative Medicine in North Carolina, USA. Scientists are also working on ways to get the body's own cells and immune system to **modify** parts of the human body for use in surgical repairs. For example, the body could generate new knee cartilage[1] that will be accepted more easily than a completely artificial knee **mechanism**.

[1] **cartilage** (n): firm, flexible tissue found in several parts of the body

B Work with a partner. Read the statements aloud and discuss whether you think they are true or false. Choose T for *True* or F for *False*. Correct the false statements.

1. If someone has a radical idea, it is similar to what many others think. T F

2. An internal medical device is located on the outside of the body. T F

3. If you undergo surgery, the surgery is done to you. T F

4. When you modify something, you change it or give it a different form. T F

5. A mechanism is a mechanical device with a certain function. T F

C 🎧 **3.6** Read and listen to the information. Notice each word in **blue** and think about its meaning.

> ### NEW ADVANCES IN PROSTHETIC DEVICES[1]
>
> - A prosthetic device can help restore movement for a person who has suffered a **severe** injury and has lost a leg, an arm, a foot, or a hand.
>
> - Advanced prosthetic arms can now be operated mentally. The user thinks about moving her hand, for example, and the **corresponding** part of the device moves.
>
> - After a patient loses an arm, **nerves** that once went to the patient's arm are surgically attached to the remaining **muscles**. The nerves move the muscles, which **transmit** electrical signals to the prosthetic arm.

[1] **prosthetic devices** (n): artificial devices that take the place of a body part such as a hand or leg

D Write each word in **blue** from exercise C next to its definition.

1. _____ (n) tissue in the body that allows feeling or sensation

2. _____ (adj) bad, causing great damage

3. _____ (v) to send a signal or message

4. _____ (n) tissues on bones that make the body move

5. _____ (adj) matching

E Read each sentence and choose the correct word form. You may use a dictionary to help you.

1. When we sneeze or cough, we may (transmit / transmission) a disease to people around us.
2. Some medicines are applied to the skin, while other medicines need to be taken (internal / internally).
3. In an emergency, a simple (modify / modification) can make a medical device for an adult work well for a child.
4. Signals that allow us to see and hear travel across (nerves / nervous) inside the head.
5. Before a strenuous workout, it is a good idea to warm up your (muscles / muscular) with gentle stretches.

F Work in a small group and discuss these questions.

1. Do you know anyone who has a prosthetic device such as an artificial knee, hip joint, or leg? Explain.
2. What ideas or feelings do you have about these examples of high-tech medicine—the "tricorder" device, regenerative medicine, and advanced prosthetic devices? For example, would you feel comfortable taking advantage of such medical science?
3. Do you feel optimistic about the future of medicine? Give reasons for your answers.

Listening A Podcast about Prosthetic Devices

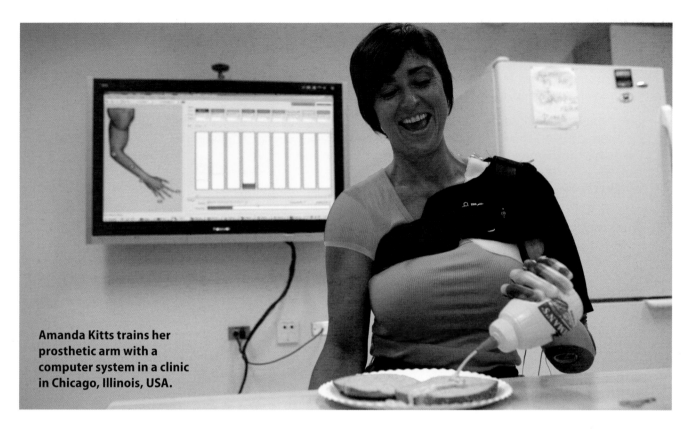

Amanda Kitts trains her prosthetic arm with a computer system in a clinic in Chicago, Illinois, USA.

BEFORE LISTENING

A Discuss these questions with a partner.

1. How do you think Amanda Kitts controls the prosthetic arm you see her wearing in the photo? What movements do you think are hard for the arm to make?
2. How would you go through your morning routine if you had only one arm? For example, how would you brush your teeth? Bathe and dress yourself? Make and eat breakfast? Discuss the steps involved in these activities and how they would be different from what you normally do.

WHILE LISTENING

LISTENING FOR
MAIN IDEAS

B 🎧 3.7 Read the questions. Then listen to the podcast and answer the questions.

1. How were older prosthetic arms operated?

_____

_____

2. What other kind of prosthetic device is mentioned, and what does it do?

_____

_____

3. How is the body modified in targeted reinnervation surgery?

_____

_____

4. How do electrodes work to make Kitts's prosthetic arm move?

_____

_____

LISTENING SKILL Listening for Supporting Details

Supporting details often include examples, an explanation of a process, numerical data, research results, and the ideas of experts. Notice how the details in bold in these sentences help us understand and trust the speakers' points.

> *Natural remedies are a common way to deal with minor health problems, for example, **drinking hot tea with honey** to ease the symptoms of a cold.*

> *Targeted reinnervation surgery was developed at the **Rehabilitation Institute of Chicago. Dr. Todd Kuiken and Dr. Gregory Dumanium** are the innovative surgeons behind the technique.*

C 🎧 3.7 Listen again and take notes on these supporting details.

LISTENING FOR DETAILS

1. How Amanda Kitts lost her arm:

_____

2. Number of people with cochlear implants:

_____

3. What doctors do in targeted reinnervation surgery:

_____

4. How Kitts's muscles make the prosthetic arm move:

_____

5. The role Kitts's brain plays in moving the prosthetic arm:

_____

AFTER LISTENING

D With a partner, discuss how the details you took notes on in exercise C helped you to understand or believe the information in the podcast.

CRITICAL THINKING: APPLYING

> *Hearing the number of people with cochlear implants helped me see that it's a very common high-tech prosthetic device. It's not something out of science fiction.*

E Discuss these questions with your partner.

1. What information from the podcast surprised you the most? Why?
2. What questions would you ask Amanda Kitts if you had the chance to speak with her?

Speaking

PRONUNCIATION Linking Vowel Sounds with /y/ and /w/

🎧 **3.8** When words that end in /i/ or /aɪ/ are followed by words that begin with a vowel sound, we can link the words together with a /y/ sound for smoother and more fluent pronunciation.

"We always" sounds like "Weyalways."

"I am" sounds like "Iyam."

With words that end in /o/ and /u/, we can link to words that begin with a vowel sound by using a /w/ sound.

"So easy" sounds like "Soweasy."

"Who is" sounds like "Whowis."

A 🎧 **3.9** Listen and choose the sound that links the words in each sentence. Then practice saying the sentences with a partner using linking.

1. She is not getting a radical kind of surgery.   /y/   /w/

2. Who else in your family has flu symptoms?   /y/   /w/

3. He asked about the new medication.   /y/   /w/

4. They did two other blood tests.   /y/   /w/

5. Three of his friends are sick.   /y/   /w/

6. Why isn't he undergoing the operation?   /y/   /w/

▶ **Aiden Kenny got two cochlear implants when he was ten months old. The implants transmit electronic signals directly to his auditory nerves and allow him to perceive sounds. Within months of the surgery, Aiden spoke the words "Mama" and "Dada."**

B 🎧 3.10 Listen to the conversation. Pay attention to the words linked with /y/ and /w/ sounds. Then practice the conversation with a partner.

A: How are you doing today?

B: I'm good, thanks. I was just listening to an incredible story about cochlear implants.

A: Sounds interesting. I always enjoy stories about new medical developments.

B: Me too! This was about a deaf child who got the implants when he was very young. His parents wanted him to be able to hear and speak normally.

A: That must have been a tough decision for the parents to make.

B: I imagine so. Well, it was nice seeing you.

EVERYDAY LANGUAGE   Ending a Conversation

To end a conversation politely, you can start with a signal word, give an explanation, and suggest a future plan.

Signal Word	Explanation	Future Plan
Well,	*I need to get going.*	*Give me a call tonight if you're not busy.*
So,	*my next class starts at 11:00.*	*I'll see you tomorrow at work.*
Anyway,	*it was nice talking to you.*	*Let's get together for coffee one of these days.*

C Think of some recent news you read or heard related to medical inventions or health news. Have a short conversation with a partner, sharing the news that you know. At the end, close the conversation politely.

D Work with a different partner.

A: *What's new with you, Marco?*

B: *Not much, but I read an interesting news article this morning.*

FINAL TASK A Presentation on Medicine and Health

You are going to give a short presentation about one of the topics from this unit that interested you or about another topic related to medicine and health.

A Work with a partner. Discuss what you learned about these topics. Brainstorm other topics related to health that interest you and add them.

BRAINSTORMING

- a traditional medicine
- a recent advance in high-tech medicine
- _____

- a plant-based medicine
- a specific prosthetic device
- _____

B **Choose a topic from your brainstorm in exercise A and follow these steps.**

1. Find an article or news story about your topic. It should be written for the general public and easy to understand.
2. Take notes on main ideas and supporting details as you read the article. Pay attention to the reasons that are given.
3. Plan a short (2-3 minute) presentation to give to your classmates.

PRESENTATION SKILL Practicing and Timing Your Presentation

Before giving a presentation, practice it several times and make sure the length is suitable. Practicing with a friend or in front of a mirror lets you work out effective ways to phrase your ideas, and timing yourself ensures that your presentation won't be too long or too short.

Many people speak faster when they feel nervous, so their actual presentation takes less time than they expected. If you tend to speak too quickly, remind yourself to speak slowly and carefully during your presentation. This will help your listeners understand you and will give them time to think about your ideas.

C **Practice and time your presentation. Try to speak in a natural way rather than reading directly from your notes. Remember to use phrases to signal reasons.**

D **In a small group, give your presentation and listen to other presentations. Give each other feedback on the timing and delivery of your presentations.**

REFLECTION

1. What two skills from the unit will be the most useful to you?

_____

_____

2. What were the most interesting things you learned about traditional and modern medicine in this unit?

_____

_____

3. Here are the vocabulary words from the unit. Check (✓) the ones you can use.

☐ associate	☐ mechanism AWL	☐ severe
☐ consistent AWL	☐ modify AWL	☐ symptom
☐ corresponding AWL	☐ muscle	☐ synthetic
☐ crucial AWL	☐ nerve	☐ transmit AWL
☐ empirical AWL	☐ radical AWL	☐ undergo AWL
☐ inhibit AWL	☐ remedy	☐ variable AWL
☐ internal AWL	☐ restore AWL	

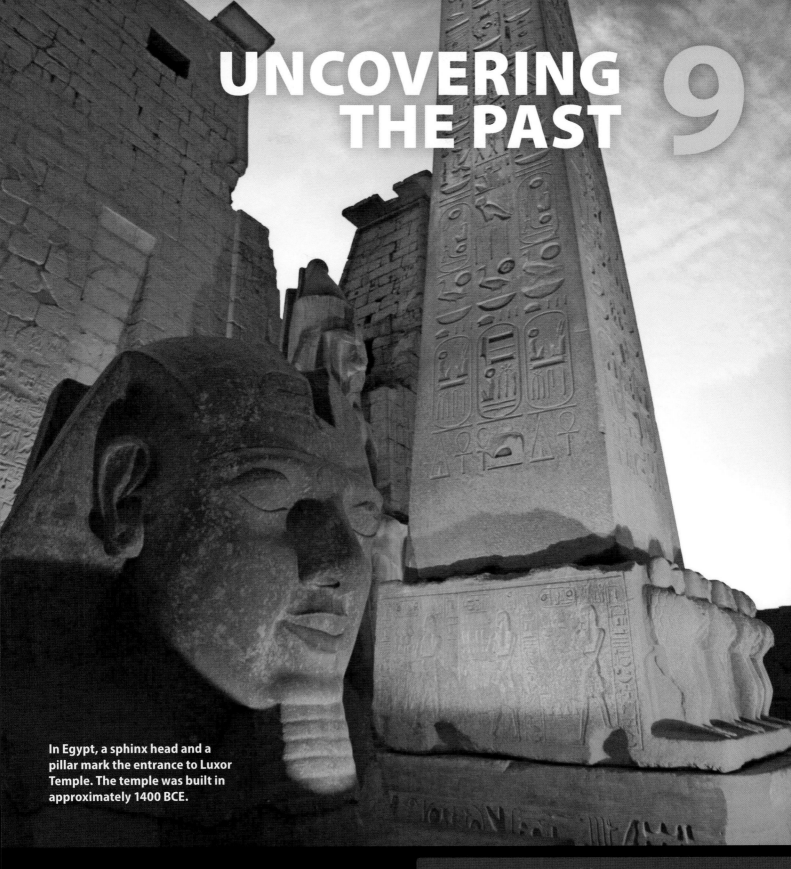

UNCOVERING THE PAST

9

In Egypt, a sphinx head and a pillar mark the entrance to Luxor Temple. The temple was built in approximately 1400 BCE.

THINK AND DISCUSS

1 What do you think might be inside the temple?
2 Would you like to enter the temple? Why or why not?
3 What famous ancient sites are in your country?

Look at the photo and read the
information. Then discuss the questions.

1. How can this digital image of a temple
   be useful to archaeologists?
2. How can it be useful to those who wish
   to repair such a place after an earthquake?
3. What ancient site would you be
   interested in visiting? Explain why.

A DEEPER LOOK

This image of an ancient temple in Bagan, Myanmar, shows a laser-scan data view by CyArk. The mission of CyArk, a non-profit organization, is to use new technologies to create a free, 3D (three-dimensional) online library of the world's cultural heritage sites. Its goal is to document important sites before they are lost to natural disasters, human activity, or the passage of time.

In Myanmar, CyArk has been working with other organizations, including Myanmar's Department of Archaeology and UNESCO, to document the more than 3,000 temples near Bagan. Built between the 10th and 14th centuries, many temples were damaged in a 2016 earthquake, illustrating the need for data to assist in conservation and reconstruction.

A Vocabulary

A 🎧 3.11 Read and listen to the sentences. With a partner, use clues in the sentences to discuss what part of speech each word in **blue** is. Then write *noun*, *verb*, or *adverb* in the space.

1. **Collaboration** (_____) is the act of working with others to produce or do something.

2. A **civilization** (_____) is a society or culture that has a high level of government, laws, art, music, and so on.

3. **Curiosity** (_____) is the feeling of wanting to know or learn more about something.

4. **Excavation** (_____) is the act of digging in the ground to look for items from the past.

5. **Participation** (_____) is the act of taking part in an activity or joining an event with other people.

6. When a person **proposes** (_____) doing something, he or she suggests a plan or idea for others to consider.

7. The **remains** (_____) of something are the parts that are left after the rest of it has been used or destroyed.

8. A **specialist** (_____) is a person with a lot of knowledge, skill, or experience in a particular field or subject.

9. To **uncover** (_____) means to find something that had been lost or hidden.

10. **Virtually** (_____) has the same meaning as the words *nearly* and *almost*.

B 🎧 3.12 Listen for these words in two conversations. Write *A* if the word is used in conversation A or *B* if it is in conversation B.

1. civilization _____   6. proposed _____

2. collaborating _____   7. remains _____

3. curious _____   8. specialists _____

4. excavated _____   9. uncovering _____

5. participate _____   10. virtually _____

Excavations continue at Angkor Wat in Cambodia, one of the largest religious sites in the world. It was built in the 12th century.

This Egyptian mummy contains the remains of a cat from about the 1st century.

C Work in a small group to answer each question. Then use a dictionary to check your answers.

1. What is the noun form of *collaborate*? _____

2. What is a noun with the same suffix as *excavation*? _____

3. What word means a person who *participates*? _____

4. What is the noun form of *propose*? _____

5. What is a noun with the same suffix as *specialist*? _____

6. What is a verb with the same prefix as *uncover*? _____

D Complete these questions with your own words. Then interview a partner. Ask follow-up questions and write answers in your notebook.

PERSONALIZING

1. Which past civilization interests you more: the Egyptians or the _____?

2. When doing homework, do you prefer to collaborate with others or _____?

3. In general, do you have more curiosity about the past or about _____?

4. Would you rather participate in a radio interview or _____?

5. What quality do medical specialists need most: ambition, intelligence, or _____?

6. What are you virtually certain to do tomorrow: study English or _____?

A Listening An Interview with an Archaeologist

Matthew Piscitelli, of the National Geographic Society, works at the 5,000-year-old archaeological site of Huaricanga in Peru.

BEFORE LISTENING

CRITICAL THINKING:
CATEGORIZING

A Make a list of five adjectives, such as *fascinating* or *exhausting*, that might describe the work of archaeologists like Matthew Piscitelli. Then share your list with two partners. Categorize the words in your lists as either positive or negative.

WHILE LISTENING

> **NOTE-TAKING SKILL** Noting Questions and Answers
>
> When you hear a question—whether it is an interview question, a question from the audience, or even a rhetorical question—make a quick note of the question itself. Then take detailed notes about the speaker's response to the question.

LISTENING FOR
MAIN IDEAS

B 🎧 3.13 Listen to the interview and take notes. Then match the summaries of Piscitelli's answers to the questions. Two of the summaries will not be used.

1. Why should people care about archaeology? _____

2. Why do you think that some cultures and some buildings inspire us more than others? _____

3. Are there any archaeological sites or ancient cultures you think people should know more about? _____

4. How can archaeology bring the past to life? _____

a. Communities can uncover useful information using archaeology.

b. It gets people interested in learning about and from the past.

c. People have always wanted to know about powerful civilizations.

d. Some famous archaeological sites are very interesting to people.

e. The participation of local people can emphasize links to the past.

f. Some ancient sites in Peru have been studied very little.

C 🎧 **3.14** Listen to excerpts from the interview. Write the referent for each pronoun or demonstrative.

LISTENING FOR REFERENTS

1. What does the pronoun *it* refer to? _____

2. What does the demonstrative *that* refer to? _____

3. What does the demonstrative *these* refer to? _____

4. What does the pronoun *they* refer to? _____

5. What does the pronoun *them* refer to? _____

AFTER LISTENING

D Read these statements by Piscitelli. Rank them in order of how much you agree with them from 1 (the most) to 4 (the least). Then discuss your rankings in a small group.

CRITICAL THINKING: RANKING

_____ Archaeology … [is] important because it inspires curiosity.

_____ The past … helps us learn more about our identity today.

_____ We need to study … ancient civilizations … [to] prepare for the future.

_____ There is so much history out here just waiting to be discovered.

Caral, Peru, a UNESCO World Heritage Site and one of the earliest cities in the Americas

A Speaking

GRAMMAR FOR SPEAKING Using Demonstratives

You can use *this*, *that*, *these*, and *those* before a noun to specify what you are talking about, such as *this assignment* or *those students*. You can also use these words as pronouns without a noun. Doing this can help you sound more natural and fluent. Here are some important points to remember.

- Use *this* and *that* to refer to singular ideas or things, and use *these* and *those* to refer to plural ideas or things.

- Generally speaking, use *this* and *these* to refer to something you mentioned recently, and use *that* and *those* to refer to something you mentioned longer ago:

    *Ancient Egyptians sometimes made <u>mummies of animals</u>. **These** have been found …*

    *People were buried with <u>many goods</u> in Ancient Egypt. Archaeologists believe **those** were intended to …*

- If using a demonstrative without a noun might confuse listeners, mention the full idea again:

    *A number of mummies were uncovered by archaeologists inside the pyramids and **these**, uh, I mean **these mummies**, were taken to a museum in …*

A Complete each sentence with your own ideas.

1. When I was a child, I lived in _____. **This** was a

    good place to live because _____

    _____.

2. A few years ago, I _____.

    I'm proud of myself for having done **that** because _____

    _____.

3. I would like to buy _____. **These** would

    help me _____

    _____.

4. _____ are some things students use daily. They use

    these to _____.

5. One of my goals – and I want to do **this** soon, if possible – is _____

    _____.

B Interview a partner. Ask questions about the sentences in exercise A.

A: *When you were a child, where did you live and why was this a good place to live?*

B: *I lived in Dubai until I was seven. This was a great place to grow up because …*

A worker uses water to wash a statue of King Sejong in Seoul, South Korea.

C Work with a partner. Read part of a history presentation. Then complete the tasks.

1. Which four of the underlined nouns could be deleted in order for the speaker to sound more natural? Which underlined noun could not be deleted? Why?
2. Take turns reading the presentation aloud. Do not say the four unnecessary nouns.

> In 1443 an important event occurred in Korean history. This <u>event</u> was the creation of an alphabet called *hangul*. This <u>alphabet</u> was developed by King Sejong the Great. *Hangul* letters are grouped into blocks, and these <u>blocks</u> can be used to write any word in the Korean language. The creation of *hangul* had a significant impact on Korea. Before this <u>invention</u>, people could only use Chinese characters that they called *hanja* to write words and phrases in Korean. These <u>characters</u> were difficult to learn. After *hangul* was invented, however, people in Korea had a stronger sense of their national identity.

D Prepare a talk following the instructions below. Make notes about what you will say in your talk. Use the paragraph in exercise C as a guide. Then rehearse your talk. Make sure that you use demonstratives correctly.

ORGANIZING IDEAS

> Speak for up to one minute about an important event from the history of your country or from the history of another country that you know well.
>
> You should say:
>
> - what the event is
> - when it happened
> - why it was important
> - what people learned from it

E Work in a small group. Follow the steps.

1. Take turns delivering your talk. When it is your turn to listen, pay attention to the demonstratives that the speaker uses.
2. After you have all delivered your talks, give each other feedback.

SPEAKING SKILL Participating in Group Discussions

Group discussions are a common feature of academic study. When taking part in such discussions, act and speak in a way that shows your respect for the other participants. This includes expressing your views calmly and respecting the opinions of others. Here are some other things to remember.

- If you disagree with what somebody has said, express your opinion politely.
  I understand what you're saying, Pedro, but isn't it true that …?
  Those are interesting points, but actually I think you'll find that …

- Keep your ideas and those of other participants focused on the topic of discussion.
  Sorry, I'm getting away from the topic.
  You've made a good argument, Yelena, but I'm not sure it's relevant.

- Avoid dominating the discussion. Encourage everyone to take turns.
  Vuong, we haven't heard from you yet. What do you think about this?
  Do you have anything to add, Maria?

- If somebody tries to interrupt you, you can prevent the interruption.
  Actually, I haven't finished what I wanted to say about that.
  Sorry, but I haven't finished what I was saying.

F Write answers to the questions about the speaking skill. Then discuss them in a small group.

1. Which of the discussion strategies do you already use?

   _____

   _____

2. Which of the strategies will you try to use more in the future?

   _____

   _____

3. What are some other ways to participate effectively in group discussions?

   _____

   _____

G Work in a group with half of the students in your class. Discuss these questions in your group. Practice using the discussion strategies you just studied and be prepared to explain your ideas.

1. What is the most important historical event that has happened in your lifetime?
2. In your opinion, which was the most interesting period of time in your country's history?

LESSON TASK Participating in a Group Discussion

An illustration of a Neolithic village at Durrington Walls in the United Kingdom shows life as it may have been over 4,500 years ago.

A In the interview, Matthew Piscitelli says that people are curious about what it was like to live 5,000 years ago. Discuss the question below in a small group. List your group's ideas in the T-chart.

CRITICAL THINKING: EVALUATING

How is modern life similar to life 5,000 years ago? How is it different?

Similar	Different

B Reflect on your group discussion and review the tips in the speaking skill box. How successfully did you participate? How can you improve your participation? Share your ideas with a partner.

CRITICAL THINKING: REFLECTING

Video

**Trajan's Column
in Rome, Italy**

How Trajan's Column Was Built

BEFORE VIEWING

A Work in a small group. Discuss the questions.

1. What monuments or structures like Trajan's Column do you have in your country?
2. In Roman times, a traditional way to remember and show respect for important people was to build a column. What are some modern ways?

B Work with a partner. Complete these definitions of words from the video with the correct word from the box. Then use a dictionary to check your answers.

carve	landmark	sophisticated	theory
conquer	lower	surface	tomb

1. A _____ is something such as a mountain that is easily seen and recognized.

2. A _____ is a place, usually underground, where a person is placed after dying.

3. A _____ is an idea that some people believe but may not be correct.

4. A machine that is _____ is advanced and works in a clever way.

5. The _____ of something is the outside or top part or layer of it.

6. To _____ something means to cut a shape, design, or pattern in it.

7. To _____ a country means to take control of it by winning a war.

8. To _____ means to move something downwards from a higher position.

WHILE VIEWING

C ▶ 1.16 Watch the video. Then number these statements in the correct order to make a summary of the video. One of the statements is not part of the summary.

UNDERSTANDING MAIN IDEAS

a. _____ It describes what the carved designs on the surface of the Column show.

b. _____ It discusses problems and solutions related to the Column's construction.

c. _____ It mentions when and why the Column was made and from what material.

d. _____ It outlines what has happened to the Column in the years since it was built.

e. _____ It summarizes one theory of how the Column was constructed.

f. _____ The video says that scholars are unsure how Trajan's Column was built.

D ▶ 1.16 Watch the video again. Take notes as you watch. Then complete each detail from the video with a number from the box. You will not use one of the numbers.

UNDERSTANDING DETAILS

12	29	77	113	126	155	656	1588

1. _____ – the length in feet of the colored design on the Column's surface

2. _____ – the maximum amount in tons that a block of marble might weigh

3. _____ – the number of blocks of marble required to build the Column

4. _____ – the number of different scenes in the Column's colored design

5. _____ – the total height of the Column in feet (three feet is about one meter)

6. _____ – the year when the Column was dedicated to the Emperor Trajan

7. _____ – the year when Trajan's statue on top of the Column was replaced

AFTER VIEWING

E In a small group, discuss each question.

CRITICAL THINKING: ANALYZING

1. In the video, a man travels back in time to see how Trajan's Column was built. What problems do you think the man would experience if he really traveled back in time?

2. If people really could travel back in time to ancient Rome, what information do you think these specialists might like to learn about Roman society?

   • a chef   • a fashion designer   • a linguist   • an architect

3. If you could travel back in time, what time period and what location would you go back to? Why?

4. If time travel really were possible, how would the world be different? Would it be better or worse?

B Vocabulary

In the Arabian Peninsula, a graduate student monitors data being received by ground-penetrating radar.

MEANING FROM CONTEXT

A 🎧 3.15 Read and listen to the information. Then complete the definitions with one of the words in **blue**. When you have finished, compare answers with a partner.

TECHNOLOGY FOR ARCHAEOLOGY

Archaeologists often use a **device** with ground-penetrating radar, or GPR, to see under the surface of the ground. It works by sending radio waves into the ground. If the waves hit an **artifact** such as a tool, they will be reflected back to the GPR machine at the surface. In this way, the device can build up a picture of what lies under the ground. GPR machines are not only useful for finding buried objects; in many cases they provide evidence of the remains of villages or other **settlements**.

Satellites are complex devices that humans send into space. They stay in orbit above Earth, often at a fixed position above the surface of the planet. They are used to send and receive large amounts of data. Many satellites have cameras that can take high-quality photos of Earth's surface. Some of them have lasers or other equipment that can **scan** objects from space. Archaeologists use this data in various ways.

1. _____ (n) an object of historical interest that was made by humans

2. _____ (v) to examine the surface or inside of something

3. _____ (n) places where groups of people have decided to live

4. _____ (n) a machine, tool, or object used for a particular task

5. _____ (n) man-made objects that go around larger objects in space

CRITICAL THINKING: ANALYZING

B Work with a partner. Take turns answering the questions and supporting your answers.

1. Which ancient artifact would you most like to discover: a tool, a pot, or a coin? Why?
2. What is one device that you use every day? Why is it so useful for you?
3. What other kinds of scanning do we use, in addition to scanning objects from space?
4. Where were some of the earliest settlements in your country? Why were they built there?

VOCABULARY SKILL Phrasal Verbs

A phrasal verb consists of a verb and either one or two prepositions or particles. The meaning of many phrasal verbs is idiomatic, so knowing the meaning of each individual word may not help you understand the meaning of the whole phrase.

Phrasal verbs are very common, and using them correctly will help you sound more natural. However, phrasal verbs are generally less formal than single-word verbs with the same meaning, so they may not be suitable in every situation.

> They **got together** to discuss the situation. (slightly less formal)
> They **gathered** to discuss the situation. (slightly more formal)

C Work in a small group. Match the **blue** phrasal verbs in these sentences to the correct definition. Then check your answers in a dictionary.

1. _____ Did you **come across** any useful data?
2. _____ This coin **dates from** the time of Caesar.
3. _____ We need to **figure out** the best schedule.
4. _____ Ana needs to **get on with** her research.
5. _____ I will **look into** how to get tickets.

a. to have existed since a specific time
b. to research or investigate
c. to see or find something unexpectedly
d. to start or continue doing
e. to understand or decide

PRONUNCIATION Stress in Phrasal Verbs

🎧 **3.16** With most phrasal verbs, the preposition or particle directly after the verb is given the main stress.

> I will **look <u>into</u>** your question.
> He **dropped <u>out</u> of** the course.

However, with some two-word phrasal verbs, the main stress is on the verb.

> Let me **<u>look</u> at** the ideas.

D 🎧 **3.17** Look at the sentences in exercise C. Mark the word in each phrasal verb that should be stressed. Then listen to check your answers. Finally, say each sentence with the correct stress.

E Work with a partner. Take turns responding to these questions.

1. When and where did you last come across something unexpected? What was it?
2. Do you or your family own something that dates from the 20th century? Describe it.
3. When have you collaborated with other people to figure something out? Explain.
4. When have you taken a very long time to get on with something? Why did it take you so long?
5. Think about a time when you looked into how to solve a problem. What solutions did you look into and why?

B Listening A Discussion about Archaeology

BEFORE LISTENING

A You are going to hear four archaeology students having a group discussion. Before you listen, preview the questions in exercise B. What will you listen for to answer each question? Share your ideas with the class.

WHILE LISTENING

LISTENING FOR
MAIN IDEAS

B 🎧 **3.18** Now listen to the discussion. Then answer the questions.

1. When are the students meeting?
   a. before class
   b. during class
   c. after class

2. What can you say about the speakers?
   a. They are very close friends.
   b. They have never met before.
   c. They know each other already.

3. What do the speakers mainly discuss?
   a. their grades on an assignment
   b. some possible ideas to research
   c. latest advances in archaeology

C 🎧 3.18 From your notes and/or memory, decide which set of notes matches the order in which the students discuss the different kinds of technology. Then listen again to check your answers.

a.

> Drones
>
> Ground-penetrating radar
>
> Lidar
>
> Robots
>
> Satellite archaeology

b.

> Lidar
>
> Robots
>
> Drones
>
> Satellite archaeology
>
> Ground-penetrating radar

c.

> Ground-penetrating radar
>
> Lidar
>
> Drones
>
> Robots
>
> Satellite archaeology

CRITICAL THINKING Drawing Conclusions

We draw conclusions from direct or indirect evidence. For example, imagine that you see many people have wet umbrellas and the ground is wet, or imagine you hear a friend say she was glad she took her umbrella yesterday. In both cases, it is logical to conclude that it rained. In the first case, this conclusion is based on direct evidence: the wet umbrellas and ground. In the second case, there is no direct evidence, but your friend's words suggest this conclusion.

D Work in a small group. Which of the questions in exercise B required you to draw a conclusion? Why do you think so? Did you get those questions right?

E 🎧 3.19 Listen to excerpts from the discussion. After each excerpt, check (✓) the conclusion or conclusions that you can draw. Discuss your answers with a partner.

1. a. _____ One of the students has another class to attend soon.
   b. _____ The students are all connected on Facebook.

2. a. _____ She has personal experience using ground-penetrating radar.
   b. _____ She thinks older technologies are more useful than newer ones.

3. a. _____ She has read the same article about lidar as the man.
   b. _____ She had heard about lidar before the man mentioned it.

4. a. _____ The tiny robots were not originally developed for use by archaeologists.
   b. _____ Both of the male students think robots are a good technology to look into.

AFTER LISTENING

F Work in a small group. List some advantages and disadvantages of researching something alone or working in a group. Discuss what the key advantage and disadvantage is for working alone or with a group.

B Speaking

A Think about the questions below. Then discuss them in a small group, using the expressions above to relate your own experience.

1. Teachers often assign students to work on group projects. Do you think working in a group is a good way to learn?
2. When you work in a group, how can you make sure that everyone contributes equally to the tasks?

CRITICAL THINKING:
RANKING

B You listened to students discuss topics to research. When you decide on a topic, what criteria do you use? Rank the criteria below, with 1 being the most important. Then add your own. Compare your criteria and ranking with a partner.

- _____ how easy it is to research or study the topic

- _____ how interesting you find the subject or topic

- _____ how useful the information might be to you in the future

- _____ how much you already know about the topic

- _____

C Work in a small group. Consider these types of technology for archaeological research: drones, lidar, robots, satellites, and ground-penetrating radar. Which one would you be most interested in researching? Explain.

D In your notebook, answer the questions, using expressions from the Everyday Language box and supporting your answers. Then interview three students. Record their answers in your notebook.

1. In your view, what is the greatest technology that humans have developed?
2. What is one way that technology has had a positive impact on your life?
3. What is one problem that you have experienced because of technology?
4. What is one technology that you hope humans will develop in the future?
5. Do you worry that technology could ever become too powerful to control?

A diver explores an archaeological site in the Adriatic Sea near Palagruza, Croatia. The ceramic jars from around 1 BCE have revealed important clues about ancient trade routes.

E Work with a partner and discuss the questions, relating information to your own experience when possible.

1. What kind of archaeological site would you be most interested in excavating? Explain. Is there a particular place you are interested in?
2. One technology that many people have dreamed about is time travel. Do you think humans will ever develop a way to travel back to the past or forward to the future? Why or why not?

FINAL TASK Presenting about Life in the Past or Future

You will give an individual presentation from a choice of topics related to some of the ideas you have studied in this unit.

A Select one of these topics for your talk, using the criteria you noted in exercise B.

- Explain why people should care about archaeology.
- If time travel were possible, say where you would go in the past or future and why.
- Say how you think life 5,000 years in the future will be the same as and different from life now.

PRESENTATION SKILL Introducing Your Talk

When giving a presentation, you should try to have a strong introduction.
An introduction can include:

- a quick message to welcome and thank your audience
- a short introduction of yourself and your background
- an overview of the things you will cover in your talk
- an explanation of your reasons for choosing your topic
- information about when people can ask you questions
- a funny story to get your audience interested in your talk

Whatever you decide to include in your introduction, be careful not to make it too long.

ORGANIZING IDEAS **B** Prepare an outline of your talk in note form. Decide what kind of introduction you will have and what information you will include in the body and in the conclusion of your talk.

C Work in a small group. Share your plan for an effective introduction. Then discuss what things you want to focus on to improve how you deliver your talk. Discuss how you can achieve those goals.

A: *I usually speak too fast, so my goal is to speak more slowly this time.*
B: *I'd like to speak slower, too, but I feel like I can't control my speed.*
C: *Have you tried pausing for longer at the end of each sentence? That helps me.*

D Rehearse your talk a few times, making sure you focus on meeting your goals.

PRESENTING **E** Present your talk to the rest of the class. After your presentation, answer questions from other students. Then watch their presentations and ask questions.

REFLECTION

1. What techniques did you learn in this unit to help you communicate more effectively in group discussions and when giving a talk?

   _____

   _____

2. What is the most useful thing you learned in this unit? How about the most interesting thing?

   _____

   _____

3. Here are the vocabulary words from the unit. Check (✔) the ones you can use.

   ☐ artifact   ☐ excavation   ☐ satellite
   ☐ civilization   ☐ figure out   ☐ scan
   ☐ collaboration   ☐ get on with   ☐ settlement
   ☐ come across   ☐ look into   ☐ specialist
   ☐ curiosity   ☐ participation AWL   ☐ uncover
   ☐ date from   ☐ propose   ☐ virtually AWL
   ☐ device AWL   ☐ remains

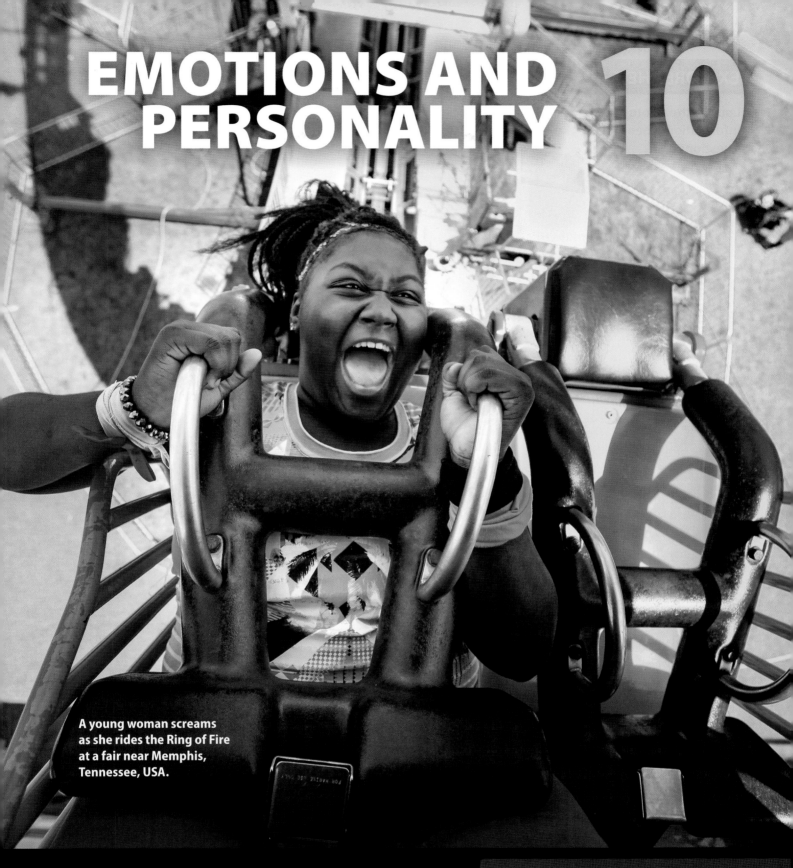

EMOTIONS AND PERSONALITY

10

A young woman screams as she rides the Ring of Fire at a fair near Memphis, Tennessee, USA.

THINK AND DISCUSS

1   What emotions do you think this woman is feeling?

2   When is the last time you screamed like this? What made you scream?

Look at the photo and read the information. Then discuss the questions.

1. Why do you imagine that this couple feels so happy?

2. What is most surprising to you about the Gallup Positive Experience Survey results?

3. How would you answer each of the questions in the Positive Experience Index?

THE GLOBAL STATE OF EMOTIONS

Where are the happiest people in the world?

The Gallup Positive Experience Poll includes the results from surveys conducted around the world. In the Positive Experience Index, people were surveyed about the feelings and emotions during their daily experiences. The results give a snapshot of our global state of emotions.

A man celebrates his 100th birthday with his wife and family in Ñeembucú, Paraguay.

Gallup Positive Experience Poll

Positive Experience Index Questions

- Did you feel well-rested yesterday?

- Were you treated with respect all day yesterday?

- Did you smile or laugh a lot yesterday?

- Did you learn or do something interesting yesterday?

- Did you experience enjoyment during a lot of the day yesterday?

Survey Results

- The Gallup Positive Experience Poll was conducted in 142 countries in 2016.

- More than 70 percent of people worldwide said they experienced a lot of enjoyment, smiled or laughed a lot, felt well-rested, and felt treated with respect.

- Fifty-one percent of people said they learned or did something interesting the day before the interview.

- Paraguay had the highest percentage of people reporting positive experiences.

- The top eleven countries were: Paraguay, Costa Rica, Panama, the Philippines, Uzbekistan, Ecuador, Guatemala, Mexico, Norway, Chile, and Colombia.

A Vocabulary

MEANING FROM
CONTEXT

A 🎧 **3.20** Read and listen to the conversation. Notice each word in **blue** and think about its meaning.

Max: Hey, Rika. What's wrong?

Rika: Nothing. I'm just reading the paper.

Max: Well, you're frowning as you read. Facial **expressions** always show your emotions. For example, frowning signals sadness or fear.

Rika: But doesn't that change depending on a person's culture? I'm Indonesian and you're Canadian. We probably just make different facial expressions.

Max: Actually, culture doesn't matter. Back in the 19th century, Charles Darwin found that all people typically make the same facial expressions. He reasoned that these expressions must be a **universal** human characteristic.

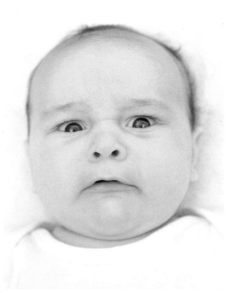

Rika: Really? Has anybody else looked into this, or was it just Darwin?

Max: Well, in the 1960s, a psychologist named Paul Ekman confirmed Darwin's theory. He conducted an experiment. He showed photos of facial expressions to people of many different cultures. The **results** showed that people across all cultures recognize—and make—the same facial expressions for the same emotions.

Rika: So culture doesn't matter then, right?

Max: Well, for *some* facial expressions. Neither Darwin nor Ekman could **confirm** that all facial expressions are universal. And Ekman also wondered whether there are things that universally **trigger** certain emotions.

Rika: So, you mean to say that what impacts our emotions is the same for everyone?

Max: Well, yes and no. Certain things are universal. For example, everyone gets scared whenever there's a sudden, unexpected movement in their field of vision.

Rika: That **makes sense**. A sudden movement might signal danger, and there's a **tendency** for humans to **react** to danger. We do it **instinctively**.

Max: Right, but not everything triggers the same emotion in different people. For example, one person might associate the smell of the sea with something enjoyable, like a vacation.

Rika: But for someone who has gotten seasick or been stung by a jellyfish, the ocean isn't so pleasant. So the smell might cause negative emotions.

Max: Exactly! Our reaction is influenced by our experience and, often, our **personality**.

B Discuss the questions with a partner.

1. Are you surprised that facial expressions are the same across cultures? Why or why not?

2. Which emotions do you feel are easiest to recognize? Which are most difficult? Explain.

C Write each word in **blue** from exercise A next to its definition.

1. _expression_ (n) ways to make your thoughts or feelings known (with gestures, writing, and so on)
2. _make sense_ (v) is logical or easy to understand
3. _result_ (n) the outcome
4. _confirm_ (v) to cause a response in someone or something
5. _react_ (adv) without having to think
6. _personality_ (n) a person's character and nature
7. _trigger_ (n) likelihood
8. _universal_ (adj) experienced by all people
9. _instinctively_ (v) to make sure something is right
10. _tendency_ (v) to respond to something or someone

D Complete each question with the correct form of a word from the box.

confirm	expression	instinctively	personality
result	trigger	universal	

1. What _trigger_ fear in you? Joy? Explain.
2. How can you _con_ an unbelievable story that you read online?
3. In addition to facial expressions, what else is _uni_ for humans?
4. What are other forms of _expr_, besides those that we make with our faces?
5. Think of a time when you tried to make something, but you didn't like the _res_. Did you ever try to make it again? Why or why not?
6. If you saw someone in danger, do you think you would _instinctively_ try to help that person? Why or why not?
7. How important is _personality_ in succeeding at a job?

E Discuss the questions from exercise D with a partner. Then use the words below to create three more questions to ask your partner.

make sense	react	tendency

A: *Do your feelings and emotions usually make sense to you?*
B: *Usually, but sometimes I don't understand why I get angry about small things.*

Listening A Lecture about Fear

A skydiver reacts as his instructor behind him opens the parachute.

BEFORE LISTENING

A Before you listen to the lecture, in your notebook make a list of five things that you fear. For each item, note whether you believe this fear is instinctive or whether it is learned.

WHILE LISTENING

LISTENING FOR
MAIN IDEAS

B 🎧 3.21 ▶ 1.17 Listen to the lecture. Then choose the best phrase to complete each sentence.

1. The lecture focuses on learning about (our ancestors' fears / the human fear response).

2. It was important for our ancestors to (react instinctively / learn a response) to things like falling rocks and hungry lions.

3. According to the lecture, our fear response can be (useful / dangerous) in certain situations, such as putting on the brakes in a car.

4. In Mineka and Davidson's experiment, the monkeys (were immediately afraid of / learned to fear) snakes.

5. Seeing a video of monkeys being fearful of flowers (impacted / didn't impact) the fear response of the monkeys in the laboratory.

NOTE-TAKING SKILL Using a Word Web

Use a word web to organize your notes as you listen. Write the main topic in the center of the web. Then as you listen, write the words you find essential to the overall message. After listening to the entire passage, go back and write any additional information you need to show how the words connect to the topic.

C 🎧 3.21 Listen to the lecture again and write notes in the word web. After you listen, add more details explaining how the ideas connect to fear.

LISTENING FOR DETAILS

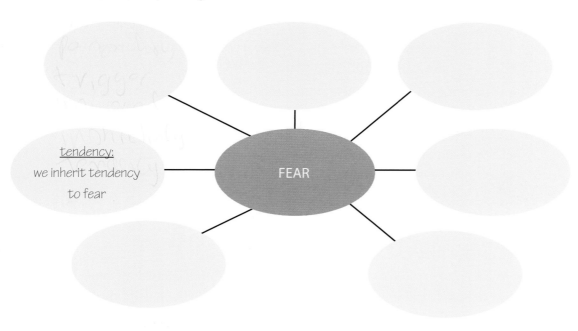

FEAR

tendency:
we inherit tendency
to fear

AFTER LISTENING

D Use your word web to complete the sentences with information from the lecture. Then compare your answers with a partner's.

1. The professor discusses _____.

2. The professor shows that some fear is inherited when he talks about _____
   _____.

3. He demonstrates that some fear is learned using the example of _____
   _____.

4. When he talks about the laboratory monkeys' lack of fear of the flowers, the professor is proving that in some cases _____.

E Work in a small group. Discuss these questions.

CRITICAL THINKING: ANALYZING

1. Look back at exercise A. Choose a fear that you identified as learned, and explain how and from whom you may have learned it.

2. Think of something that many people fear, such as flying. Why do you think it causes so much fear? Do you think it is learned or instinctive? Explain.

3. How can you overcome a fear? Explain with examples.

A Speaking

PERSONALIZING **A** Read the summary below. Then discuss the questions with a partner.

HOW DOES THE TEENAGE BRAIN AFFECT BEHAVIOR?

- During the teenage years, an area of the brain called the *prefrontal cortex* is still developing. This part of the brain is essential for decision-making and self-control. Because this part of the brain doesn't mature until adulthood, teenagers typically have weaker reasoning skills and more social anxiety than adults.

- The changes in the brain are evolutionary. They help teens prepare to leave home and go out into the world on their own. The teenage brain is in the process of adapting.

- Parents and teachers often notice the negative behaviors caused by these changes. However, changes in the brain also bring positive behaviors, such as a willingness to try new things and a desire to connect with friends—both necessary skills for adulthood.

1. In general, did you engage in risky behavior as a teen? Why or why not?
2. As a teen, who did you prefer spending time with more—friends or family? Why?
3. According to the information above, was your behavior typical of a teenager, or were you different from the average teen? Explain.

CRITICAL THINKING Making Judgments

When you make a judgment, you use various pieces of information to analyze a situation. You may combine new information with your own knowledge and previous experiences. For example, you can make a judgment about why an accident happened and support your judgment with reasons.

The driver is distracted while looking at the map on the cell phone.

B Read each situation below. Make judgments about how the teens' brains are affecting their actions. Discuss your ideas in a small group.

1. Fernando was driving too fast and crashed his father's car into a tree.

2. Lara's teacher asked her to work out a math problem on the board, but she refused. When the teacher asked her again, Lara got angry and walked out of the classroom.

3. Jian spends every evening at his best friend's house, instead of at home with his family. This hurts his mother's feelings.

4. Rachel's volleyball teammates didn't ask her to join them for pizza after the game. Rachel didn't go to volleyball practice the following day.

C Work with a partner. Explain a situation when, as a teenager, you acted in a way that was risky or showed poor judgment. Draw conclusions about what was happening in your brain that may have caused this behavior.

> *Once, I skateboarded down a steep staircase, without a helmet. I knew that it would be fun. I wasn't thinking about the risk, just the reward.*

GRAMMAR FOR SPEAKING *Used To* and *Would*

Use *used to* and *would* followed by a verb to talk about events or situations in the past that happened over a certain period of time, but no longer happen.

Both *used to* and *would* can be used to talk about repeated past actions.
> I **used to** worry about what other people thought.
> I **would** worry about what other people thought.

Use only *used to* to talk about past states or conditions.
> She **used to** like watching cartoons on Saturdays.
> We **used to** live in Ontario.
> They **used to** be best friends.

In questions and negatives, do not use *-d* on *use to*.
> **Did** you **use to** fight with your sister?
> No, I **didn't use to** fight with her. We **used to** get along well.

Don't confuse *used to* + verb with *be used to* + noun, which means "familiar with."
> **Are** you **used to** your new neighborhood yet?

D Complete each question with the correct form of *use to* or *would*. Then answer them with a partner.

1. What TV show ___I used to___ like as a child?

2. ___Did you use to___ live someplace other than where you live now? Where?

3. Where ___would you___ go to play with your friends? What ___I used to___ play?

4. Where ___did you use to___ go on vacation when you were younger?

5. What class ___didn't you use to___ like most in high school? Least?

6. What family member ___used to___ enjoy spending time with most? What ___you would___ do together?

E Work with a partner to discuss the topics below. Use *use(d) to* or *would* to talk about being younger. Give examples.

1. take risks
2. fight with family members
3. spend time away from home
4. feel left out
5. your own idea

A: *Did you use to take risks when you were younger?*
B: *Yes, I would take risks. For example, I used to go up on the roof every night.*

F Think about your life as a child and as a teenager. In the T-chart below, add notes about what you used to do, who you used to spend time with, and what you used to like or dislike. Write at least three things in each column.

As a Child	As a Teenager

EVERYDAY LANGUAGE   Asking Follow-Up Questions

When you're having a conversation, you can use the following expressions to learn more about what the other person is saying.

What is/was that like?   *What do you mean by that?*
Why do you think that is/was?   *What else can you tell me about … ?*

G Work with a partner. Using your notes from exercise F, take turns describing yourself both as a child and as a teenager. Use *used to* and *would* in your discussion. When appropriate, use follow-up questions to learn more about your partner.

H In a small group, discuss the questions.

1. How did your behavior change in your teenage years? How does this compare with other members of the group?
2. What stayed the same between your childhood and teenage years? Explain.
3. How can researchers use information about the teenage brain to help parents and teachers better understand and relate to teenagers?

LESSON TASK Presenting Survey Results

A Follow these steps. Take notes in the chart below.

1. Choose a negative emotion to ask about and complete the questions.
2. Add one more question about this emotion.
3. Ask a classmate the questions and take notes on the answers.
4. Repeat with two more classmates.

Survey Questions	Name: _____	Name: _____	Name: _____
1. How often do you feel _____? (i.e., once a day, several times a week.)			
2. What triggers _____ in you?			
3. How do you show that you feel _____? (i.e., facial expressions, certain behaviors.)			
4. What behavior related to this emotion do you think you have learned?			
5. _____ _____			

B Use your survey results to prepare a short summary. In your summary you will describe common triggers of the emotion as well as how people respond to it, without giving names.

C Form a small group with two or three classmates that you did *not* interview in your survey. Present what you learned about the classmates that you surveyed, without providing personal details or names. Then listen as group members share their results. Ask follow-up questions to learn more.

PRESENTING

> *The emotion that I asked about in my survey was jealousy. Many people felt it every day . . .*

Video

Cory Richards photographed himself moments after an avalanche on Gasherbrum II in the Himalayas on the border of Pakistan and China.

A Tribute to Discomfort

BEFORE VIEWING

CRITICAL THINKING:
CATEGORIZING

A Work with a partner. Discuss the meaning of some words you will hear in the video. Use a dictionary if needed. Then categorize the words as generally positive (+) or negative (–). Some words can go in either category.

adventure (n)	experience (n)	triumph (v)
avalanche (n)	hurt (v)	unknown (adj)
comfortable (adj)	stress (n)	
confusing (adj)	struggle (n)	

B Read the information about Cory Richards. What kind of person do you think he is? What adjectives would you use to describe him? List four adjectives.

_____

> **MEET CORY RICHARDS.** Mountain climber, photojournalist, and visual storyteller, National Geographic Photographer Cory Richards has traveled from the peaks of Antarctica to the Himalayas to capture the soul of adventure and the beauty of our world. He was named 2012 National Geographic Adventurer of the Year. He is one of the world's leading adventure photographers.

WHILE VIEWING

C ▶ 1.18 Watch the video and choose the best answers.

UNDERSTANDING MAIN IDEAS

1. For Richards, photography is a way to _____.
   a. communicate what it means to be human
   b. document incredible and dangerous adventures
   c. share beautiful images from around the world

2. Richards is motivated to _____.
   a. photograph world problems and issues
   b. go to the highest peaks in the world
   c. explore what is unknown to him

3. The purpose of this video is _____.
   a. to inspire others to climb mountains
   b. to explain what motivates him to take photographs
   c. to tell the story of his life

D ▶ 1.18 Watch the video again. Complete the sentences with the words you hear.

UNDERSTANDING DETAILS

1. I think _____ is anything that puts us outside our comfort zone.

2. When I _____ that I had not died, I turned the camera on myself and took an image.

3. I've never been _____ in the place that I'm in. I can't stop and sit.

4. I've seen faces that are just years and years of history all wrapped into one single _____ .

5. My job is to communicate a _____ , raw, visceral[1] experience.

6. I mean, life is _____ .

7. This started as a way for me to communicate what I was _____ .

[1]**visceral** (adj): deeply felt feelings that are difficult to control

AFTER VIEWING

E In a small group, discuss the questions below.

CRITICAL THINKING: ANALYZING

1. Read statements 1, 3, and 6 in exercise D. Are any of them true for you? How would you change any statements to make them true for you?
2. Look at how you categorized the words in exercise A. How do you think Cory Richards would categorize them? Discuss and explain your reasons.
3. Think about the title of the video: A Tribute to Discomfort. A tribute shows admiration or respect for something or someone. In what way might Richards respect or admire discomfort? What is your attitude toward discomfort?
4. Have you (or someone you know) had an experience that changed your life? Describe it.

Vocabulary

A   Make a list of words to describe your personality (e.g., curious, shy, agreeable).

_____   _____   _____

_____   _____   _____

MEANING FROM
CONTEXT

B   🎧 3.22   Read and listen to the information. Notice each word in **blue** and think about its meaning.

INTROVERT AND EXTROVERT

Modern psychology offers many models to explain personality types, but nearly all of them include two terms made popular by Carl Jung in the early 20th century: **introvert** and **extrovert**. These two personality types have very different characteristics, and while almost everyone has some aspects of both in their own personality, one type is usually stronger.

In general, introverts prefer activities they can do alone, such as reading or playing video games. For most people, being an introvert simply means preferring less frequent social contact with smaller numbers of people—going out with friends one-on-one, instead of in a large group, for example. In more extreme cases, introverts may feel **awkward** in social situations and may even feel so much **anxiety** that they avoid socializing altogether.

Extroverts **differ** from introverts in several ways. Extroverts **thrive** on interaction with others and feel energized at big social gatherings. They often have jobs in which they collaborate with others—teachers and politicians tend to be extroverts, for example. While people often find extroverts charming, some can be too talkative and **outgoing**, to the point that others may feel uncomfortable around them. Extroverts often become **upset** when they **lack** human contact on the job or in their social lives. Sometimes feelings of being alone can even **lead to** depression. In general, extroverts tend to feel best about themselves in the company of others.

C   Look at the words you wrote to describe yourself in exercise A. Are you more of an introvert, extrovert, or a combination? Discuss with a partner.

D Write each word in **blue** from exercise B next to its definition.

1. _____ (adj) unhappy or disappointed

2. _____ (v) to vary, be different from

3. _____ (v ph) to result in

4. _____ (n) a feeling of extreme nervousness or worry

5. _____ (v) to have too little of

6. _____ (n) a person who prefers to spend time alone or in small groups

7. _____ (adj) friendly, enjoys meeting others

8. _____ (v) to be motivated, energized by

9. _____ (n) a person who prefers to spend time with other people

10. _____ (adj) uncomfortable and embarrassed

VOCABULARY SKILL Identifying Latin Prefixes and Suffixes

Many words in English take prefixes and suffixes that originate from Latin. Here are some Latin prefixes and suffixes commonly used in English.

Prefix	Meaning	Suffix	Meaning
co-	*together*	-able, -ible	*capable, able to*
inter-	*between, among*	-er, -or	*one who (does something)*
intro-	*inward*	-ion, -sion, -tion	*act of, result of*
pre-	*before*	-ive	*having a tendency to*
re-	*again*	-logy	*the study of*

E Notice the prefix and/or suffix in each word. Then write another word with that same word part. Use a dictionary if necessary.

1. intro verted *introspective*

2. depress ion _____

3. talk ative _____

4. psycho logy _____

5. comfort able _____

6. teach er _____

7. co llaborate _____

8. inter action _____

9. pre teen _____

10. re confirm _____

F Work with a partner. Discuss these questions.

1. Describe someone you know who is very outgoing. What are some other personality characteristics of the person?

2. Describe situations in which people often feel awkward. Explain why they may feel that way.

3. Why do people suffer from anxiety in today's world? Give at least three reasons.

Listening A Conversation about Food and Emotions

BEFORE LISTENING

PERSONALIZING

A You are going to hear a conversation about how eating is connected with personality and emotions. How do your emotions affect what you eat? Does what you eat affect your emotions? Write your ideas. Then discuss them with a partner.

WHILE LISTENING

> **LISTENING SKILL** Listening for Consequences
>
> It is important to understand the relationship between actions and the consequences (results). Here are some words and phrases that often signal consequences.
>
> *if* clauses
> > **If** you get more exercise, you will sleep better at night.
>
> *when* clauses
> > **When** I sleep well, I wake up in a good mood the next day.
>
> *because* clauses
> > She got lost **because** she wasn't paying attention.
>
> *lead to*
> > Long-term job stress can **lead to** health problems.

B 🎧 3.23 Complete each statement with your own idea of a consequence. Then listen to find out what the person actually says. Were your consequences different?

1. I have a tendency to _____ when I'm stressed.

2. If you eat healthy foods today, you'll _____.

3. If you're in a good mood, you'll feel more _____.

4. Diets that contain a lot of sugar can lead to _____.

5. Extroverts eat _____ because they're always socializing.

LISTENING FOR
MAIN IDEAS

C 🎧 3.24 Listen to the first part of the conversation. Write answers to the questions in your notebook. Then compare with a partner.

1. How does Sam feel? Why?

_____

2. Why does Mae want him to throw out his snack?

_____

3. What does Mae say about eating unhealthy food?

_____

4. How does Sam react to Mae's suggestions?

_____

D 🎧 3.25 Listen to the second part of the conversation. Mark the statements T for *True* or F for *False*. Correct the false statements.

LISTENING FOR DETAILS

1. Foods you eat can affect how you feel a few days later.   T   F

2. Your personality has nothing to do with your diet.   T   F

3. Extroverts have a tendency to be healthy eaters.   T   F

4. In some cases, picky eating can be a sign of anxiety.   T   F

AFTER LISTENING

E 🎧 3.26 Listen to each person talk about his or her emotions. Then write the letter of the food that each person might eat based on what you hear. Compare your answers with a partner. Explain the inferences you made for each.

CRITICAL THINKING: MAKING INFERENCES

1. _____   2. _____   3. _____   4. _____

a.

b.

c.

d.

F Work in a small group. Discuss the questions.

CRITICAL THINKING: EVALUATING

1. Look at your responses for exercise A. Did the new information change your ideas about the relationship between eating and emotions for you? Explain.

2. What unusual eating habits do you have? For example, do you eat all of one type of food before starting another? Do you eat special kinds of food? Are you willing to try really unusual foods? What do you think these habits say about your personality?

3. What else affects how and what you eat? What can you change to be healthier? How might those changes, in turn, affect your personality?

B Speaking

A Discuss the questions in small groups.

1. Look back at your list of personality traits from the vocabulary section of this lesson. How many of these attributes are positive? Negative?
2. If you could change one thing about your personality, what would it be? Why?

CRITICAL THINKING:
APPLYING

B 🎧 3.27 Look at the graphic and listen to the description. Then read the description of each person below. Identify which of the Big 5 aspects each person is most associated with and discuss your answers with a partner.

The Big 5 Personality Aspects

1. Lisa is working toward a promotion at her job. She comes early and stays late every day, and her boss knows that he can depend on Lisa to get the job done.
2. Daigo is so popular! It feels like everyone on campus knows him. I don't know how he does it.
3. Hector is hard to be around. He seems annoyed by everything I say! He always seems nervous or stressed about something.
4. Ana just signed up for a course on acrobatics! And last year, she learned to go deep-sea fishing. She is always doing something unusual.
5. Giselle is a very generous person. She's always doing volunteer work in the community. Her neighbors' well-being is really important to her.

CRITICAL THINKING:
JUDGING

C Look at the graphic in exercise B. Rate your personality (or that of a family member) for each of the five aspects. Rate 1 for *not very* up to 5 for *very*.

_____ Openness   _____ Agreeableness

_____ Dependability   _____ Neuroticism

_____ Extroversion

D With a partner, give examples of behavior that demonstrate your ratings in exercise C.

> *I really like trying new things! For example, last week, I went skydiving. I must be strong in the "openness" category. Maybe I'm a 5?*

PRONUNCIATION Using Punctuation Marks

When you're reading aloud, use the punctuation marks to guide how you pronounce sentences. When you see:

. → use falling intonation

, / ; / : / . . . → pause

? → use rising or falling intonation to show a question

! → use stress to show emphasis

" " → add emphasis to that word

E With a partner, read the conversation model in exercise D aloud, focusing on the correct pronunciation for each punctuation mark. Then write down one of the answers that you gave in exercise D and read it aloud.

F 🎧 **3.28** Listen to the conversation about changing your personality. Then discuss the questions with a partner.

1. In a research study, what percent of people were satisfied with their personality? Are you surprised at this number? Explain.
2. What do Luis and Alma want to change about their personalities?
3. According to the article Alma read, how can you change your personality?

SPEAKING SKILL Defending an Opinion

When you give your opinion, you should provide facts to make your argument stronger. Use the phrases below to introduce facts to defend your opinion.

I read that *the teenage brain is less developed than the adult brain.*

Most people would agree that *extroverted people are fun to be around.*

As far as I know, *fear is a learned behavior.*

Research suggests that *personality can change over time.*

G In exercise F, you heard about how personality changes. Give your opinion of how the life events below can change you and defend your opinion.

CRITICAL THINKING: ANALYZING

1. getting a job that you really like
2. having a baby
3. getting married
4. moving to a new place

FINAL TASK Presenting Research

You and a partner are going to research one of the topics below and prepare an interactive presentation on the topic for the class:

- the effects of sleep on the brain
- how different genders show the same emotions
- the relationship between personality type and exercise
- behavior and emotions in young children

PRESENTATION SKILL Interacting with the Audience

When giving a presentation, try to engage your audience. You can do this in any of the following ways:

- Ask audience members what they already know about the topic.
- Ask for volunteers to share personal stories that relate to your topic.
- Hold a question-and-answer session at the end of your presentation.

Here are three important tips:

- After someone participates, follow up by relating what he or she said directly to your topic.
- Don't hesitate to politely interrupt an audience member if what he or she is saying is off topic.
- Only call on a person who volunteers to answer.

A Work with a partner. Select one of the topics above to research. Before you begin researching, write five questions that you want to answer in your research.

ORGANIZING IDEAS **B** With your partner, compile your research into a presentation. Organize the subtopics according to the five questions you wrote in exercise A. Then for one or two of the subtopics, write a relevant question for the audience.

PRESENTING **C** With your partner, give your presentation. Take turns engaging your audience and responding to their input.

REFLECTION

1. What information about psychology are you most likely to remember? Why?

_____

_____

2. What is the most useful thing you learned in this unit?

_____

_____

3. Here are the vocabulary words from the unit. Check (✓) the ones you can use.

☐ anxiety	☐ introvert	☐ result
☐ awkward	☐ lack	☐ tendency
☐ confirm AWL	☐ lead to	☐ thrive
☐ differ	☐ make sense	☐ trigger AWL
☐ expression	☐ outgoing	☐ universal
☐ extrovert	☐ personality	☐ upset
☐ instinctively	☐ react AWL	

Independent Student Handbook

Table of Contents

LISTENING SKILLS

Predicting

Speakers giving formal talks usually begin by introducing themselves and their topic. Listen carefully to the introduction of the topic so that you can predict what the talk will be about.

Strategies:

- Use visual information including titles on the board or on presentation slides.
- Think about what you already know about the topic.
- Ask yourself questions that you think the speaker might answer.
- Listen for specific phrases that indicate an introduction (e.g., *My topic is…*).

Listening for Main Ideas

It is important to be able to tell the difference between a speaker's main ideas and supporting details. It is more common for teachers to test understanding of main ideas than of specific details.

Strategies:

- Listen carefully to the introduction. Speakers often state the main idea in the introduction.
- Listen for rhetorical questions, or questions that the speaker asks, and then answers. Often the answer is the statement of the main idea.
- Notice words and phrases that the speaker repeats. Repetition often signals main ideas.

Listening for Details (Examples)

A speaker often provides examples that support a main idea. A good example can help you understand and remember the main idea better.

Strategies:

- Listen for specific phrases that introduce examples.
- Listen for general statements. Examples often follow general statements.

Listening for Details (Cause and Effect)

Speakers often give reasons or list causes and/or effects to support their ideas.

Strategies:

- Notice nouns that might signal causes/reasons (e.g., *factors, influences, causes, reasons*) or effects/results (e.g., *effects, results, outcomes, consequences*).
- Notice verbs that might signal causes/reasons (e.g., *contribute to, affect, influence, determine, produce, result in*) or effects/results (often these are passive, e.g., *is affected by*).

Understanding the Structure of a Presentation

An organized speaker uses expressions to alert the audience to important information that will follow. Recognizing signal words and phrases will help you understand how a presentation is organized and the relationship between ideas.

Introduction

A good introduction identifies the topic and gives an idea of how the lecture or presentation will be organized. Here are some expressions to introduce a topic:

I'll be talking about . . .   *My topic is . . .*

There are basically two groups . . .   *There are three reasons . . .*

Body

In the body of a lecture, speakers usually expand upon the topic. They often use phrases that signal the order of events or subtopics and their relationship to each other. Here are some expressions to help listeners follow the body of a lecture:

The first/next/final (point/reason) is . . .   *First/Next/Finally, let's look at . . .*

Another reason is . . .   *However, . . .*

Conclusion

In the conclusion of a lecture, speakers often summarize what they have said. They may also make predictions or suggestions. Sometimes they ask a question in the conclusion to get the audience to think more about the topic. Here are some expressions to give a conclusion:

In conclusion, . . .   *In summary, . . .*

As you can see. . .   *To review, + (restatement of main points)*

Understanding Meaning from Context

When you are not familiar with a word that a speaker says, you can sometimes guess the meaning of the word or fill in the gaps using the context or situation itself.

Strategies:

- Don't panic. You don't always understand every word of what a speaker says in your first language, either.
- Use context clues to fill in the blanks. What did you understand just before or just after the missing part? What did the speaker probably say?
- Listen for words and phrases that signal a definition or explanation (e.g., *What that means is…*).

Recognizing a Speaker's Bias

Speakers often have an opinion about the topic they are discussing. It's important for you to know if they are objective or subjective about the topic. Objective speakers do not express an opinion. Subjective speakers have a bias or a strong feeling about the topic.

Strategies:

- Notice words like adjectives, adverbs, and modals that the speaker uses (e.g., *ideal, horribly, should, shouldn't*). These suggest that the speaker has a bias.
- Listen to the speaker's voice. Does he or she sound excited, angry, or bored?
- Notice if the speaker gives more weight or attention to one point of view over another.
- Listen for words that signal opinions (e.g., *I think…*).

NOTE-TAKING SKILLS

Taking notes is a personalized skill. It is important to develop a note-taking system that works for you. However, there are some common strategies to improve your note taking.

Before You Listen

Focus

Try to clear your mind before the speaker begins so you can pay attention. If possible, review previous notes or think about what you already know about the topic.

Predict

If you know the topic of the talk, think about what you might hear.

Listen

Take Notes by Hand

Research suggests that taking notes by hand rather than on a computer is more effective. Taking notes by hand requires you to summarize, rephrase, and synthesize information. This helps you *encode* the information, or put it into a form that you can understand and remember.

Listen for Signal Words and Phrases

Speakers often use signal words and phrases (e.g., *Today we're going to talk about…*) to organize their ideas and show relationships between them. Listening for signal words and phrases can help you decide what information to write in your notes.

Condense (Shorten) Information

- As you listen, focus on the most important ideas. The speaker will usually repeat, define, explain, and/or give examples of these ideas. Take notes on these ideas.

    Speaker: *The Itaipu Dam provides about 20% of the electricity used in Brazil and about 75% of the electricity used in Paraguay. That electricity goes to millions of homes and businesses, so it's good for the economy of both countries.*

    Notes: Itaipu Dam → electricity: Brazil 20%, Paraguay 75%

- Don't write full sentences. Write only key words (nouns, verbs, adjectives, and adverbs), phrases, or short sentences.

    Full sentence: *Teachers are normally at the top of the list of happiest jobs.*

    Notes: teachers happiest

- Leave out information that is obvious.

  Full sentence: *Photographer Annie Griffiths is famous for her beautiful photographs. She travels all over the world to take photos.*

  Notes: A. Griffiths famous for photos; travels world
- Write numbers and statistics using numerals (9 bil; 35%).
- Use abbreviations (e.g., *ft., min., yr*) and symbols (=, ≠, >, <, %, →).
- Use indenting. Write main ideas on the left side of the paper. Indent details.
  Benefits of eating ugly foods
  > *Save $*
  >> *10-20% on ugly fruits & vegs. at market*
- Write details under key terms to help you remember them.
- Write the definitions of important new words.

After You Listen
- Review your notes soon after the lecture or presentation. Add any details you missed.
- Clarify anything you don't understand in your notes with a classmate or teacher.
- Add or highlight main ideas. Cross out details that aren't important or necessary.
- Rewrite anything that is hard to read or understand. Rewrite your notes in an outline or other graphic organizer to organize the information more clearly.
- Use arrows, boxes, diagrams, or other visual cues to show relationships between ideas.

ORGANIZING INFORMATION

You can use a graphic organizer to take notes while you are listening, or to organize your notes after you listen. Here are some examples of graphic organizers:

Flowcharts are used to show processes, or cause/effect relationships.

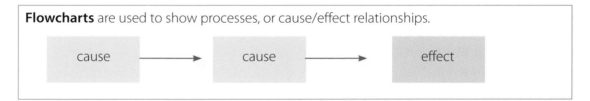

Mind maps show the connection between concepts. The main idea is usually in the center with supporting ideas and details around it.

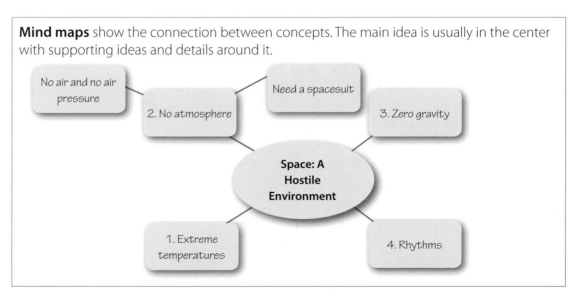

Outlines show the relationship between main ideas and details.

To use an outline for taking notes, write the main ideas at the left margin of your paper. Below the main ideas, indent and write the supporting ideas and details. You may do this as you listen, or go back and rewrite your notes as an outline later.

> **I. Introduction:** How to feed the world
>
> **II. Steps**
>
> Step One: Stop deforestation
>
> a. stop burning rainforests
>
> b. grow crops on land size of South America

T-charts compare two topics.

Climate Change in Greenland	
Benefits	**Drawbacks**
shorter winters	rising sea levels

Timelines show a sequence of events.

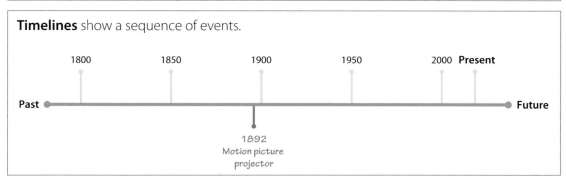

1800   1850   1900   1950   2000 **Present**

Past   Future

1892
Motion picture
projector

Venn diagrams compare and contrast two or more topics. The overlapping areas show similarities.

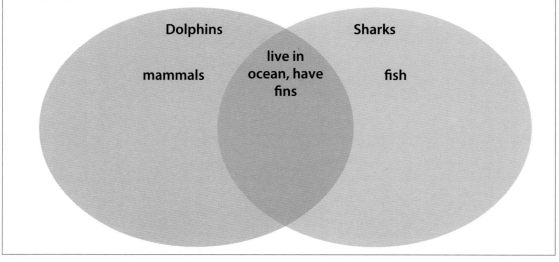

Dolphins   Sharks

mammals   live in ocean, have fins   fish

SPEAKING: COMMON PHRASES

Phrases for Expressing Yourself

Expressing Opinions

I think…
I believe…
I'm sure…
In my opinion/view…
If you ask me,…
Personally,…
To me,…

Expressing Likes and Dislikes

I like…
I prefer…
I love…
I can't stand…
I hate…
I really don't like…
I don't care for…

Giving Facts

There is evidence/proof…
Experts claim/argue…
Studies show…
Researchers found…
The record shows…

Giving Tips or Suggestions

Imperatives (e.g., Try to get more sleep.)
You/We should/shouldn't…
You/We ought to…
It's (not) a good idea to…
I suggest (that)…
Let's…
How about… + (noun/gerund)
What about… + (noun/gerund)
Why don't we/you…
You/We could…

Agreeing

I agree.
True.
Good point.
Exactly.
Absolutely.
I was just about to say that.
Definitely.
Right!

Disagreeing

I disagree.
I'm not so sure about that.
I don't know.
That's a good point, but I don't agree.
I see what you mean, but I think that…

Phrases for Interacting with Others

Clarifying/Checking Your Understanding

So are you saying that…?
So what you mean is…?
What do you mean?
How's that?
How so?
I'm not sure I understand/follow.
Do you mean…?
I'm not sure what you mean.

Asking for Clarification/Confirming Understanding

Sorry, I didn't catch that. Could you repeat it?
I'm not sure I understand the question.
I'm not sure I understand what you mean.
Sorry, I'm not following you.
Are you saying that…?
If I understand correctly, you're saying that…
Oh, now I get it. You're talking about…, right?

Checking Others' Understanding

Does that make sense?
Do you understand?
Do you see what I mean?
Is that clear?
Are you following/with me?
Do you have any questions?

Asking for Opinions

What do you think?
We haven't heard from you in a while.
Do you have anything to add?
What are your thoughts?
How do you feel?
What's your opinion?

Taking Turns

Can/May I say something?
Could I add something?
Can I just say…?
May I continue?
Can I finish what I was saying?
Did you finish your thought?
Let me finish.
Let's get back to…

Interrupting Politely

Excuse me.
Pardon me.
Forgive me for interrupting…
I hate to interrupt but…
Can I stop you for a second?

Asking for Repetition

Could you say that again?
I'm sorry?
I didn't catch what you said.
I'm sorry. I missed that. What did you say?
Could you repeat that please?

Showing Interest

I see.	*Good for you.*
Really?	*Seriously?*
Um-hmm.	*No kidding!*
Wow.	*And? (Then what?)*

That's funny / amazing / incredible / awful!

SPEAKING: PHRASES FOR PRESENTING

Introduction

Introducing a Topic

I'm going to talk about…
My topic is…
I'm going to present…
I plan to discuss…
Let's start with…

Today we're going to talk about…
So we're going to show you…
Now/Right/So/Well, (pause), let's look at…
There are three groups/reasons/effects/ factors…
There are four steps in this process.

Body

Listing or Sequencing

First/First of all/The first (noun)/To start/To begin,…
Second/Secondly/The second/Next/Another/ Also/Then/In addition,…
Last/The last/Finally,…
There are many/several/three types/kinds of/ ways…

Signaling Problems/Solutions

One problem/issue/challenge is…
One solution/answer/response is…

Giving Reasons or Causes

Because + (clause): Because the climate is changing…
Because of + (noun phrase): Because of climate change…
Due to + (noun phrase)…
Since + (clause)
The reason that I like hip-hop is…
One reason that people listen to music is…
One factor is + (noun phrase)
The main reason that…

Giving Results or Effects

so + (clause): so I went to the symphony
Therefore, + (sentence): Therefore, I went to the symphony.
As a result, + (sentence)
Consequently, + (sentence)
…causes + (noun phrase)
…leads to + (noun phrase)
…had an impact/effect on + (noun phrase)
If…then…

Giving Examples

The first example is…
Here's an example of what I mean…
For instance,…
For example,…
Let me give you an example…
…such as…
…like…

Repeating and Rephrasing

What you need to know is…
I'll say this again…
So again, let me repeat…
The most important point is…

Signaling Additional Examples or Ideas	Signaling to Stop Taking Notes
Not only…, but	*You don't need this for the test.*
Besides…	*This information is in your books/on your handout/on the website.*
Not only do…, but also	*You don't have to write all this down.*
Identifying a Side Track	**Returning to a Previous Topic**
This is off-topic,…	*Getting back to our previous discussion,…*
On a different subject,…	*To return to our earlier topic…*
As an aside, …	*OK, getting back on topic…*
That reminds me…	*So to return to what we were saying,…*
Signaling a Definition	**Talking about Visuals**
Which means…	*This graph/infographic/diagram shows/explains…*
What that means is…	*The line/box/image represents…*
Or…	*The main point of this visual is…*
In other words,…	*You can see…*
Another way to say that is…	*From this we can see…*
That is…	
That is to say…	

Conclusion

Concluding	
Well/So, that's how I see it.	*To sum up,*
In conclusion,	*As you can see,…*
In summary,	*At the end,…*
	To review, (+ restatement of main points)

PRESENTATION STRATEGIES

You will often have to give individual or group presentations in your class. The strategies below will help you to prepare, present, and reflect on your presentations.

Prepare

As you prepare your presentation:

Consider Your Topic

- **Choose a topic you feel passionate about.** If you are passionate about your topic, your audience will be more interested and excited about your topic, too. Focus on one major idea that you can bring to life. The best ideas are the ones your audience wants to experience.

Consider Your Purpose

- **Have a strong start.** Use an effective hook, such as a quote, an interesting example, a rhetorical question, or a powerful image to get your audience's attention. Include one sentence that explains what you will do in your presentation and why.
- **Stay focused.** Make sure your details and examples support your main points. Avoid sidetracks or unnecessary information that takes you away from your topic.
- **Use visuals that relate to your ideas.** Drawings, photos, video clips, infographics, charts, maps, slides, and physical objects can get your audience's attention and explain ideas effectively. For example, a photo or map of a location you mention can help your audience picture a place they have never been. Slides with only key words and phrases can help emphasize your main points. Visuals should be bright, clear, and simple.
- **Have a strong conclusion.** A strong conclusion should serve the same purpose as a strong start—to get your audience's attention and make them think. Good conclusions often refer back to the introduction, or beginning of the presentation. For example, if you ask a question in the beginning, you can answer it in the conclusion. Remember to restate your main points, and add a conclusion device such as a question, a call to action, or a quote.

Consider Your Audience

- **Use familiar concepts.** Think about the people in your audience. Ask yourself these questions: Where are they from? How old are they? What is their background? What do they already know about my topic? What information do I need to explain? Use language and concepts they will understand.
- **Share a personal story.** Consider presenting information that will get an emotional reaction; for example, information that will make your audience feel surprised, curious, worried, or upset. This will help your audience relate to you and your topic.
- **Be authentic (be yourself!).** Write your presentation yourself. Use words that you know and are comfortable using.

Rehearse

- **Make an outline** to help you organize your ideas.
- **Write notes on notecards.** Do not write full sentences, just key words and phrases to help you remember important ideas. Mark the words you should stress and places to pause.
- **Review pronunciation.** Check the pronunciation of words you are uncertain about with a classmate, a teacher, or in a dictionary. Note and practice the pronunciation of difficult words.
- **Memorize the introduction and conclusion.** Rehearse your presentation several times. Practice saying it out loud to yourself (perhaps in front of a mirror or video recorder) and in front of others.
- **Ask for feedback.** Note and revise information that doesn't flow smoothly based on feedback and on your own performance in rehearsal. If specific words or phrases are still a problem, rephrase them.

Present

As you present:

- **Pay attention to your pacing** (how fast or slow you speak). Remember to speak slowly and clearly. Pause to allow your audience to process information.
- **Speak at a volume loud enough to be heard** by everyone in the audience, but not too loud. Ask the audience if your volume is OK at the beginning of your talk.

- **Vary your intonation.** Don't speak in the same tone throughout the talk. Your audience will be more interested if your voice rises and falls, speeds up and slows down to match the ideas you are talking about.
- **Be friendly and relaxed with your audience**—remember to smile!
- **Show enthusiasm for your topic.** Use humor if appropriate.
- **Have a relaxed body posture.** Don't stand with your arms folded, or look down at your notes. Use gestures when helpful to emphasize your points.
- **Don't read directly from your notes.** Use them to help you remember ideas.
- **Don't look at or read from your visuals too much.** Use them to support your ideas.
- **Make frequent eye contact** with the entire audience.

Reflect

As you reflect on your presentation:

- **Consider what you think went well** during your presentation and what areas you can improve upon.
- **Get feedback** from your classmates and teacher. How do their comments relate to your own thoughts about your presentation? Did they notice things you didn't? How can you use their feedback in your next presentation?

PRESENTATION OUTLINE

When you are planning a presentation, you may find it helpful to use an outline. If it is a group presentation, the outline can provide an easy way to divide the content. For example, one student can do the introduction, another student the first idea in the body, and so on.

1. Introduction

Topic: _____

Hook: _____

Statement of main idea: _____

2. Body

First step/example/reason: _____

    Supporting details: _____ _____ _____

Second step/example/reason: _____

    Supporting details: _____ _____ _____

Third step/example/reason: _____

    Supporting details: _____ _____ _____

3. Conclusion

Main points to summarize: _____ _____

Suggestions/Predictions: _____ _____

Closing comments/summary: _____ _____

PRONUNCIATION GUIDE

Sounds and Symbols

Vowels

Symbol	Key Words
/ɑ/	hot, stop
/æ/	cat, ran
/aɪ/	fine, nice
/i/	eat, need
/ɪ/	sit, him
/eɪ/	name, say
/ɛ/	get, bed
/ʌ/	cup, what
/ə/	about, lesson
/u/	boot, new
/ʊ/	book, could
/oʊ/	go, road
/ɔ/	law, walk
/aʊ/	house, now
/ɔɪ/	toy, coin

Consonants

Symbol	Key Word	Symbol	Key Word
/b/	boy	/t/	tea
/d/	day	/tʃ/	cheap
/dʒ/	job, bridge	/v/	vote
/f/	face	/w/	we
/g/	go	/y/	yes
/h/	hat	/z/	zoo
/k/	key, car		
/l/	love	/ð/	they
/m/	my	/θ/	think
/n/	nine	/ʃ/	shoe
/ŋ/	sing	/ʒ/	measure
/p/	pen		
/r/	right		
/s/	see		

Source: *The Newbury House Dictionary plus Grammar Reference,* Fifth Edition, National Geographic Learning/Cengage Learning, 2014.

Rhythm

The rhythm of English involves stress and pausing.

Stress

- English words are based on syllables—units of sound that include one vowel sound.
- In every word in English, one syllable has the primary stress.
- In English, speakers group words that go together based on the meaning and context of the sentence. These groups of words are called *thought groups*. In each thought group, one word is stressed more than the others—the stress is placed on the syllable with the primary stress in this word.
- In general, new ideas and information are stressed.

Pausing

- Pauses in English can be divided into two groups: long and short pauses.
- English speakers use long pauses to mark the conclusion of a thought, items in a list, or choices given.
- Short pauses are used in between thought groups to break up the ideas in sentences into smaller, more manageable chunks of information.

English speakers use intonation, or pitch (the rise and fall of their voice), to help express meaning. For example, speakers usually use a rising intonation at the end of *yes/no* questions, and a falling intonation at the end of *wh-* questions and statements.

VOCABULARY BUILDING STRATEGIES

Vocabulary learning is an on-going process. The strategies below will help you learn and remember new vocabulary words.

Guessing Meaning from Context

You can often guess the meaning of an unfamiliar word by looking at or listening to the words and sentences around it. Speakers usually know when a word is unfamiliar to the audience, or is essential to understanding the main ideas, and often provide clues to its meaning.

- Repetition: A speaker may use the same key word or phrase, or use another form of the same word.
- Restatement or synonym: A speaker may give a synonym to explain the meaning of a word, using phrases such as *in other words, also called, or…, also known as*.
- Antonyms: A speaker may define a word by explaining what it is NOT. The speaker may say *Unlike A/In contrast to A, B is…*
- Definition: Listen for signals such as *which means* or *is defined as*. Definitions can also be signaled by a pause.
- Examples: A speaker may provide examples that can help you figure out what something is. For example, **Mascots** *are a very popular marketing tool. You've seen them on commercials and in ads on social media –* **cute, brightly colored creatures that help sell a product**.

Understanding Word Families: Stems, Prefixes, and Suffixes

Use your understanding of stems, prefixes, and suffixes to recognize unfamiliar words and to expand your vocabulary. The stem is the root part of the word, which provides the main meaning. A prefix comes before the stem and usually modifies meaning (e.g., adding *re-* to a word means "again" or "back"). A suffix comes after the stem and usually changes the part of speech (e.g., adding *-ion*, *-tion*, or *-ation* to a verb changes it to a noun). Words that share the same stem or root belong to the same word family (e.g., *event, eventful, uneventful, uneventfully*).

Word Stem	Meaning	Example
ann, enn	year	anniversary, millennium
chron(o)	time	chronological, synchronize
flex, flect	bend	flexible, reflection
graph	draw, write	graphics, paragraph
lab	work	labor, collaborate
mob, mot, mov	move	automobile, motivate, mover
port	carry	transport, import
sect	cut	sector, bisect

Prefix	Meaning	Example
dis-	not, opposite of	disappear, disadvantages
in-, im-, il-, ir-	not	inconsistent, immature, illegal, irresponsible
inter-	between	Internet, international
mis-	bad, badly, incorrectly	misunderstand, misjudge
pre-	before	prehistoric, preheat
re-	again; back	repeat; return
trans-	across, beyond	transfer, translate
un-	not	uncooked, unfair

Suffix	Meaning	Example
-able, -ible	worth, ability	believable, impossible
-en	to cause to become; made of	lengthen, strengthen; golden
-er, -or	one who	teacher, director
-ful	full of	beautiful, successful
-ify, -fy	to make or become	simplify, satisfy
-ion, -tion, -ation	condition, action	occasion, education, foundation
-ize	cause	modernize, summarize
-ly	in the manner of	carefully, happily
-ment	condition or result	assignment, statement
-ness	state of being	happiness, sadness

Using a Dictionary

Here are some tips for using a dictionary:

- When you see or hear a new word, try to guess its part of speech (noun, verb, adjective, etc.) and meaning, then look it up in a dictionary.

- Some words have multiple meanings. Look up a new word in the dictionary and try to choose the correct meaning for the context. Then see if it makes sense within the context.

- When you look up a word, look at all the definitions to see if there is a basic core meaning. This will help you understand the word when it is used in a different context. Also look at all the related words, or words in the same family. This can help you expand your vocabulary. For example, the core meaning of *structure* involves something built or put together.

> **structure** /ˈstrʌktʃər/ *n.* **1** [C] a building of any kind: *A new structure is being built on the corner.* **2** [C] any architectural object of any kind: *The Eiffel Tower is a famous Parisian structure.* **3** [U] the way parts are put together or organized: *the structure of a song‖a business's structure*
> –*v.* [T] **-tured, -turing, -tures** to put together or organize parts of s.t.: *We are structuring a plan to hire new teachers.*
> –*adj.* **structural.**

Source: *The Newbury House Dictionary plus Grammar Reference*, Fifth Edition, National Geographic Learning/Cengage Learning, 2014

Multi-Word Units

You can improve your fluency if you learn and use vocabulary as multi-word units: idioms (*go the extra mile*), collocations (*wide range*), and fixed expressions (*in other words*). Some multi-word units can only be understood as a chunk—the individual words do not add up to the same overall meaning. Keep track of multi-word units in a notebook or on notecards.

Vocabulary Note Cards

You can expand your vocabulary by using vocabulary note cards or a vocabulary building app. Write the word, expression, or sentence that you want to learn on one side. On the other, draw a four-square grid and write the following information in the squares: definition; translation (in your first language); sample sentence; synonyms. Choose words that are high frequency or on the academic word list. If you have looked a word up a few times, you should make a card for it.

definition:	first language translation:
sample sentence:	synonyms:

Organize the cards in review sets so you can practice them. Don't put words that are similar in spelling or meaning in the same review set as you may get them mixed up. Go through the cards and test yourself on the words or expressions. You can also practice with a partner.

VOCABULARY INDEX

Word	Page	CEFR† Level	Word	Page	CEFR† Level	Word	Page	CEFR† Level
perceive *	125	C1	resources*	124	B2	substance	34	B2
personality	184	B2	response*	94	B2	sufficient*	14	B2
pessimism	134	off list	responsibility	24	B2	survive*	54	B2
philosophy*	104	B2	restore*	144	B2	sustainable*	104	C1
poverty	84	B2	result (n)	184	B2	symptom	144	B2
predators	24	C1	retail	4	C1	synthetic	144	off list
preserve	74	B2	sacrifice	125	C1	tendency	184	C1
pressure	64	B2	satellite	174	B2	territory	24	B2
primary *	34	B2	satisfaction	114	B2	threaten	24	B2
principle*	104	C1	scan	174	C1	thrive	194	C1
profits	84	B2	settle	44	B2	transfer*	34	B1
propose	164	B2	settlement	174	C1	transmit*	155	C1
prospect*	54	B2	severe	155	B2	trigger*	184	C1
purchase*	4	B2	shelter	34	B2	uncover	164	C1
radical*	154	C1	solar	54	B2	undergo*	154	C1
react*	184	B2	sophisticated	114	B2	unique *	64	B2
relocate*	54	C1	source*	134	B2	universal	184	B1
remains	164	B2	specialist	164	B2	upset	194	B1
remedy	144	B2	specialize /	34	B2	variable*	144	C1
renewable	134	C1	specialise			virtually*	164	B2
reproduce	24	C2	stability*	44	C1	voluntary*	44	C1
resemble	34	C1	struggle	24	B2			

†The Common European Framework of Reference for Languages (CEFR) is an international standard for describing language proficiency. Pathways Level 3 is intended for students at CEFR level B2. The target vocabulary is at the CEFR levels as shown.

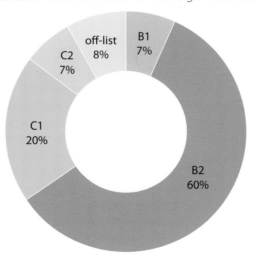

*These words are on the Academic Word List (AWL). The AWL is a list of the 570 highest-frequency academic word families that regularly appear in academic texts. The AWL was compiled by researcher Averil Coxhead based on her analysis of a 3.5-million-word corpus (Coxhead, 2000).

RUBRICS

UNIT 1   Lesson B Final Task

Check (✓) if the presenters did the following:	Name		
1. described app benefits, features, and name	☐	☐	☐
2. described how it would solve a problem	☐	☐	☐
3. included a rhetorical question	☐	☐	☐
4. kept presentation to within 60 seconds	☐	☐	☐
5. spoke clearly and at an appropriate pace	☐	☐	☐
6. used appropriate vocabulary	☐	☐	☐
OVERALL RATING Note: 1 = lowest; 5 = highest	1　2　3　4　5	1　2　3　4　5	1　2　3　4　5
Notes:			

UNIT 2   Lesson B Final Task

Check (✓) if the presenters did the following:	Name		
1. clearly explained the film focus and the scenes	☐	☐	☐
2. in introduction, explained who would talk about what	☐	☐	☐
3. included transitions between speakers	☐	☐	☐
4. each person spoke for about the same amount of time	☐	☐	☐
5. spoke clearly and at an appropriate pace	☐	☐	☐
6. used appropriate vocabulary	☐	☐	☐
OVERALL RATING Note: 1 = lowest; 5 = highest	1　2　3　4　5	1　2　3　4　5	1　2　3　4　5
Notes:			

UNIT 3   Lesson B Final Task

Check (✓) if the presenters did the following:	Name		
	_____	_____	_____
1. presented a clear viewpoint on colonization	☐	☐	☐
2. supported points with reasons and details	☐	☐	☐
3. used adjectives and adverbs in strong opinions	☐	☐	☐
4. used appropriate visuals	☐	☐	☐
5. kept presentation to within 5 minutes	☐	☐	☐
6. used appropriate vocabulary	☐	☐	☐
OVERALL RATING Note: 1 = lowest; 5 = highest	1 2 3 4 5	1 2 3 4 5	1 2 3 4 5
Notes:			

UNIT 4   Lesson B Final Task

Check (✓) if the presenter did the following:	Name		
	_____	_____	_____
1. report included advantages and disadvantages, popular ecotourism packages, and possible destinations	☐	☐	☐
2. referenced research that was done	☐	☐	☐
3. each presenter had approximately equal time	☐	☐	☐
4. maintained eye contact with audience	☐	☐	☐
5. kept presentation within two minutes	☐	☐	☐
6. used appropriate vocabulary	☐	☐	☐
OVERALL RATING Note: 1 = lowest; 5 = highest	1 2 3 4 5	1 2 3 4 5	1 2 3 4 5
Notes:			

UNIT 5   Lesson B Final Task

Check (✓) if the presenters did the following:	Name		
	_____	_____	_____
1. gave information about a company, including three interesting facts	☐	☐	☐
2. gave three facts about its social responsibility	☐	☐	☐
3. looked up while speaking	☐	☐	☐
4. spoke clearly and at an appropriate pace	☐	☐	☐
5. answered audience questions appropriately	☐	☐	☐
6. used appropriate vocabulary	☐	☐	☐
OVERALL RATING Note: 1 = lowest; 5 = highest	1　2　3　4　5	1　2　3　4　5	1　2　3　4　5
Notes:			

UNIT 6   Lesson B Final Task

Check (✓) if the presenters did the following:	Name		
	_____	_____	_____
1. gave a clear description of steps in a process	☐	☐	☐
2. included information on improvements made	☐	☐	☐
3. made good use of gestures and facial expressions	☐	☐	☐
4. maintained good posture and faced audience	☐	☐	☐
5. spoke clearly and at an appropriate pace	☐	☐	☐
6. used appropriate vocabulary	☐	☐	☐
OVERALL RATING Note: 1 = lowest; 5 = highest	1　2　3　4　5	1　2　3　4　5	1　2　3　4　5
Notes:			

UNIT 7   Lesson B Final Task

Check (✓) if the presenters did the following:	Name		
1. presented a clear concept for a film	☐	☐	☐
2. described what would be in the 60-second video	☐	☐	☐
3. included at least one visual, possibly a storyboard	☐	☐	☐
4. made sure that everyone had a chance to speak	☐	☐	☐
5. spoke clearly and at an appropriate pace	☐	☐	☐
6. used appropriate vocabulary	☐	☐	☐
OVERALL RATING Note: 1 = lowest; 5 = highest	1 2 3 4 5	1 2 3 4 5	1 2 3 4 5
Notes:			

UNIT 8   Lesson B Final Task

Check (✓) if the presenter did the following:	Name		
1. presented a topic; supported it with information from an article	☐	☐	☐
2. supported main points with reasons and details	☐	☐	☐
3. spoke at a good pace and not too quickly	☐	☐	☐
4. kept presentation within 2-3 minutes	☐	☐	☐
5. used appropriate vocabulary	☐	☐	☐
OVERALL RATING Note: 1 = lowest; 5 = highest	1 2 3 4 5	1 2 3 4 5	1 2 3 4 5
Notes:			

UNIT 9   Lesson B Final Task

Check (✓) if the presenter did the following:	Name		
	_____	_____	_____
1. presented a clear topic related to life in the past or future	☐	☐	☐
2. had a strong introduction that wasn't too long	☐	☐	☐
3. had a clear conclusion	☐	☐	☐
4. spoke clearly and at an appropriate pace	☐	☐	☐
5. answered audience questions appropriately	☐	☐	☐
6. used appropriate vocabulary			
OVERALL RATING Note: 1 = lowest; 5 = highest	1 2 3 4 5	1 2 3 4 5	1 2 3 4 5
Notes:			

UNIT 10   Lesson B Final Task

Check (✓) if the presenters did the following:	Name		
	_____	_____	_____
1. presented a clear topic; supported points with research	☐	☐	☐
2. included questions for audience during presentation	☐	☐	☐
3. encouraged audience interaction at the beginning or end of presentation	☐	☐	☐
4. spoke clearly and at an appropriate pace	☐	☐	☐
5. answered audience questions appropriately	☐	☐	☐
6. used appropriate vocabulary	☐	☐	☐
OVERALL RATING Note: 1 = lowest; 5 = highest	1 2 3 4 5	1 2 3 4 5	1 2 3 4 5
Notes:			

ACKNOWLEDGEMENTS

The Authors and Publisher would like to acknowledge the teachers around the world who participated in the development of the second edition of *Pathways*.

A special thanks to our Advisory Board for their valuable input during the development of this series.

ADVISORY BOARD

Mahmoud Al Hosni, Modern College of Business and Science, Muscat; **Safaa Al-Salim**, Kuwait University, Kuwait City; **Laila AlQadhi**, Kuwait University, Kuwait City; **Julie Bird**, RMIT University Vietnam, Ho Chi Minh City; **Elizabeth Bowles**, Virginia Tech Language and Culture Institute, Blacksburg, VA; **Rachel Bricker**, Arizona State University, Tempe, AZ; **James Broadbridge**, J.F. Oberlin University, Tokyo; **Marina Broeder**, Mission College, Santa Clara, CA; **Shawn Campbell**, Hangzhou High School, Hangzhou; **Trevor Carty**, James Cook University, Singapore; **Jindarat De Vleeschauwer**, Chiang Mai University, Chiang Mai; **Wai-Si El Hassan**, Prince Mohammad Bin Fahd University, Dhahran; **Jennifer Farnell**, University of Bridgeport, Bridgeport, CT; **Rasha Gazzaz**, King Abdulaziz University, Jeddah; **Keith Graziadei**, Santa Monica College, Santa Monica, CA; **Janet Harclerode**, Santa Monica Community College, Santa Monica, CA; **Anna Hasper**, TeacherTrain, Dubai; **Phoebe Kamel Yacob Hindi**, Abu Dhabi Vocational Education and Training Institute, Abu Dhabi; **Kuei-ping Hsu**, National Tsing Hua University, Hsinchu; **Greg Jewell**, Drexel University, Philadelphia, PA; **Adisra Katib**, Chulalongkorn University Language Institute, Bangkok; **Wayne Kennedy**, LaGuardia Community College, Long Island City, NY; **Beth Koo**, Central Piedmont Community College, Charlotte, NC; **Denise Kray**, Bridge School, Denver, CO; **Chantal Kruger**, ILA Vietnam, Ho Chi Minh City; **William P. Kyzner**, Fuyang AP Center, Fuyang; **Becky Lawrence**, Massachusetts International Academy, Marlborough, MA; **Deborah McGraw**, Syracuse University, Syracuse, NY; **Mary Moore**, University of Puerto Rico, San Juan; **Raymond Purdy**, ELS Language Centers, Princeton, NJ; **Anouchka Rachelson**, Miami Dade College, Miami, FL; **Fathimah Razman**, Universiti Utara Malaysia, Sintok; **Phil Rice**, University of Delaware ELI, Newark, DE; **Scott Rousseau**, American University of Sharjah, Sharjah; **Verna Santos-Nafrada**, King Saud University, Riyadh; **Eugene Sidwell**, American Intercon Institute, Phnom Penh; **Gemma Thorp**, Monash University English Language Centre, Melbourne; **Matt Thurston**, University of Central Lancashire, Preston; **Christine Tierney**, Houston Community College, Houston, TX; **Jet Robredillo Tonogbanua**, FPT University, Hanoi.

GLOBAL REVIEWERS

ASIA

Antonia Cavcic, Asia University, Tokyo; **Soyhan Egitim**, Tokyo University of Science, Tokyo; **Caroline Handley**, Asia University, Tokyo; **Patrizia Hayashi**, Meikai University, Urayasu; **Greg Holloway**, University of Kitakyushu, Kitakyushu; **Anne C. Ihata**, Musashino University, Tokyo; **Kathryn Mabe**, Asia University, Tokyo; **Frederick Navarro Bacala**, Yokohama City University, Yokohama; **Tyson Rode**, Meikai University, Urayasu; **Scott Shelton-Strong**, Asia University, Tokyo; **Brooks Slaybaugh**, Yokohama City University, Yokohama; **Susanto Sugiharto**, Sutomo Senior High School, Medan; **Andrew Zitzmann**, University of Kitakyushu, Kitakyushu

LATIN AMERICA AND THE CARIBBEAN

Raul Billini, ProLingua, Dominican Republic; **Alejandro Garcia**, Collegio Marcelina, Mexico; **Humberto Guevara**, Tec de Monterrey, Campus Monterrey, Mexico; **Romina Olga Planas**, Centro Cultural Paraguayo Americano, Paraguay; **Carlos Rico-Troncoso**, Pontificia Universidad Javeriana, Colombia; **Ialê Schetty**, Enjoy English, Brazil; **Aline Simoes**, Way To Go Private English, Brazil; **Paulo Cezar Lira Torres**, APenglish, Brazil; **Rosa Enilda Vasquez**, Swisher Dominicana, Dominican Republic; **Terry Whitty**, LDN Language School, Brazil.

MIDDLE EAST AND NORTH AFRICA

Susan Daniels, Kuwait University, Kuwait; **Mahmoud Mohammadi Khomeini**, Sokhane Ashna Language School, Iran; **Müge Lenbet**, Koç University, Turkey; **Robert Anthony Lowman**, Prince Mohammad bin Fahd University, Saudi Arabia; **Simon Mackay**, Prince Mohammad bin Fahd University, Saudi Arabia.

USA AND CANADA

Frank Abbot, Houston Community College, Houston, TX; **Hossein Aksari**, Bilingual Education Institute and Houston Community College, Houston, TX; **Sudie Allen-Henn**, North Seattle College, Seattle, WA; **Sharon Allie**, Santa Monica Community College, Santa Monica, CA; **Jerry Archer**, Oregon State University, Corvallis, OR; **Nicole Ashton**, Central Piedmont Community College, Charlotte, NC; **Barbara Barrett**, University of Miami, Coral Gables, FL; **Maria Bazan-Myrick**, Houston Community College, Houston, TX; **Rebecca Beal**, Colleges of Marin, Kentfield, CA; **Marlene Beck**, Eastern Michigan University, Ypsilanti, MI; **Michelle Bell**, University of Southern California, Los Angeles, CA; **Linda Bolet**, Houston Community College, Houston, TX; **Jenna Bollinger**, Eastern Michigan University, Ypsilanti, MI; **Monica Boney**, Houston Community College, Houston, TX; **Nanette Bouvier**, Rutgers University – Newark, Newark, NJ; **Nancy Boyer**, Golden West College, Huntington Beach, CA; **Lia Brenneman**, University of Florida English Language Institute, Gainesville, FL; **Colleen Brice**, Grand Valley State University, Allendale, MI; **Kristen Brown**, Massachusetts International Academy, Marlborough, MA; **Philip Brown**, Houston Community

College, Houston, TX; **Dongmei Cao**, San Jose City College, San Jose, CA; **Molly Cheney**, University of Washington, Seattle, WA; **Emily Clark**, The University of Kansas, Lawrence, KS; **Luke Coffelt**, International English Center, Boulder, CO; **William C Cole-French**, MCPHS University, Boston, MA; **Charles Colson**, English Language Institute at Sam Houston State University, Huntsville, TX; **Lucy Condon**, Bilingual Education Institute, Houston, TX; **Janice Crouch**, Internexus Indiana, Indianapolis, IN; **Charlene Dandrow**, Virginia Tech Language and Culture Institute, Blacksburg, VA; **Loretta Davis**, Coastline Community College, Westminster, CA; **Marta Dmytrenko-Ahrabian**, Wayne State University, Detroit, MI; **Bonnie Duhart**, Houston Community College, Houston, TX; **Karen Eichhorn**, International English Center, Boulder, CO; **Tracey Ellis**, Santa Monica Community College, Santa Monica, CA; **Jennifer Evans**, University of Washington, Seattle, WA; **Marla Ewart**, Bilingual Education Institute, Houston, TX; **Rhoda Fagerland**, St. Cloud State University, St. Cloud, MN; **Kelly Montijo Fink**, Kirkwood Community College, Cedar Rapids, IA; **Celeste Flowers**, University of Central Arkansas, Conway, AR; **Kurtis Foster**, Missouri State University, Springfield, MO; **Rachel Garcia**, Bilingual Education Institute, Houston, TX; **Thomas Germain**, University of Colorado Boulder, Boulder, CO; **Claire Gimble**, Virginia International University, Fairfax, VA; **Marilyn Glazer-Weisner**, Middlesex Community College, Lowell, MA; **Amber Goodall**, South Piedmont Community College, Charlotte, NC; **Katya Goussakova**, Seminole State College of Florida, Sanford, FL; **Jane Granado**, Texas State University, San Marcos, TX; **Therea Hampton**, Mercer County Community College, West Windsor Township, NJ; **Jane Hanson**, University of Nebraska – Lincoln, Lincoln, NE; **Lauren Heather**, University of Texas at San Antonio, San Antonio, TX; **Jannette Hermina**, Saginaw Valley State University, Saginaw, MI; **Gail Hernandez**, College of Staten Island, Staten Island, NY; **Beverly Hobbs**, Clark University, Worcester, MA; **Kristin Homuth**, Language Center International, Southfield, MI; **Tim Hooker**, Campbellsville University, Campbellsville, KY; **Raylene Houck**, Idaho State University, Pocatello, ID; **Karen L. Howling**, University of Bridgeport, Bridgeport, CT; **Sharon Jaffe**, Santa Monica Community College, Santa Monica, CA; **Andrea Kahn**, Santa Monica Community College, Santa Monica, CA; **Eden Bradshaw Kaiser**, Massachusetts International Academy, Marlborough, MA; **Mandy Kama**, Georgetown University, Washington, D.C.; **Andrea Kaminski**, University of Michigan – Dearborn, Dearborn, MI; **Phoebe Kang**, Brock University, Ontario; **Eileen Kramer**, Boston University CELOP, Brookline, MA; **Rachel Lachance**, University of New Hampshire, Durham, NH; **Janet Langon**, Glendale Community College, Glendale, CA; **Frances Le Grand**, University of Houston, Houston, TX; **Esther Lee**, California State University, Fullerton, CA; **Helen S. Mays Lefal**, American Learning Institute, Dallas, TX; **Oranit Limmaneeprasert**, American River College, Sacramento, CA; **Dhammika Liyanage**, Bilingual Education Institute, Houston, TX; **Emily Lodmer**, Santa Monica Community College, Santa Monica Community College, CA; **Ari Lopez**, American Learning Institute Dallas, TX; **Nichole Lukas**, University of Dayton, Dayton, OH; **Undarmaa Maamuujav**, California State University, Los Angeles, CA; **Diane Mahin**, University of Miami, Coral Gables, FL; **Melanie Majeski**, Naugatuck Valley Community College, Waterbury, CT; **Judy Marasco**, Santa Monica Community College, Santa Monica, CA; **Murray McMahan**, University of Alberta, Alberta; **Deirdre McMurtry**, University of Nebraska Omaha, Omaha, NE; **Suzanne Meyer**, University of Pittsburgh, Pittsburgh, PA; **Cynthia Miller**, Richland College, Dallas, TX; **Sara Miller**, Houston Community College, Houston, TX; **Gwendolyn Miraglia**, Houston Community College, Houston, TX; **Katie Mitchell**, International English Center, Boulder, CO; **Ruth Williams Moore**, University of Colorado Boulder, Boulder, CO; **Kathy Najafi**, Houston Community College, Houston, TX; **Sandra Navarro**, Glendale Community College, Glendale, CA; **Stephanie Ngom**, Boston University, Boston MA; **Barbara Niemczyk**, University of Bridgeport, Bridgeport, CT; **Melody Nightingale**, Santa Monica Community College, Santa Monica, CA; **Alissa Olgun**, California Language Academy, Los Angeles, CA; **Kimberly Oliver**, Austin Community College, Austin, TX; **Steven Olson**, International English Center, Boulder, CO; **Fernanda Ortiz**, University of Arizona, Tucson, AZ; **Joel Ozretich**, University of Washington, Seattle, WA; **Erin Pak**, Schoolcraft College, Livonia, MI; **Geri Pappas**, University of Michigan – Dearborn, Dearborn, MI; **Eleanor Paterson**, Erie Community College, Buffalo, NY; **Sumeeta Patnaik**, Marshall University, Huntington, WV; **Mary Peacock**, Richland College, Dallas, TX; **Kathryn Porter**, University of Houston, Houston, TX; **Eileen Prince**, Prince Language Associates, Newton Highlands, MA; **Marina Ramirez**, Houston Community College, Houston, TX; **Laura Ramm**, Michigan State University, East Lansing, MI; **Chi Rehg**, University of South Florida, Tampa, FL; **Cyndy Reimer**, Douglas College, New Westminster, British Columbia; **Sydney Rice**, Imperial Valley College, Imperial, CA; **Lynnette Robson**, Mercer University, Macon, GA; **Helen E. Roland**, Miami Dade College, Miami, FL; **Maria Paula Carreira Rolim**, Southeast Missouri State University, Cape Girardeau, MO; **Jill Rolston-Yates**, Texas State University, San Marcos, TX; **David Ross**, Houston Community College, Houston, TX; **Rachel Scheiner**, Seattle Central College, Seattle, WA; **John Schmidt**, Texas Intensive English Program, Austin, TX; **Mariah Schueman**, University of Miami, Coral Gables, FL; **Erika Shadburne**, Austin Community College, Austin, TX; **Mahdi Shamsi**, Houston Community College, Houston, TX; **Osha Sky**, Highline College, Des Moines, WA; **William Slade**, University of Texas, Austin, TX; **Takako Smith**, University of Nebraska – Lincoln, Lincoln, NE; **Barbara Smith-Palinkas**, Hillsborough Community College, Tampa, FL; **Paula Snyder**, University of Missouri, Columbia, MO; **Mary; Evelyn Sorrell**, Bilingual Education Institute, Houston TX; **Kristen Stauffer**, International English Center, Boulder, CO; **Christina Stefanik**, The Language Company, Toledo, OH; **Cory Stewart**, University of Houston, Houston, TX; **Laurie Stusser-McNeill**, Highline College, Des Moines, WA; **Tom Sugawara**, University of Washington, Seattle, WA; **Sara Sulko**, University of Missouri, Columbia, MO; **Mark Sullivan**, University of Colorado Boulder, Boulder, CO; **Olivia Szabo**, Boston University, Boston, MA; **Amber Tallent**, University of Nebraska Omaha, Omaha, NE; **Amy Tate**, Rice University, Houston, USA; **Aya C. Tiacoh**, Bilingual Education Institute, Houston, TX; **Troy Tucker**, Florida SouthWestern State College, Fort Myers, FL; **Anne Tyoan**, Savannah College of Art and Design, Savannah, GA; **Michael Vallee**, International English Center, Boulder, CO; **Andrea Vasquez**, University of Southern Maine, Portland, ME; **Jose Vasquez**, University of Texas Rio Grande Valley, Edinburg, TX; **Maureen Vendeville**, Savannah Technical College, Savannah, GA; **Melissa Vervinck**, Oakland University, Rochester, MI; **Adriana Villarreal**, Universided Nacional Autonoma de Mexico, San Antonio, TX; **Summer Webb**, International English Center, Boulder, CO; **Mercedes Wilson-Everett**, Houston Community College, Houston, TX; **Lora Yasen**, Tokyo International University of America, Salem, OR; **Dennis Yommer**, Youngstown State University, Youngstown, OH; **Melojeane (Jolene) Zawilinski**, University of Michigan – Flint, Flint, MI.

CREDITS

PHOTOS

Front Matter: iii AP Images/Caroline Seidel, **iv (tl)** Suzi Eszterhas/Minden Pictures, **(bl1)** DEREK GRIGGS/500PX/National Geographic Creative, **(bl2)** ©Emotiv, **vi (tl1)** Bloomberg/Getty Images, **(tl2)** ARNOLD,COREY/National Geographic, **(cl)** ©Karsten Moran/The New York Times/Redux, **(bl)** MICHAEL MELFORD/National Geographic Creative.

Cover (c) AP Images/Caroline Seidel, **001** (c) ©Mark Henley/Panos, **002** (br) ©7-11 Corporate Communications, **002** (bc) Science History Images / Alamy Stock Photo, **002-003** (c) Bettmann/Getty Images, **003** (bl) Carl Clark / Alamy Stock Photo, **003** (br) Maksym Yemelyanov / Alamy Stock Photo, **004** (t) Kelly Cheng/Getty Images, **006** (t) ©GMB Akash/Panos, **011** (t) Jon Hicks/Getty Images, **012** (t) Bloomberg/Getty Images, **015** (t) Jeffrey Blackler / Alamy Stock Photo, **017** (b) Bloomberg/Getty Images, **019** (b) ZUMA Press, Inc. / Alamy Stock Photo, **021** (c) Suzi Eszterhas/Minden Pictures, **022-023** (c) ©Mark Moffett/Minden Pictures, **023** (br) DESIGN PICS INC/National Geographic Creative, **023** (tr) ©Norbert Wu/Minden Pictures, **024** (t) JOHN EASTCOTT AND YVA MOMATIUK/National Geographic Creative, **024** (br) Cengage Learning, Inc., **026** (t) ©Steve Winter/National Geographic Creative, **029** (tl) Pixeljoy/Shutterstock.com, **029** (tr) STOCKTREK IMAGES/National Geographic Creative, **029** (cr) Justin Guariglia/National Geographic Image Collection, **029** (cl) STOCKTREK IMAGES/National Geographic Creative, **029** (bl) Tim Graham/Getty Images, **029** (br) Tim Graham/Getty Images, **031** (c) LU ZHI/National Geographic Creative, **032** (t) Kip Evans / Alamy Stock Photo, **032** (cr) Cengage Learning, Inc., **034** (bc) Christian Ziegler/National Geographic, **036** (t) RAYMOND GEHMAN/National Geographic Creative, **038** (t) REZA/National Geographic Image Collection, **041** (c) ©Doug Gimesy, **042-043** (c) National Geographic Maps, **045** (tr) Cengage Learning, Inc., **045** (t) Bloomberg/Getty Images, **046** (cl) Mike Goldwater / Alamy Stock Photo, **046** (cr) CHRIS JOHNS/National Geographic Creative, **049** (t) Fernando Vazquez Miras/Getty Images, **050** (t) Olena Suvorova / Alamy Stock Photo, **052** (t) ©JR/Redux, **055** (t) STANLEY MELTZOFF / SILVERFISH PRESS/National Geographic Creative, **057** (t) ©NASA/JPL-Caltech/Univ. of Arizona, **059** (t) ©NASA/National Geographic Creative, **059** (t) NASA/National Geographic Creative, **061** (c) DEREK GRIGGS/500PX/National Geographic Creative, **062-063** (c) MICHAEL NICHOLS/National Geographic Creative, **064** (tl) ©Mark Chivers/Robert Harding/Aurora Photos, **064** (tr) CARSTEN PETER/National Geographic Creative, **064** (cl) ©M. Schmidt/F1 Online/Aurora Photos, **064** (cr) JOHN STANMEYER/National Geographic Creative, **066** (cr) ©Fernando G. Baptista/National Geographic Creative, **068** (bc) MARTIN GRAY/National Geographic Creative, **070** (bc) ©Jeffrey Murray/Aurora Photos, **071** (tl) Andrea Obzerova / Alamy Stock Photo, **071** (tr) Mathew Alexander/Shutterstock.com, **072** (tc) PETE MCBRIDE/National Geographic Creative, **072** (br) PETE MCBRIDE/National Geographic Creative, **077** (c) ©Monica and Michael Sweet/Pacific Stock/Aurora Photos, **078** (bc) DESIGN PICS INC/National Geographic Creative, **081** (c) ©Emotiv, **082-083** (c) Monique Jaques/Getty Images, **083** (br) ALEX TREADWAY/National Geographic Creative, **083** (cr) Greg Balfour Evans / Alamy Stock Photo, **083** (tr) XPACIFICA/National Geographic Creative, **085** (tr) cbphotoart / Alamy Stock Photo, **086** (tr) ARUN SANKAR/Getty Images, **088** (bl) age fotostock / Alamy Stock Photo, **089** (cl) AP Images/MARY ANN CHASTAIN, **091** (b) Barcroft Media/Getty Images, **092** (t) Bloomberg/Getty Images, **094** (bc) ZUMA Press, Inc./Alamy Stock Photo, **097** (b) Jemal Countess/Getty Images, **099** (tr) ©Lauren Tobias, **101** (c) Bloomberg/Getty Images, **102-103** (c) CATHERINE KARNOW/National Geographic Creative, **104** (tl) ART on FILE/Getty Images, **104** (tr) Science & Society Picture Library/Getty Images, **106** (t) Vince Talotta/Getty Images, **110** (bl) YOSHIKAZU TSUNO/Getty Images, **110** (br) JOEL SAGET/Getty Images, **112** (t) ©Robert Clark/National Geographic Creative, **116** (t) www.phdcomics.com, **118** (bc) Bagiuiani Constantin/Alamy Stock Photo, **121** (c) ARNOLD, COREY /National Geographic, **122–123** (c) Bancroft Media/Contributor, **123** (br) Anand Varma/National Geographic Creative, **123** (tr) Sangay Sherpa/AFP/GettyImages, **126** (tl) ©Mark Thiessen/National Geographic Creative, **126** (tr) ©Mark Thiessen/National Geographic Creative, **127** (br) ©Tierney Thys, **130** (cl) Cengage Learning, Inc., **130** (cr) Cengage Learning, Inc., **131** (tl) Education Images/Getty Images, **132** (t) ©Kees Veenenbos/National Geographic Creative, **133** (bl) Rachel Murray/Getty Images, **135** (bl) ©DesignPics/National Geographic Creative, **137** (tr) Rene Johnston/Getty Images, **137** (cr) ©Adeline Tiffanie Suwana, **138** (b) Blend Images / Alamy Stock Photo, **139** (t) Cecilie_Arcurs/Getty Images, **141** (c) ©Karsten Moran/The New York Times/Redux, **142-143** (c) ©Evgeni Dinev/Aurora Photos, **143** (tr) DESIGN PICS INC/National Geographic Creative, **143** (br) Cseh Ioan / Alamy Stock Photo, **143** (cr) JILL SCHNEIDER/National Geographic Creative, **144** (cl) Paul Vinten / Alamy Stock Photo, **144** (cr) blickwinkel / Alamy Stock Photo, **149** (t) Feliciano dos Santos, **152** (t) Winfried Wisniewski/ Minden Pictures/National Geographic Creative, **153** (bc) MICHAEL NICHOLS/National Geographic Creative, **154** (tl) Kim Kulish/Getty Images, **154** (cl) XPACIFICA/National Geographic Creative, **156** (tc) MARK THIESSEN/National Geographic Creative, **158** (bc) Mark Thiessen/National Geographic Creative, **161** (c) MICHAEL MELFORD/National Geographic Creative, **162-163** (c) ©Cyark, **165** (tl) ©Robert Clark/National Geographic Creative, **165** (tr) Lanmas / Alamy Stock Photo, **166** (t) ©Matthew Piscitelli, **167** (b) age fotostock / Alamy Stock Photo, **169** (t) JUNG YEON-JE/Getty Images, **171** (tl) KAZUHIKO SANO/National Geographic Creative, **172** (t) KENNETH GARRETT/National Geographic Creative, **174** (tr) Pool DEVILLE/AFSM/Getty Images, **176** (tr) Weekend Images Inc./Getty Images, **179** (t) WaterFrame / Alamy Stock Photo, **181** (c) ©Kyle Kurlick, **182-183** (c) AFP/Getty Images, **184** (cr) Tiago Zegur/Alamy Stock Photo, **186** (t) Graiki/Getty Images, **188** (bc) Nico De Pasquale Photography/Getty Images, **192** (t) CORY RICHARDS/National Geographic Creative, **194** (bl) Mariusz Szczawinski / Alamy Stock Photo, **194** (br) Jessica Lia/Getty Images, **197** (cl) gkrphoto/Shutterstock.com, **197** (cr) vanillaechoes/Shutterstock.com, **197** (cl) Prostock-studio/Shutterstock.com, **197** (br) Matt Benoit/Shutterstock.com.

End Matter: 201 ©Emotiv.

Maps

24 National Geographic Maps; **32** Mapping Specialists; **42–43** Adapted from *National Geographic Atlas of the World, Tenth Edition*, page 48–49, Salopek, Paul, Washington, DC: National Geographic Society, 2015; **45** Mapping Specialists; **66** National Geographic Maps

Illustrations/Infographics

8 Adapted from "What would winners do?": https://www.visioncritical.com/emerging-lottery-trends/; **16** Adapted from https://i.ytimg.com/vi/OrAytLkEBMU/hqdefault.jpg; **29** Created by MPS; **42–43** Adapted from *National Geographic Atlas of the World, Tenth Edition*, page 48-49, Salopek, Paul, Washington, DC: National Geographic Society, 2015; **66** "Living on a Razor's Edge" by Neil Shea, National Geographic Magazine, November 2009; **95** Adapted from "Our Story," https://www.givebackbox.com/story; **130** Created by MPS; **198** Adapted from "Big Five Plus Personality Inventory (BigFive+)," http://thepsychometricworld.com/psychometric-tests/big-five-plus-personality-inventory.html

Listening and Text Sources

2 Sources: Chronology of the Sears Catalog: http://www.searsarchives.com/catalogs/chronology.htm; The Birth of Convenience Retailing: http://corp.7-eleven.com/corp-BAK/history; **6** Source: *Why We Buy: The Science of Shopping*, Paco Underhill, Simon and Schuster, 2009; **16** Sources: "He Buys, She Shops: A Study of Gender Differences in The Retail Experience,": http://www.verdegroup.com/wp-content/uploads/2012/10/He-Buys-She-Shops.pdf; 'Men Buy, Women Shop': The Sexes Have Different Priorities When Walking Down the Aisles: http://knowledge.wharton.upenn.edu/article/men-buy-women-shop-the-sexes-have-different-priorities-when-walking-down-the-aisles/; **18** Sources: Customer Service Facts, Quotes & Statistics: https://www.helpscout.net/75-customer-service-facts-quotes-statistics/; "Valuable Variables: Consumers want more than low prices from retailers," http://www.nielsen.com/eu/en/insights/news/2016/valuable-variables-consumers-want-more-than-low-prices-from-retailers.html; "The impact of customer service on customer lifetime value," https://www.zendesk.com/resources/customer-service-and-lifetime-customer-value/; **24** Source: "Every Bird a King" by Tom O'Neill, National Geographic Magazine, September 2009; **29** Source: "Recipe for a Resurrection" by Tom Mueller, National Geographic Magazine, May 2009; **34** Source: "Love & Lies (Orchids)" by Michael Pollan, National Geographic Magazine, September 2009; **42–43** Source: National Geographic Atlas of the World, Tenth Edition, page 48-49, Salopek, Paul, Washington, DC: National Geographic Society, 2015; **45** Sources: "Romania," http://focus-migration.hwwi.de/Romania.2515.0.html?&L=1; "Romania: Settlement Patterns," https://www.britannica.com/place/Romania/Settlement-patterns#toc42845; **50** Source: "The world's most liveable cities," https://www.economist.com/blogs/graphicdetail/2016/08/daily-chart-14; **53** Source: "Questions Asked of Immigrants at Ellis Island," https://ntieva.unt.edu/pages/about/newsletters/vol_11/issue1/questions.htm; **58–59** Sources: "SpaceX's Mars Colony Plan: By the Numbers," https://www.space.com/34234-spacex-mars-colony-plan-by-the-numbers.html; "World Population projections revised upwards by the U.N.," http://www.worldometers.info/news/; **63** Sources: "Booming Tourism Becomes a Stress Test for Yellowstone," http://www.nationalgeographic.com/magazine/2016/05/yellowstone-national-parks-tourism/; "Yellowstone By The Numbers," http://www.yellowstonenationalparklodges.com/connect/yellowstone-hot-spot/infographic-yellowstone-by-the-numbers/; **66** Source: "Living on a Razor's Edge" by Neil Shea, National Geographic Magazine, November 2009; **69–70** Sources: "Bryce Canyon," https://www.nps.gov/brca/index.htm; *Painters of Utah's Canyons and Deserts*, Donna Poulton, Vern Swanson, Gibbs Smith, 2009, page 154; **72** Source: https://petemcbride.com/INFO/bio/1; **85** Source: "Inca Traditions Pay Off for Peruvian Weavers," http://news.nationalgeographic.com/news/2002/04/0430_020430_TVincatextiles.html; **86–87** Source: "India Snake Hunters find Antidote to Joblessness" by Pallava Bagla, National Geographic News, February 2003; **88–89** Source: "Kudzu Entrepreneurs find Gold in Green Menace" by John Roach, National Geographic News, April 2005; **90** Sources: https://www.census.gov/data/tables/2014/econ/susb/2014-susb-annual.html, https://www.sba.gov/sites/default/files/advocacy/SB-FAQ-2016_WEB.pdf; **95** Source: "Our Story," https://www.givebackbox.com/story; **96** Source: "Study: 81% of Consumers Say They Will Make Personal Sacrifices to Address Social, Environmental Issues," http://www.sustainablebrands.com/news_and_views/stakeholder_trends_insights/sustainable_brands/study_81_consumers_say_they_will_make_; **96–97** Sources: "Change the World," http://fortune.com/change-the-world/gsk/, "Going Beyond the Bag," https://www.statebags.com/pages/2017-give-back-pack; **104** Source: "The Power of Good Design," https://www.vitsoe.com/us/about/good-design; **110** Source: http://www.chindogu.com/?page_id=336; **122–123** Source: https://www.nationalgeographic.org/explorers-festival/2016/emerging-explorers/; **126–127** Sources: http://www.nationalgeographic.com/explorers/bios/kenny-broad/; http://www.nationalgeographic.com/explorers/bios/tierney-thys/; **136–137** Sources: "Meet Madhav Rajaram Subrahmanyam," http://www.sanctuaryasia.com/people/interviews/3372-meet-madhav-rajaram-subrahmanyam.html; "Call Me Hannah," http://callmehannah.ca/about/; "9 young inventors who may just save the world," https://www.mnn.com/green-tech/research-innovations/blogs/9-young-inventors-who-may-just-save-the-world; "How kids are saving the planet," http://earth911.com/home/family/how-kids-are-saving-the-planet/; **144** Source: "Nature's RX" by Joel Swerdlow, nationalgeographic.com (Republished from the pages of National Geographic Magazine); **146** Source: "The Drug Development Process," https://www.fda.gov/forpatients/approvals/drugs/; **149** Source: "Feliciano Dos Santos Musician and Activist," www.nationalgeographic.com/field/explorers; **150** Source: https://www.cdc.gov/nchs/fastats/default.htm; **154** Sources: "Repairing and Replacing Body Parts: What's Next," http://news.nationalgeographic.com/news/2012/13/130415-replacement-body-parts-longevity-medicine-health-science/; "The hospital of the future may be a tiny, high-tech medical kit," http://www.popsci.com/doctor-future-may-be-personal-high-tech-medical-box; **156–157** Source: "Bionics," Fischman, Josh, and Mark Thiessen, National Geographic Magazine, January 2010; **169** Source: "Answers from Angkor" by Richard Stone, National Geographic Magazine, November 2009; **174** Source: "Ground Penetrating Radar in Archaeology," http://www.archaeologyexpert.co.uk/groundpenetratingradarinarchaeology.html; **182** Source: "Gallup 2017 Global Emotions Report," Gallup, Inc. Reprinted by Permission; **188** Sources: "Beautiful Teenage Brains" by Dobbs, David, and Kitra Cahana, National Geographic Magazine, October 2011; "That Teenage Feeling," http://www.apa.org/monitor/apr07/teenage.aspx; **196** Source: "Our Foods, Our Moods," https://www.theatlantic.com/health/archive/2014/03/our-moods-our-foods/284238/; **198** Source: "Big Five Plus Personality Inventory (BigFive+)," http://thepsychometricworld.com/psychometric-tests/big-five-plus-personality-inventory.html

Definitions for glossed words and vocabulary exercises: *The Newbury House Dictionary Plus Grammar Reference, Fifth Edition*, National Geographic Learning/Cengage Learning, 2014

INDEX OF EXAM SKILLS AND TASKS

Pathways Listening, Speaking, and Critical Thinking 2nd Edition is designed to provide practice for standardized exams, such as IELTS and TOEFL. Many activities in this book practice or focus on **key exam skills** needed for test success. Here is an index of activities in Level 3 that are similar to common questions types found in these tests.

Listening

Key Exam Skills	IELTS	TOEFL	Page(s) / Exercise(s)
Listening for a speaker's purpose	X	X	127 D
Listening for content words	X	X	36 LS, 36 A
Listening for inferences	X	X	107 LS, 107 E, 109 CT
Listening for key details	X	X	6 B, 17 C, 37 C, 57 C, 107 D, 126 C, 157 NT, 177 C, 197 D
Listening for main ideas	X	X	6 A, 16 B, 26 B, 37 B, 46 B, 66 B, 76 B, 106 C, 116 B, 126 B, 146 B, 156 B, 166 B, 176 B, 186 B, 196 C
Listening for questions and answers	X	X	166 NT, 166 B
Listening for similarities and contrasts	X	X	96 LS, 97 C
Listening for causes and effects	X	X	196 LS, 196 B, 196 C
Listening for steps in a process	X	X	117 NT, 117 C
Listening for the order of events	X	X	56 LS, 56 B
Making inferences or drawing conclusions	X	X	136 B, 177 CT, 177 D, 177 E
Predicting what speakers might say	X	X	56 A
Recognizing a speaker's attitude		X	7 LS, 7 E
Recognizing digressions	X	X	67 LS, 67 D, 67 E
Taking notes about different speakers' opinions	X	X	27 NT, 27 C, 126 C
Taking notes about contrasting ideas	X	X	46 NT, 47 C
Taking notes effectively	X	X	136 NT, 136 C, 147 NT
Understanding referents	X	X	167 LS, 167 C

KEY

CT   Critical Thinking
LS   Listening Skill
NT   Note-Taking Skill

Common Question Types for Listening	IELTS	TOEFL	Page(s) / Exercise(s)
Connecting content		X	17 C, 56 B, 107 D, 146 B
Diagram completion	X		66 C, 117 C
Matching	X		166 B
Multiple choice	X	X	16 B, 37 B, 87 C, 116 B, 127 D, 176 B
Multiple response		X	6 C, 6 D, 46 B, 106 C, 126 B, 146 B
Note completion	X		47 C, 87 B, 96 B, 147 C
Sentence completion	X		97 C, 187 D
Summary completion	X		57 C, 66 B, 137 D
Short answer	X		76 C, 156 B, 157 C, 196 C

INDEX OF EXAM SKILLS AND TASKS

Speaking

Key Exam Skills	IELTS	TOEFL	Page(s) / Exercise(s)
Answering questions effectively	X		69 SS, 69 D
Brainstorming ideas	X	X	19 A, 38 A, 39 A, 53 F, 58 B, 71 A, 93 F, 111 A, 120 A, 131 A, 139 A, 150 G, 159 A, 171 A
Comparing and contrasting	X	X	108 GFS, 108 B
Describing a process	X	X	120 C
Discussing pros and cons	X	X	10 CT, 10 EL, 10 E, 10 F, 91 A, 177 F
Expressing agreement or disagreement	X	X	25 E, 78 EL, 107 F
Expressing likelihood	X	X	59 D
Expressing opinions and/or reasons	X	X	5 D, 11 B, 37 D, 51 EL, 51 B, 57 D, 60 PS, 73 D, 75 C, 95 D, 113 E, 137 D, 150 SS, 150 F, 151 B, 199 SS, 199 G
Expressing preferences	X	X	27 D
Expressing probability and possibility	X	X	58 SS, 58 A
Linking	X	X	49 PRON, 50 D, 158 PRON, 158 A, 159 B
Making suggestions	X	X	38 A, 38 SS, 39 B
Organizing your ideas	X	X	140 B
Pausing effectively	X	X	118 PRON, 119 B
Pronouncing numbers correctly	X	X	90 PRON, 90 E
Speaking about abstract concepts	X	X	4 A, 7 G, 13 F, 29 D, 31 A, 59 E, 89 D, 97 D, 138 B, 178 D
Speaking about conditional situations	X	X	8 GFS, 8 A, 8 B, 45 D, 47 D, 53 E, 117 D, 173 E
Speaking about familiar, everyday topics	X	X	10 E, 15 B, 39 B, 48 A, 50 E, 50 F, 69 C, 105 B, 109 C, 148 B, 188 A
Speaking about historical events	X	X	169 D, 170 E
Speaking about likes and/or dislikes	X	X	55 F, 115 D
Speaking about personal experiences or feelings	X	X	105 B, 107 F, 138 A, 149 E, 165 E, 175 E, 178 EL, 178 A, 185 E, 191 B, 193 E
Speaking about past actions or situations	X	X	138 A, 189 GFS, 189 D, 190 E, 190 F, 190 G, 190 H
Speaking about the views of others	X	X	17 E, 33 E, 129 CT, 129 C, 193 E
Speaking about your life or your job	X	X	99 D, 99 E
Summarizing what you have heard		X	13 E, 133 G
Using correct stress and emphasis	X	X	28 PRON, 28 A, 28 B, 78 PRON, 78 A, 79 B
Using descriptive language	X	X	109 SS, 109 C
Using statistics to support your views	X	X	18 SS, 18 A, 18 D, 88 SS, 88 A, 88 B

KEY

CT	Critical Thinking
EL	Everyday Language
GFS	Grammar for Speaking
LS	Listening Skill
NT	Note-Taking Skill
PRON	Pronunciation
PS	Presentation Skill
SS	Speaking Skill

Pathways	CEFR	IELTS Band	TOEFL Score
Level 4	C1	6.5–7.0	81–100
Level 3	**B2**	**5.5–6.0**	**51–80**
Level 2	B1–B2	4.5–5.0	31–50
Level 1	A2–B1	0–4.0	0–30
Foundations	A1–A2		

2-> want furniture that can build itself.

1- Skylar Tibbits creates material that self

various object transform themselves.

3. The high tech material are trigger by
time and slightest touch

4- they respond to the same triggers that notice dvs

5- self assembles material can be used for
airplane and even shoes clothing and
sporting goods are different material.